BIG JIM

Crusading Territory
newspaper editor, Jim Bowditch

Peter Simon

Peter Simon: Author.
Big Jim: Crusading Territory newspaper editor, Jim Bowditch.
Text © Peter Simon 2022.
Photographs: Unless otherwise indicated, photographs and newspaper clippings are
from the collection of the author.

ISBN: 978-0-646-85630-8

Design and layout by Michael Pugh: michael.pugh@bigpond.com.

Subjects:
> Northern Territory newspapers
> Aboriginal Advancement and Land Rights
> White Australia Policy
> NT Political reform
> Indentured labour
> Cyclone Tracy
> World War II
> Z Special Unit
> Australian Security Intelligence Organisation (ASIO)

Front Cover:
The quintessential Jim; cigarette and phone. *Darwin Star* c. 1975. Photo by
Kerry Byrnes.

Contact: petersimonbooks@gmail.com

A catalogue record for this
book is available from the
National Library of Australia

NATIONAL
LIBRARY
OF AUSTRALIA

Dedication

This book is dedicated to Betty Bowditch, a 90-year-old Arabana elder and dear long-term friend. Betty, a strong and resilient woman is recognised by many as both a loving, patient and long-suffering wife to Jim who, for all his flaws, deeply loved her and his family. Jim's story is Betty's legacy as she was there for much of the journey.

Warning: This book contains some language and terms which were in general usage at the time they were expressed but are no longer considered acceptable.

Indigenous readers are advised that the book contains photographs and names of people who have died.

Contents

INTRODUCTION

Fleeing the grime of London and its oppressive social order, an unusual teenager, Jim Bowditch, sailed for Australia in 1937 in search of a new life. Throughout his time in Australia he fought the establishment and relentlessly championed the cause of the underdog. Even during his distinguished war service, which saw him perform repeated acts of bravery against enormous odds, he clashed with officers, military police of several nations and incurred so many fines that he often organised gambling and other lurks to get spending money. After the war he built a reputation as a fearless, crusading journalist. From ramshackle newspaper buildings with clapped-out equipment, he fought to right many wrongs.

It mattered not if you were regarded by society as a mental defective, an escapee on the run from police, a woman with children facing eviction or a member of one of the richest families on earth, Bowditch was prepared to take instant—often daring—action to help or rescue you. One request he did turn down was to use his wartime knowledge of explosives to blow up a bridge to disrupt the production of uranium in the Northern Territory.

Apart from covering the news himself, his exploits often became headline news throughout Australia. His campaigns helped shape the nation's attitude on such issues as the White Australia Policy, indentured labour, Northern Territory political reform, Aboriginal advancement and land rights.

While not hiding his flaws, this book is a tribute to a man who, with great courage, flair and undoubted cost to his family, relentlessly fought for humanity in general. With the passage of time, his so-called larrikinism tended to overshadow and detract from the greatness of the man. In a self-deprecating way he described his wayward behaviour as "naughty" or being "a bit bent". For the first time, as this book explains, there is a detailed medical explanation for his excesses.

This book also provides an unusual insight into Australia's Cold War period when Bowditch and many of his associates, exercising the rights and freedoms of individuals in a democracy, were closely watched by the nation's security network, ASIO, the Australian Security Intelligence Organisation.

Peter Simon
14 Compass Crescent,
Nelly Bay
Magnetic Island, 4082
February 2022

1. A BOY CALLED BOADICEA

A certain amount of printer's ink coursed through the veins of Frederick James Bowditch when he was born in Lewisham, south-east London, on 27 July 1919. The second oldest of five children, he had been named after his maternal grandfather, Frederick Manning, who lived in and ran a printery in a large building in the Lewisham High Street. Grandfather Manning had an uncle and cousin in the printing and stationery trade. In the 1881 British census Manning was listed as being 17 years of age and a bookbinder. He grew into a large, tall man, and was dubbed "Frederick the Great".

As young Jim grew his family called him "Big Jim", not because of any outstanding physical characteristic, but simply because he was slightly bigger than most boys, though lean. Like all the children in the family, four boys and a girl, Jim inherited his mother's somewhat prominent nose. He was very fond of his mother a gentle, placid, but tenacious woman, bullied by his father.

About age five Jim was found to have anaemia, a condition common on his father's side of the family, including his father. As a result, Jim was placed on an iron-rich diet of chopped raw liver and watercress. The removal of his tonsils and adenoids in an operation on the kitchen table frightened him. His mother and father stood beside him to make sure he did not jump about while the doctor held a funnel doused with anaesthetic over his face.

Immediately, he began to dream that he was in a canoe on a very long, fast flowing river. Somewhere up ahead was a waterfall, and he was going straight over the edge. He awoke on the kitchen table in excruciating pain, hardly able to breathe or swallow.

Because of his similar sounding surname of Bowditch, schoolmates nicknamed him after a prominent figure in British history, Boadicea, the legendary warlike Queen of the Iceni tribe. Popularly depicted carrying a shield and trident, she defiantly fought the Roman invaders. Like the warrior queen, Bowditch had an impressive mop of hair.

The early childhood years were fairly affluent for the Bowditch family. His father, Captain Hugh Bowditch, once a British Army boxing champion, was an electrical engineer in a large company, Philips, and earned good money, enabling them to move to a wooded estate in Sidcup, Kent. Captain Bowditch wanted one of his sons to continue the family name in the ring. Boxing gloves were kept at home, and he often sparred with his sons, strongly urging them to pursue the "manly art". Because of his bigger build, Jim was pressed into the school boxing team and for each win his father rewarded him with five shillings. He received a mind-scarring thrashing from one particularly good boxer with whom his father had matched him to encourage the necessary "backbone" to become a fighter.

Violence, in many forms, would stalk Jim throughout his life. Captain Bowditch, in the Royal Fusiliers, had been awarded the Military Cross in World War I. He boasted of quelling a revolt by Indian troops by shooting dead several of the unfortunate men on or near the front line.

Much to the consternation of neighbours, Captain Bowditch blazed away at cats with his service revolver, which he had kept. Even when police called to investigate the shots, he was able to bluff them out of taking any action, certainly not confiscating his trusty revolver.

Manliness, his form of manliness, was extolled, and the eldest son, John, because he was artistically and musically inclined, had a difficult time at home.

Captain Bowditch liked his drop. Under the influence of liquor he would indulge his peculiar sense of humour. At random, he would select a name he considered "funny" from the telephone directory. Smelley, a common name in Britain, gave him considerable entertainment. Late at night, in his cups, Captain Bowditch would call up a Smelley. "Are you Smelley?" he would demand in a deep military voice.

When the surprised person answered in the affirmative, Captain Bowditch would then bellow, "Well, what are you going to do about it?!" He would then, in Jim's words, "laugh himself silly." The Smelleys of London were not the only ones to receive such annoying calls from his intoxicated father.

The estate at Sidcup was ringed by a high stone wall and the Bowditch boys used to indulge in a disgusting pastime. They would lie on top of the wall and spit on hats going by. Top hats were a favoured target because they were bigger, and there was less chance of the spittle being noticed. Other entertainment for the boys included conker fights and they swung their chestnuts with great gusto. They also kept pet rabbits. It was at Sidcup while he was in the boy scouts that Jim first came in contact with what, on reflection, he thought was homosexuality. There was a scoutmaster who used to keep some of the boys behind at night. He would pull down his trousers and display a scar near his penis, which he said "the Huns" had inflicted on him with a bayonet. He would then invite the boys to touch the scar. It was through the scouts that Jim joined a gang of boys who used to play up on the streets.

One of the nastiest pieces of violence took place when the gang decided that a lad from another gang in the same scout group had done something wrong. They ambushed the boy outside the scout hall, bound him tightly to a stepladder and then gagged him. The ladder was placed against the main entrance door to the scout hall so that the scoutmaster unwittingly sent the boy crashing to the floor on his face when it opened. The hapless victim received facial injuries and all members of the gang were severely punished.

Scouting also gave Jim his first understanding of the immense poverty in London. Each Christmas the scouts would get donations of food from their parents, parcel them up and distribute gifts in wheelbarrows and billycarts to the poor and needy. Those who received the gifts lived in deplorable slums. Most of the homes consisted of one large room with a fireplace; there was no plumbing. Communal toilets and taps were in the courtyards. The scouts, bearing the gifts, would approach the hovels blowing whistles. The object of all the noise-making, in Jim's opinion, was more to bolster the spirits of the scouts than to let the unfortunate recipients of this Christian charity know they were coming. "We used to think that these strange people we had seen emerging from these places on previous occasions might be dangerous to us," he said. "The real tragedy of the situation was that the people could not afford to refuse the food, but they hated us. They would emerge from their filthy rooms, snatch the bread and dripping, or whatever, from our hands and slam the door in our faces."

The squalor of the fetid residences compared with the leafy estate upon which he lived made a vivid impression on young Bowditch. At home Jim said it was wrong that people had to live that way. From time to time he also spoke out about other things he thought were wrong in society, causing his parents to jokingly call him "our little socialist." His brother Peter was also in the scouts and they went on annual camps, looking very much alike because of their hair. Jim was supposed to take care of Peter, because he was older, but never did. They performed in the annual scout concert, *The Gang Show*, taking part in singing, sketches and dressing up as girls. The two had frequent fist fights.

On several occasions Jim stood up to his father over the way he treated his mother. Responding to being chipped by Jim, Captain Bowditch once chased his son, who climbed a chestnut tree and spent most of the day and part of a chilly night out on a limb. Jim's elder daughter, Ngaire, recalls a different version of this story in which Jim landed, legs spread-eagled, in a bramble bush and was left in some discomfort for hours. Either way it was an ignominious situation for a boy called Boadicea and doesn't show his father in a very good light. During an interview in Australia, Jim's sister Mary Bowditch said their father had been a "gay blade", an expression which at that time indicated a person who enjoyed partying, drinking and smoking with his friends.

At some stage the Bowditch family had a typewriter which Mary thought had been given them by a workmate of their father, "Uncle" Bill Glass. With this typewriter the boys played at bringing out a newspaper on a desk in the lounge room, selling copies to family members. Jim had a major part in its production and the paper ran local news. It was produced on and off for several years. Jim, the chief reporter, did everything with a flourish. It had been Mary's task to keep the boys supplied with cups of tea when they were working on the paper.

Jim's first interest in Australia began when a suntanned man addressed the scouts about "the colonies"—Australia, New Zealand and Canada. He painted a glowing picture of open space, adventure and opportunity—a vision which entranced Jim. Jim attended the Lee County Council School and Colfe's Grammar School, the latter founded by the Reverend Abraham Colfe, Vicar of Lewisham from 1610 to 1657. At Colfe's, Jim had his own gang, Boadicea's. His gang attained what could be called official approval when the headmaster became upset by the schoolboy prank of "flying"—ripping trouser fly buttons out with a quick movement of the hand. He called in Jim to combat the trouble. Jim described the event thus: "The headmaster asked to see me one day and we had a long conversation about my gang. He was not concerned about the gang fighting with other kids. The headmaster discussed an episode in which my gang had beaten up a gigantic lad called Gas. Believe it or not, Gas had a friend, Kettle, and they were fairly repulsive lads. Gas had consistently bullied the Divinity teacher. I, personally, would not have been able to handle Gas, but I got the gang together and we beat him up.

"The headmaster said he had received a lot of complaints from parents and pupils about flying. He asked if I would take up the role of being the flying vigilante. It appealed to my ego, so I spoke to the lads and they thought it would be a good laugh. We just passed the word around: flying was out and thumped anybody who broke the edict. After a little while, the flying epidemic was broken by the Boadicea Gang."

With the arrival of the Depression, life became harder for the Bowditch family. When his mother was short of money, often because of his father's failure to pay bills, she was able to get help from her father. It was grandfather Manning who paid for the education of the boys. Sister Mary said Captain Bowditch squandered everything. She said her father preferred being out with his wartime pals and others, drinking and smoking. However, when the economic crash came their life changed. Captain Bowditch kept his job, but had to take a cut in pay. Grandfather Manning also felt the pinch. The Bowditch family was forced to move from their comfortable house to a small council dwelling at Lee, about seven miles south-east of London, and their lifestyle changed dramatically. Jim's mother, although named Edith Mary, was mostly called "Tina" and actively supported St Margaret's Anglican Church, Lee. As she strode purposefully up the path to the church with her four sons, the vicar often remarked, "Here is Tina with her disciples." Young Jim, with a mop of golden curls, and his brother Peter, who had platinum locks, looked angelic, and both served as choir boys.

Through a friend at the grammar school Jim got to know a farming family at Little Marlow in the Buckinghamshire area. Often he would cycle to the farm for the weekend, hanging on to the side of trucks for a tow along the way. On the farm he helped to milk cows, plough fields, handle equipment and look after livestock. Although a small farm, the people ate well and seemed better off than his family. A desire to become a farmer when he grew up developed in Jim.

Returning late one Sunday from a pleasant time on the farm, Jim found a disturbing situation at home. His mother, crumpled and crying, was sitting on the floor in the corner of the dining room. The entire house had been stripped by heartless bailiffs. Recalling the event, he said: "There was nothing in the way of furniture, no knives, no forks, no towels, no sheets—the house was stripped bare and she [Mother] was enormously distressed. I can remember trying to comfort her, and she told me that as a result of bills not being paid by my father the bailiffs had come around and taken away all our possessions.

"I was furious. Over the years, I have campaigned strongly against racial discrimination, but I must admit that then I had a deep hatred for the Jews because they were bailiffs. I raced around on my bike and got relatives and friends to provide bedding, pots and pans and other household needs.

"But I had already determined to get revenge on the bailiffs. In those days, chemistry sets were popular and you could get the ingredients for gunpowder. I found out where the bailiffs lived, and set to work making flying bombs. Using cardboard and plywood, doorknobs filled with gunpowder, live matches and pieces of matchbox, I made primitive gliders which exploded on impact. At night I would ride pretty fast past a bailiff's house, launch the flying bomb and ride off quickly; there was a pretty big explosion. The aim was to terrorise the bailiffs and pay them back for their act of cruelty on my mother. It is a wonder that I did not blow myself up in the process. Nobody got hurt as far as I know. It was revenge for an act of total brutality on a human being."

While it might be thought strange that Bowditch engaged in such activity against bailiffs, a popular British boys' magazine of the time urged children to buy aerial bombs called whiz bangs, gliders with an explosive tip. These were described as ideal to scare policemen, old ladies and postmen. The idea was to sneak up on your target, launch the glider and the resultant explosion would frighten your victim. Advertisements for these bombs carried drawings of a little old lady with a walking stick, a tubby policeman and a tired looking postie carrying a heavy mail sack.

The campaign against bailiffs lasted about three months, during which time he enlisted the help of some gang members. As if bailiffs were not bad enough, Jim had to contend with a thankless headmaster. Caught by prefects puffing a cigarette, he was hauled before the same headmaster who had enlisted his help to wipe out flying. Instead of getting a mild reprimand, as Jim expected, the headmaster decided to make an example of him. The headmaster, carrying a cane, took him on stage in front of the entire school assembly and said smoking had to stop. He then called the porter up and Jim was told to jump on his back and put his arms around his shoulders. The headmaster then pulled up Jim's shirt and took down his trousers. He then "got into" Jim with the birch. "It must have been a ludicrous sight," said Bowditch, "because the headmaster was this strange little monkey-like man, very small indeed, whaling away at me sitting on the back of the porter. After that, he left the stage and summoned me to the study where he gave me a lecture on why he had done what he did. Then he told me to go home and not return until the next day."

It had been an enormous indignity being beaten before so many people, but he did not smoke again until he joined the Australian Army. Recurring nightmares about being chained to a block of ice caused him to wonder if they were caused by that public flogging.

His memories of school were mainly ones of scuffling and fighting. He had no clear memory of learning much at all and came to distrust "almost everything" a few years after leaving school. In particular, he discovered that what he had been taught at school about China had been misleading: "I can remember being taught by this geography teacher, a strange man whose form of punishing kids was to stand them in a corner and throw pieces of chalk at their heads. Anyway, he told us that the lesson on China was brief, and he really meant brief. The book he quoted from dismissed China as a very big area of land with so many people in it nobody had ever been able to count the population. He said the country was subject to serious drought every year which killed millions of people, and that was China."

2. LIFE IN A LOLLY FACTORY

The economic grind and Jim's disenchantment with school combined to encourage him leave school at 14. Fortunately, while still at school, he had made the acquaintance of a remarkable man, Pat Martin, an early exponent of time and motion studies. A "mathematical wizard" and "humanist", Martin was in his early twenties, and he and Jim were close. It is not known how they met, but Jim's sister Mary recalled that she had been a babysitter for the Martins. Presumably, Martin, a quietly spoken Irishman, had been a friend of the family. Martin said he wanted Jim to work in a new industrial psychology department he was about to open in C. & E. Morton Pty Ltd, a huge canning works on East India Dock Road, Mill Wall, London, where they canned fish, meat, jam and produced a wide range of confectionery, including acid drops.

Morton's wanted a bonus system introduced similar to the one devised by Frenchman Charles Eugene Bedaux, who gained notoriety as an exploiter of the workforce. In America the Bedaux technique had substantially increased output by offering workers a bonus payment for greater production. It became a method of weeding out slower workers, and there was much union suspicion about the time and motion study techniques from across the Atlantic. Jim said he believed the distrust of the Bedaux system was responsible for Australian trade unions being antagonistic to all bonus systems.

So Jim went to work for Martin in the cannery. Men and women in the vast works were apprehensive about Martin, his time and motion studies and the young men, including Jim, who worked for him. According to Jim, Martin firmly believed that his mathematical variations on the Bedaux system would give the workers a greater share in the company's profits. Martin explained to the workers, he was a great speaker "but not a used car type", that while the aim was to increase productivity, it would not be done at the expense of jobs. He gave an undertaking that workers who could not reach the production norm would be given more suitable jobs and not be fired. It was agreed the study should go on trial for some months.

Armed with a stopwatch and clipboard, Jim went to work as a time and motion observer in a confectionery packing section. He noted that girls on the production line were on their feet 10 hours a day. The monotonous work involved taking jars or bottles from a production line, laying them on a bench, sticking on labels, then placing them back on the conveyor belt. Because the girls and women were on their feet so long, they experienced sore legs and extreme fatigue.

Jim told Martin the staff should have adjustable chairs to sit on to take the weight off their legs. He also pointed out the process of taking a container from a production belt to be labelled took a large amount of time. As a result of his suggestions and observations, chairs were supplied and the production line was adjusted to make labelling easier and faster, resulting in increased production. What is more, the girls received more pay. Some of them showed their appreciation by offering to take gawky Jim behind the chocolate box stack for a quick cuddle, but he was too shy to avail himself of the offers by the saucy London lasses. Jim was given a bonus payment for his work and his wage went up to seven shillings and sixpence (75 cents) a week.

As he cycled to work he observed the grubby surroundings. His income helped his family in those tough times. Martin influenced Jim's thinking as he often had him at home discussing working conditions, workers' pay and enlightened industrial psychology.

Despite the interesting and rewarding work, Jim wanted to move on. The grime of London, which he described as a nauseating place, and the poverty of the people bore down heavily on him. One of his abiding memories of London was the stench from glue factories where the workers, overcome by the putrid smell, rushed outside to vomit, and then returned to the fetid interiors.

His longing to leave developed into a hatred for London and what it did to people who lived in the sprawling city. Tension at home with his father added to the desire to get away. The seductive colonies seemed to call him. He still had this overwhelming desire to be a farmer or an agricultural worker: "I had a mad desire to milk cows, ride horses and plough fields. I hated London, this filthy, smog-filled, poverty-ridden bugger of a place." After deciding that he would "flee" to either New Zealand or Australia, he found that it was sometimes possible to work your passage to these distant Meccas.

However, he was told that the colonies required that you had six pounds in your pocket when you landed. That was a lot of money in those days. Martin readily provided Jim with a glowing reference in the hope that he could find work in the colonies in industrial psychology. Nobody could tell him if industrial psychology was even used in NZ or Australia, but he was prepared to give it go. Before Jim left the cannery, Martin arranged a meeting with the boss of Morton's, hoping that he might even contribute to his passage money. However, the head man delivered a lecture for about half an hour during which he never mentioned money and warned that the colonies were rough places. Honesty and the virtue of hard work were emphasised.

Jim's depression at not being able to raise funds lifted when a rich relative, Uncle Joshua Cornelius, who part-owned or had shares in Welsh coalmines, asked to see him. "Uncle Corny", whose name was mentioned in hushed tones in the Bowditch household because of his wealth, lived in a mansion near Blackheath. Uncle Corny opened proceedings with another long lecture which warned about bad women, keeping your nose clean and the necessity to work hard. Jim's heart began to thump when his uncle put his hand in his pocket—and pulled out a mere five shillings. This was much less than he had hoped for. It fell to Jim's maternal grandfather, the man after whom he had been named, to provide the necessary hard cash to enable Jim to muster the money for a passage to a new life. It was not ingratitude that made Jim sign the necessary papers for his trip in the name of James Frederick Bowditch instead of Frederick James Bowditch. Everybody knew him as Jim, and he really did not like being called Fred.

3. ESCAPE FROM LONDON

His passage to Australia in 1937 might have been arranged through the Anglican Big Brother organisation. His sister suggested their mother could have used her church connections to help him. The day he was supposed to board the *Port Dunedin*, sister Mary, upset at him leaving, put her head under the blanket when he entered her bedroom to say goodbye. His mother was emotional and tearful at the thought of her teenage son leaving home and going far away. His father gave him a hearty slap on the back. Jim felt lonely and was secretly fearful of the voyage ahead, partly because he suffered from sea sickness. Not only that, he suffered from motion sickness. Sitting in the back of a car made him ill and facing towards the back of transport also made him queasy. Eventually he left carrying a kitbag but was back in half an hour. Word had come through that the ship's departure had been delayed and there was no need for him to go aboard. Next day there was another farewell. This time there was no return and he never saw his parents again, his father supposedly dying of a heart attack in the arms of his secretary during "a dirty weekend".

Aboard ship, Jim was put to work under the chief steward, a tired-eyed homosexual. The steward grabbed him by the hair, made comments about his arse and tried to rape Jim, whose boxing experience and fitness enabled him to fight off the man. The tussle took place in a cabin and they crashed about for five minutes until the steward gave up. The early part of the voyage was a nightmare because of Jim's seasickness and the fear of further attacks by the steward. He and another young lad also working his passage polished brass, washed dishes, prepared vegetables, chipped at rust and painted. There was a short stopover in Cape Town, South Africa, where Jim bought souvenir postcards and sent them home. Magnificent albatrosses glided alongside the ship and Jim threw them titbits. Sailors regaled him with stories about what happened to people who shot the birds.

New Zealand, he felt, seemed the desirable destination for him. Crewmen backed his desire to go there, saying it was more British than Britain. However, when the ship passed through Sydney Heads the wonderful vista made him feel Australia was the country for him. Besides, he had been given the name of a man in a Sydney suburb, Stanmore, as a contact.

Because it was his job to clean up, Jim was one of the last to leave the ship; he found the officials at the wharf gate did not care where he was going and nobody asked him if he had the six pounds which had been so difficult to raise. With a kitbag slung over a shoulder, he went looking for the contact, only to find the man had moved on. Not only had the man moved, but the residence had been replaced by a baker's shop owned by a Frenchman. The Frenchman, amused by Jim's story, gave him a job as a dough stirrer and provided accommodation. The hospitable Frenchman showed him around Sydney and helped him look for jobs on hearing of Jim's desire to go on the land.

The New South Wales state government advertised for young people to work on an experimental farm at Glen Innes, in New England. No pay was offered, but the rudiments of farming were taught and free dormitory accommodation and food were provided. This was a dream come true for Jim, and off he went to Glen Innes, where he ploughed fields, rode horses, ripped out lantana, milked cows, looked after sheep and cattle dogs and learned how to use farm machinery. It was paradise in his estimation.

He played rugby league as scrum half and five-eighth for the Glen Innes team in what was a fierce competition. After working at the farm he got casual work at Inverell and Warialda, where he was a wheat lumper, lifting heavy bags. This hard work contributed to his physical development and capacity to work for long hours. He discovered by working on farms that Pommies got paid less than Australians. On one farm where he and an Australian lad looked after 80 cows, Jim got 10 shillings ($1) a week and the other fellow got one pound ($2). From then on Jim disguised his English accent and said he came from Queensland. Cow cockies, he found, led a dour, hard existence, even though they were better off from the tucker point of view. On reading of a Queensland job paying 1 pound, twelve shillings and sixpence ($3.25) a week and keep at Gamarren Station, owned by the King family, he applied for and got the job. The position mainly entailed killing and dressing sheep, clearing trees and even helping the laundry maid. Feeding 14 dogs was another chore.

One stockman on the station, Mick Kane, owned a superb kelpie bitch which was outstanding at working sheep. Named Toy, the dog would obey only Kane's instructions. An event took place involving Toy and his master which left an indelible mark on Jim's memory. Some sheep were being mustered and several kept breaking away and sending up a large cloud of dust. The dog was working hard to round up the sheep, but they kept breaking away. Kane, normally patient, was weary and lost his temper with the dog. For some reason, the "magic combination" between the man and dog finally failed. In a towering rage, Kane leapt from his horse, grabbed Toy by the back legs, swung her round his head and smashed her against the main gate post. She lay whimpering on the ground. Kane immediately sat beside her and burst into tears. Nobody was game to interfere; he was a tough egg, Mick. "We just left him there," said Jim. "Kane sat for many days and nights with Toy, nursing her back to health. In a remarkably short time she was back on deck again. And our regard for this man hadn't lessened at all. It was a relationship between animal and man that taught me a great deal."

Jim clashed with a contract horse breaker, Joe Copel, over the way he handled horses. Copel, according to Jim, hated horses and was paid 30 shillings ($3) a head to break them in. "The way he walked and moved, you could see he had suffered much from his horse breaking.

"Many bones had been broken over the years. He was bent and battered. His whole body was distorted. Joe would start off breaking a horse by hitting it in the head with a bag, choking it down and pouring water in its ears. Before mounting, he would go to a corner of the yard and urinate. After getting the saddle on, he would stamp around the yard and steel himself for the task. You could feel the horse quiver as Joe mounted. We opened the gate, and the animal pig-rooted, bucked and spun. Joe suffered many falls. He was a great rider and could break in eight or 10 a day. When he was thrown off he would urinate again and climb back on."At a dance, Jim told Joe that he did not like the way he broke horses and a fight broke out. Joe fought like a wild horse.

Ten months after Jim joined the hired hands on the station, another young stockman, Jack Green, from the Miles area of Queensland, was engaged. Tall, strong and raw-boned, he and Jim got along well. After a time they came to the common conclusion that working long hours and being treated "like shit" was not much of a life. They decided to go gold prospecting at Wellington, NSW, and seek their fortune. Jim had a pushbike and Jack went to Cunnamulla and bought himself one. They then made up swags, gave notice, and pedalled off for El Dorado.

When they arrived in Wellington they went to the pub and store and asked for instructions about how to prospect for gold. An old bloke showed them how to make a sluice box from timber, with ripple irons and coconut matting. The old-timer kindly gave them his own coconut matting to put in the sluice box as long as they promised to give it back when they decided to leave. Fair enough. Eager and fit, the two began digging and soon had the sluice box working. Because funds were low, they shot rabbits, which were boiled, fried and even fricasseed when there was enough money from prospecting to afford potatoes and onions. So many rabbits did they eat that they began to smell like rabbits. Whatever gold they found was exchanged for tea, flour, tinned meat and vegetables. Because little gold was being found, they decided to pull down their tents, pack their swags and pedal off once more. The coconut matting was returned with thanks to its kindly owner. Days later they were told by another prospector that matting held about 50 per cent of the fine gold put through a sluice and the only way of getting it out was to burn it. Jim and Jack realised that they had probably been set up by the helpful prospector who, no doubt, had burned the matting when they returned it to him.

During his travels Jim sent home excited letters to his family. His sister had reason to recall one letter because Jim described killing snakes by grabbing them by the tail and cracking them like a whip.

There were many other people on the track seeking work and food. Rations were doled out by the government in those days. The travelling dole was a little more than five shillings worth of rations a week; tea, sugar, flour, maybe vegetables and a can or two of meat. To be eligible for the dole, you had to have travelled at least 20 miles from the last point where you got help. As towns in the outback were a long way apart it kept the jobless on the move. It also stopped them from getting organised.

At Moree, Jim and Jack joined a large number of men gathered under a railway bridge. Because it was so hot, many of the men who were on foot did not want to go on. This is Bowditch's account of what happened: "We were fairly tired and yarned about the lack of money and the injustice of the dole system, we decided to go *en masse* and ask the sergeant of police for permission to stay on and collect the dole instead of having to move off again. I was a bit opinionated in those days and had my bit to say. As a result, I was elected to be the spokesman. I had this firm belief in the basic kindness of the human race. After a feed of damper and treacle, about 80 of us marched up to the police station. The police had been warned in advance about our coming. We trudged up to the station and there was a gigantic red-headed sergeant who came out and confronted us with a revolver and a rifle. He demanded to know what we wanted. I gave a speech in which I said that we were tired, that it was more than 20 miles to the next town and we would like to spend another week in town, so we would appreciate him handing out five shillings and tuppence (52 cents) worth of rations. He refused in a very belligerent and emphatic manner. Lurking behind him were two other police with rifles. I kept on talking, arguing you might say, with all this crowd pushing behind me. Finally, the copper did his block, stepped forward and drove his fist right into my face, breaking a tooth in half. Other teeth were damaged and had to be eventually removed. I went down in a welter of blood. Everyone scattered. You have no basis from which to argue when the police are armed. I staggered to my feet and made it back to the camp. Fellows there patched me up and advised me not to stand too close to a policeman in the future."

Battered Bowditch and his mate Jack rode off on their bicycles. They headed for Jack's hometown, Miles. There they got contract work ringbarking wattle and ironbark. Times were so tough the going rate for ringbarking was two shillings and sevenpence (27 cents) an acre. They were able to get a contract for 2/8 (28 cents) an acre for a large area, but that was only because it was a more difficult block to cut. It was hard, grinding work. Jack could handle up to five and a half acres a day. Jim was hard pressed doing half an acre at first. There was plenty of water and the area abounded with wallabies which they trapped with wire loop snares.

However, they ate so much wallaby, johnny cakes and treacle, Jim developed spots before his eyes. A doctor told him this was due to grease in the johnny cakes which affected his liver. Occasionally they were able to vary their diet with eggs and poultry from Jack's parents. One thing he learned while roaming the outback was to always wash your dishes at night, never leave them with food attached as they became hard to wash in the morning. It was a habit he followed for the rest of his life.

When war broke out, news spread quickly in the bush. Jim felt the British would surely stop the Germans. He wrote to his parents and suggested he should come home and join the army. When Dunkirk was evacuated in 1940 he knew the situation was grave and that his family was under threat. His brother John, a pacifist at heart, was at Dunkirk when the German blitzkrieg swept the British into the sea. John went on to become a parachutist with the Red Devils commandos. Peter went straight from Colfe's Grammar School at Greenwich into the RAF as a tail gunner and was badly injured when his plane, returning from a bombing raid, crashed and burst into flames at Lincoln. Young David was evacuated to a safe area with his school and when his mother rang up to ask after him she was told he had run away five days previously and had joined the merchant navy by telling them he was 17 instead of 15.

He was subsequently on a ship which was dive bombed and after that shock he told his officers his real age and asked to go home. He returned to the family in disgrace and the school and other people got into trouble.

Jim decided to join up in Australia, and jumped a rattler to Brisbane so he could enlist. He travelled in a railway truck with some swagmen in a load of stinking hides. The train pulled into a siding and he could hear something striking canvas. It was a policeman with a truncheon trying to flush out non-paying passengers. The whacking noise got closer and closer; occasionally there was a yelp. Fearing he would have his head split open, he revealed himself to the policeman, a large smiling man, who took him and others to the lock-up. The officer proved to be friendly. Jim chopped some wood for the policeman's wife and received bacon, eggs and toast for breakfast. Cell doors were left open. And the officer told Jim where he could catch another train, a mile down the track, where it had to slow down. Another bit of advice from the cop was that he should jump off the train before it got into Brisbane because of further police checks.

Acting on that advice, he jumped from the train just before Brisbane and spent the first night camped in a park. Next day he went to the Redbank Recruiting Centre and enlisted on 1 July 1940. He was 21 and 5ft 8½ inches tall. Though slightly built, during his medical examination the military men remarked on his physical development, the hard life had made him muscular.

4. ARMY STRIFE

On his first day in the army, Private James Bowditch, QX 13703, after having been put through the quartermaster's store and shouted at from all sides, was lined up with the other raw recruits and inspected by a sergeant-major. This man passed uncomplimentary remarks to his aides as he inspected the intake. When he came to Jim with his mop of hair which he had let grow wild, he said, "First thing, haircut for you." Jim responded by saying he had not joined the army to get a haircut. The SM pulled up with a jerk and delivered a fierce lecture. Jim's account of what followed went this way: "While I did not use words like get stuffed or up your arse, I used terms which amounted to that." This resulted in him being confined to barracks for seven days. Paraded before an officer, he was told that he had to do as he was told from then on. Disregarding the confinement order, he slipped out of the camp, and was caught. His clash with the army brass would last a long time.

A fresh-faced Jim joins the Army.
Bowditch family collection.

Monotonous was how Bowditch described early training. There was much guarding of flagpoles and marching, marching, marching. Because of his fitness he was made a Bren gunner, a Bren being a light machine gun. On leave, he and mates lived it up in Brisbane. He was introduced to beer, which filled him with gas and made him belch, so he bought creme de menthe and creme de cacao for one shilling a nip. He had an affair with a skinny young woman who already had a child. With the likelihood of him soon being sent overseas on active duty, she suggested they get married. Jim agreed and, because regulations required approval from superiors before any soldier could marry, applied for clearance. An officer said the woman must come to the camp for an interview and discuss the marriage proposal. After the interview, the officer called Bowditch in and told him the marriage could not be approved because she was a camp follower. The officer said he had seen the woman hanging around the camp before and believed she had had affairs with other soldiers.

She was just a good-time girl. Furthermore, the officer said he would not be surprised to learn that she had been "hitched" to several troops. So shocked was Bowditch that he wanted to fight the officer and refused to accept what he had said about her. Bowditch then went out and began asking questions about the woman and discovered that what he had been told by the officer was true. After this disturbing disclosure he was keen to get away and fight. This was not to be because just when it appeared he was about to be sent overseas it was discovered he was suffering from non-specific urethritis. Many troops departed but he was left behind. What annoyed him was that the troopship he should have sailed on went via England and he was denied the opportunity to see his family.

Placed in a pool of troops, he was eventually assigned to the 2/9th Battalion of the AIF led by Major-General George "Piggy" Wootten. He was sent to Sydney and boarded the *Queen Mary* which had been stripped below decks except for a section allocated to officers. His deep antipathy to authority grew when he saw the special privileges and conditions officers enjoyed. He reasoned that when "the shit hit the fan" and they faced death they were all equal, so why should any section be treated differently? The troops were packed in hammock to hammock and the stench from vomit was overpowering. Seasickness once more claimed him.

They disembarked in the Middle East in 1941 and quickly went into action. He was in two companies diverted to the fort at Giarabub, Libya, which was held by about 1200 Italians. It was a bloody and unpleasant conflict. Contrary to popular myth, Bowditch said the Italians fought very bravely, but realised they could not win and surrendered. Between 50 and 100 had been captured. When the troops were told to quickly move to another area where fierce fighting was going on they were told to shoot the Italians. This would be denied by authorities, Bowditch said, but it definitely took place. "We were instructed to mow down these prisoners and that, in fact, is what was done. It was contrary to conventions and all the rules governing war."

The troops then moved to Tobruk, which was caught up in what was the longest siege in modern warfare up to that time.

Tobruk had been held by Italians before it was seized by Australians in January 1941 and was ringed by wire and minefields. The Allies were keen to keep Tobruk at all costs to protect the important naval base at Alexandria in Egypt. During the eight-month siege in which the German Field Marshal Erwin "The Desert Fox" Rommel did his utmost to dislodge the Allies, more than 47,000 men including wounded and prisoners were taken out of Tobruk while 43,000 men and 34,000 tons of supplies were brought in. A total of 34 warships and merchant ships were sunk and another 33 damaged.

A sun-baked hellhole raked by enemy fire, Tobruk had underground dugouts where men could rest from the relentless sun and bullets to have a smoke. The desert was alive with scorpions, fleas, lice, flies and other insect pests. Soldiers poured petrol around the dugouts as an insecticide. Bowditch was resting in a shelter when somebody lit a cigarette which ignited petrol fumes and the place exploded in a ball of flame. He remembered with horror that as he scrambled to get out he was kicking the man behind him who was also frantic to escape. Several men died in the explosion and although his clothing was set alight, Jim escaped with minor burns. One man suffered severe burns from his feet to his waist.

There was not enough water to drink, and that supplied was salty. Because of the constant dust, all clothing was covered. Temperatures rose to 130 degrees Fahrenheit (54 degrees Celsius) and there was stunted vegetation in the surrounding country which troops called camel bush. The soil was rocky and sandy and digging trenches was hard work. Sand permeated footwear and clothing.

Frequent dive bombing by the Germans added to the hell of Tobruk. The British traitor William Joyce, Lord Haw Haw, who made radio propaganda broadcasts for the Nazis, said the Australians were like rats in a trap. This led to the Australians proudly boasting to be the Rats of Tobruk. Naval ships running the gauntlet to Tobruk came at night with supplies of food and ammunition, quickly unloaded, took on wounded, and zigzagged out to try to dodge aerial bombardment. The harbour became littered with wrecks. The Germans stepped up the bombardment of Tobruk and poured tanks in. Bowditch used "sticky bombs" to knock out several tanks. These bombs looked like toffee apples and were a ball about twice the size of a baseball, filled with high explosives. When the outside wrapping was torn from the bomb there was a sticky substance which enabled them to be attached to tanks. Many men got shot down running up to tanks with sticky bombs. Jim would lie in a trench and let the tanks run over the top. In a quick movement, he applied the bomb to the bottom of the tank and it would pass on and eventually explode.

Because of his skill with the Bren gun, he was placed near the perimeter in the thick of fighting. An enemy machine gun caused havoc because it opened up on the barbed wire perimeter at night when men were stretching their legs and standing about. Jim suggested he and Tom Clark, an older Queenslander, should try to pinpoint the gun and have it put out of action. On a dark night they advanced into no-man's land and took up a position in a bomb crater and waited for daylight. Such night time listening posts were a regular feature of the warfare and small groups would venture out and try to pick up noises from the enemy. With the help of a periscope, Bowditch and his comrade found the machine gun and made other observations. They quietly discussed many things out there in no-man's land. The Queenslander spoke about his family and life in the bush; Jim told him about London and the way of life there. Sex was another topic.

Their periscope was obviously detected because late in the day their crater was mortared. For two terrifying hours they cringed in the hole as shells rained down around them. Like the sound of machine gun fire, Bowditch said being subjected to a constant mortar barrage was frightening. They were eventually able to sneak back to their own lines in the dark and the company commander congratulated them. As a result of their observations the sector containing the machine gun was heavily bombarded. Clark later trod on a booby trap and barbed wire was driven into his leg. He was evacuated and Jim never heard of him again.

Bowditch further tempted fate by raiding the well-guarded food dumps at Tobruk. The noncoms (non commissioned officers) were annoyed that officers got tinned fruit and they did not. Baked beans and biscuits were apparently deemed adequate for the common troops.

Raiding the food dumps was every bit as dangerous as attacking machine gun nests because guards were ordered to shoot first and ask questions later. Some guards had also been seriously injured by night-time raiders. Bowditch was in a party of about 10 which raided the food supply one night with the officers' tins of fruit the target. Jim incurred much derision by bringing back tins of baked beans as well as fruit. "I used to have simple tastes," he explained, "and I liked baked beans."

As each month passed at Tobruk he increasingly began to wonder when his number would come up. "Something in your brain tells you the numbers game is being played and it is only a matter of time before you get killed." For a month he was ill, vomiting and feeling bad. He hardly ate. When he went to the Medical Orderly, known as "March On" McGregor, he got no sympathy. McGregor seemed to have little feeling for soldiers and it appeared his duty was to get men back to their section even on their hands and knees. He accused Bowditch of cowardice and told him he just wanted to be evacuated. Still feeling terrible, Jim went back to fighting. He was delighted to hear they were going to be relieved by fresh Polish troops.

The 1st Carpathian Brigade duly arrived, all wearing Bombay bloomers, baggy shorts like the British, and all looking "mad". "I did not understand what the Germans had done to their country," said Bowditch. "They had lost their families, wives and kids, their land. They filed in before us and shook our hands. Very few could speak English. As we left, the Poles shot off every weapon they could at the enemy. Had their officers not stopped them they would have exhausted the entire ammunition supply of Tobruk. They just wanted to kill every German in the area to get revenge for what had been done to their homeland."

Bowditch was by now so ill he really did not care and dragged himself aboard an RAN vessel. Stukas flew overhead and at one stage he did not dive for cover because he felt so sick. When they disembarked they prepared to entrain for eventual action in Syria. However, Bowditch collapsed and was taken to hospital. He woke to find an aristocratic doctor standing over him, his hand pressing on his liver saying: "The poor bastard's got jaundice." Many troops at Tobruk fell victim to jaundice. Bowditch also had a desert sore on his leg which had eaten to the bone and refused to heal. Under treatment, he gradually came good but a skin graft was needed to overcome the desert sore. In the skin graft ward he saw a man who had been badly burned in the dugout explosion at Tobruk. The drugged man was lowered into a regular saline bath by four orderlies. Despite sedation, the man would scream and sometimes pass out. The graft specialist, Dr Rank, called in four times a day and would never show emotion as he looked over the terrible victims of burns and appalling wounds. The doctor would look at extensive afflicted areas, probe rotting flesh and sinews and point out where they would have to start the rebuilding process. Bowditch told the doctor he felt ashamed occupying a bed while all he had was a desert sore. Dr Rank gave him a short lecture and told him not to be silly. Because of his spell in hospital he missed the Syrian campaign in which many of his comrades were killed.

A wild escapade in Palestine landed him in serious trouble. During a bout of drinking with mates they ran out of money. A large businessman wearing a fez was seen sitting in what looked like a garage. Jim went over and asked the man if he would like to make a donation to their drinking funds. He refused, so Jim took down a sword, one of two crossed on the wall, and chased the man. In the uproar, British, military police, Red Caps, became involved and a brawl erupted. Bowditch was hit with the book and spent 48 days in a military prison awaiting trial and forfeited 49 days' pay. Although soldiers were paid six shillings a day, Bowditch said he averaged about one shilling a day for his first three years of service because of his fines.

5. HOME AND AWAY

On the return voyage to Australia, Bowditch became enraged in Bombay when he saw young girls in cages being offered to the soldiers. He called on the men not to have anything to do with the prostitution of children and even tried to get through to them by saying they would return home with the pox. Similar thinking men joined him and there was a fight with others who were eager to get at the caged girls. During the voyage he was given medical treatment and back in Australia was treated for bronchitis, traumatic sinusitis and malaria. He also faced charges of conduct prejudicial to good order and military discipline, drunkenness, using insubordinate language and resisting an escort whose duty it was to apprehend him.

Bowditch, with other troops brought back from the Middle East, was sent to do jungle training in North Queensland to prepare them for action against the Japanese. Then Bowditch boarded the *Katoomba* in Townsville and sailed to Port Moresby, to take part in the fierce fighting for the strategically important Milne Bay which would result in the first defeat of Japanese on land. The seemingly invincible Japanese had landed at Gona. Two squadrons of RAAF Kittyhawks arrived at Milne Bay to bolster the battle against the Japanese sweeping down towards them. Nine vessels landed 1250 seasoned Japanese marines on the coast accompanied by a naval bombardment. Rumours came through that the Japanese had broken through. Fighting was so ferocious Bowditch saw men go to pieces under the strain. The enemy came to an important airfield, where the canteen was blown up to prevent it falling into enemy hands. Bowditch saw RAAF men, probably ground crew, white and terrified, running away.

He was involved in the savage combat which saw corporal Jack French posthumously awarded the Victoria Cross. This is Jim's account, which varies slightly from official records. In the circumstances it's perfectly understandable: "I was with the platoon next to that of French, a burly, blond fellow; we were advancing along this coastal area. There were camouflaged machine guns and snipers all over the place. Bullets were flying everywhere. Somebody started to shout, 'Retreat! Retreat! Retreat!', and it caught on like a wave. We turned and we were running back. One fellow ran past me and ran into a tree, dropped his gun and kept on running. French started to sing out, 'Hold it! Hold it! Hold the line!'. I think he was angry. I saw him take the first machine gun nest. He just lobbed a grenade, fired his gun and appeared to bayonet someone. I saw him go for the second nest and that was when I think he got hit because he appeared to stagger when running at the nest. He went down throwing a grenade into a third nest. In my view, that stopped the retreat from Milne Bay. If it had continued there would have been a debacle. After that brave effort by French we got on top."

There was, however, more ferocious fighting ahead. The older Japanese, he said, fought like "kamikaze" soldiers, but as they were killed the younger enemy became less fanatical. The smell of death was everywhere as the Australians continued to mop up the enemy. Bowditch was so exhausted at the end of a day's fighting he slumped down on what he thought was a log and found it was the putrefying body of an enemy soldier. Early in the advance a handsome young officer he had known in the Middle East had half his face blown away and it was obvious he was going to die despite the fact that he was still walking with blood spurting from a horrible wound.

Out front one day with his Bren gun at the ready, Jim saw Japanese up in the hills looking down on the platoon. One of them produced a white flag and advanced towards him. Bowditch asked his commanding officer what he should do. The officer, in the middle of the platoon, said to signal the soldier to come down: "I did. We did not know what to expect as we had heard how they had pretended to surrender and would then shoot people dead. We had seen where they had tied people to trees and set them alight with petrol. Women had also been staked out and raped. I signalled this kid in and he was knocking at the knees. He had hardly got past me than the officer drew his revolver and started shooting at him. He missed a couple of times but eventually hit this kid who went down. I finished him off with a quick burst from my Bren gun and actually swung around in a rage and pointed it at the officer. I was nearly going to shoot him. I don't know how I restrained myself. That senseless act probably cost the lives of hundreds of Australians because the Japanese then fought to the last man."

Bowditch was in the Milne Bay area for about a month continuing the coastal sweep through Buna and Sanananda and had many grisly experiences. When they took enemy first aid posts they shot wounded Japanese because they were instructed to take no prisoners. However, there was one prisoner who stuck in his memory because he was more than six feet tall. This man was brought in for interrogation, but bit his own tongue off rather than talk.

Dysentery swept through the troops on both sides and the Japanese, because they had little in the way of medical supplies, often fought without their soiled trousers. The bodies of some 2/9th Battalion men were found on wire frames, mutilated from being used for bayonet practice.

The Australians learnt early in the piece not to peer into enemy trenches because the Japanese would lie there pretending to be dead and shoot your head off. It was safer to lob grenades into trenches. Bowditch recounted how one day while Australian soldiers were resting on a beach, a Japanese holding a sword in his mouth was seen swimming toward them. On reaching shore he took the sword from his mouth and rushed, shouting, up the beach towards the soldiers who shot him to pieces. At Buna, on the northeast coast of Papua, the Allies sent in 660 men from corvettes who linked up with tanks in further battles for strategic airstrips. The Japanese had many camouflaged bunkers and there were snipers in trees. At times they threw back hand grenades hurled into their bunkers. In 14 days of fierce fighting at Buna the 2/9th lost more officers and men of other ranks than in four months at Tobruk.

But there was no end to their fighting for the battalion then had to march 15 miles to Sanananda along a rough truck through swamps, creeks, small rivers and kunai grass. The tanks sent in ahead of them were picked off by heavy Japanese guns. Once again, many enemy were trouserless, but fought with fanatical fury. After all he had been through, Bowditch was made a lance corporal.

6. SECRET SERVICE

While resting at Port Moresby, Bowditch said he found the troops, especially those who had been in the Middle East and Syria, were battle hardened but war weary. When volunteers were sought for a select commando group, the Z Special Unit, many men in New Guinea, Bowditch included, jumped at the opportunity to escape the steamy jungles and get back to Australia. He believed officers took the opportunity to "get rid of" men who bucked authority. Bowditch was selected for Z Special Unit and was flown back to Australia on 29 October 1943. A spot of well-earned and much needed leave followed and then he joined the Z Special Unit on 17 December.

Training included a stint on Fraser Island, Queensland, where the unarmed combat instructor would attack at any hour of the day or night to test the readiness of his men. "You would be coming out of your tent first thing in the morning, hear a noise, and it was the unarmed combat instructor flying at you feet first. It was like Peter Sellers playing the crazy Inspector Clouseau and his oriental servant who tried to catch him off guard." This person, a professional wrestler, Major Reg McCissock, had run a gymnasium in Perth. He was a strong, bear-sized man, weighing nearly 20 stone (nearly 130 kilograms). His tent on the island was near a sandbagged sandpit in which he plied his trade.

West Australian Z Special Unit member Jack Sue recounted an episode with McCissock. Sue's cousin, Peter Wong, was on Fraser Island when "mad screaming" was heard coming from McCissock's tent. The instructor suddenly came tearing out with a rifle to which was attached a bayonet and threw it at Wong. Wong, much smaller than his assailant, but versed in unarmed combat, stepped aside, caught and threw the rifle into the sandpit. At some stage McCissock had Wong in a Boston crab wrestling hold in the sandpit. He told the surrounding soldiers that when they had "a bastard" down they should rub his head into the sand, and proceeded to do so. Wong had sand in his ears, eyes and nostrils. This caused him to "do his block", and he threw McCissock out of the pit. The instructor said he was delighted to see some spirit from Wong, and rushed back in to grapple with him once more. After he was thrown out three times, McCissock said, "Okay, Wong, you're a better man than I am Gunga Din."

Bowditch also went to Camp Z near Sydney, where emphasis was on weaponry, explosives, navigation, map reading, cliff climbing, long distance running and living off the land, which included eating bats. At the Richmond RAAF base in NSW, Bowditch attended the Australian Parachute Training Unit and qualified as a parachutist.

After all the training they were sent in groups to be briefed and further evaluated at the Batman Avenue, Melbourne, headquarters of the secret Z Special Unit organisation, where he met Major (later Lieut. Colonel) Ivan Lyon, MBE, DSO, of the Gordon Highlanders, and Lieutenant Davidson, DSO, RNVR, who organised operations in Europe after the Dunkirk catastrophe. Bowditch's group received a preliminary briefing from Major Lyon for a special operation behind the enemy lines. Both Lyon and Davidson were inspirational men, said Bowditch, who convinced you of your ability to succeed and the importance of your part in the war effort. Both men had led the incredibly successful Operation Jaywick in which the small vessel *Krait* sailed from Perth to Singapore with a raiding party and blew up shipping with limpet mines.

Then in June 1944 Bowditch was in a group of six flown to Darwin to the East Arm flying boat base which was used by intelligence groups. After some training in the harbour, they assembled their equipment, folboats (light, folding, two-man canoes), guns, explosives, ammunition, food and radios which were loaded aboard the Dutch submarine *K XIV*. Leader of the operation was Lieutenant V.D. "Dave" Prentiss, who at 6ft 4inches Bowditch felt was too big for paddling a small canoe. Their destination was

Dutch Submarine of the K XIV Class believed to be that which took
Bowditch and his group into Batanta Island in Dutch New Guinea
(now West Papua).

Batanta Island, Dutch New Guinea, where they were to watch
Sorong Harbour, a busy Japanese port, and a nearby airfield where
Betty bombers were based which could have been used to attack
places as far away as Townsville.

As the submarine stealthily approached their destination the
crew was forced to spend 18 hours on the bottom in cramped and
stifling conditions with enemy patrol vessels moving overhead.
Eventually the submarine surfaced, the canoes were prepared on
deck and the commandos paddled off into the unknown. After
three days' hard paddling they set up an observation post high on
Batanta Island and supplied radio messages about enemy shipping
and aircraft movements which were relayed back to Batchelor, near
Darwin. Then under the cover of darkness, Bowditch paddled
into Sorong Harbour and attached mines to shipping. He heard
explosions later but was unable to find out what damage had been
done. At night the Japanese often were out patching up the runways
which had been bombed; Jim's group could hear machinery
and pinpoint its location. The information they radioed through
enabled further bombing raids. The Japanese knew they were there
and tried to hunt them down.

At times the commandos used a heavily wooded island near
the airstrip as a daytime resting spot, as much of their work involved
exploring at night. The island afforded the opportunity to swim
and relax while always being on the alert. Bowditch and another
operative, Stan Taylor, a house painter from Sydney, paddled to
the pleasant island one day and found a slit trench and cans from a
Japanese party which had been on patrol.

A supply drop to them included six bottles of Johnnie Walker Black Label whisky. The resultant booze up brought some personal tensions to the surface and there were clashes with Captain Prentiss. Bowditch wrote that he and two others "nearly shot Captain Prentiss."

The Australian commandos were in the area from 20 June to 28 September 1944 when they were taken out by PT boats crewed by young, trigger-happy Americans who shot up huts along the way. Bowditch remonstrated with the Americans for strafing the huts saying that they probably belonged to "natives" friendly towards the Allies. At the American base the party was feted and then flown back to Townsville for debriefing. In December, Bowditch was again charged for non-military conduct and his service record shows he was "severely reprimanded" by the commanding officer.

In another unusual wartime operation, Bowditch was sent to a Z Special Unit establishment near Toowoomba with operative George Carter, a former Victorian wrestling champion, to develop a new technique of parachuting men from Liberator bombers. Parachute drops were usually made from DC3 aircraft and when the Japanese saw one of these planes they went on the alert for parachutists. It also made them wonder if there were Allied troops on the ground receiving supplies. It was thought that a good way to insert small groups of operatives into an area would be to have them drop from a bomber. The bomber could fly into a target, unload some bombs, and on the way out drop parachutists for behind-the-line operations. Bowditch and Carter first practised sliding out of a chute in the bottom of a fuselage mock-up. Then came the real test but after a night of heavy drinking in the mess, Bowditch was not feeling the best, and when he entered the chute he jumped prematurely from the bomber, ending up miles from the drop target. He made his way to a road, was picked up by a farmer and asked to be taken to the nearest pub. While the military were out trying to find their missing parachutist he was having a "hair of the dog". Carter, who revelled in physical fitness, enjoyed the jumps more than Bowditch. And he was such a good chess player that he played Bowditch with his back turned.

During a break in parachuting tests they got a lift into Toowoomba with an officer Bowditch described as a real "Colonel Blimp" type; fat, pompous and nasty. The officer, who had a chauffeur driven car, picked up a young girlfriend and took her to the pictures. Carter and Bowditch headed to the pub. When they ran out of drinking money, Bowditch went to the picture theatre and got them to flash a message across the screen for the officer.

The officer, probably thinking there was an invasion on, rushed out and was most annoyed when Bowditch bit him for some drinking money. Driving back to camp in the officer's car, Bowditch asked the driver to stop so he could relieve himself. The gruff officer told the man to drive on. Bowditch reached across and grabbed the driver by the throat and the car skidded to a halt. Jim jumped from the car, climbed up on the bonnet, and urinated on the windscreen. He got back in and they drove off without a word being said by the officer, who just stared straight ahead.

The next day Bowditch was told a recommendation had been made to send him to officers' training college, but he had blown it by urinating on the officer's car the night before. Even though he missed the opportunity to become an officer and a gentleman, he described the urination as one of the most satisfying pisses in his life. In one grand act it had shown the officer what he felt about his chauffeur, his car and his "dolly bird".

Bowditch was sent to Morotai in the Philippines and worked with Americans who were flying "Black Cats", Catalinas painted black. The slow, highly manoeuvrable amphibians were used to pluck frightened fishermen from their boats to gain intelligence about the Japanese. Ammunition barges were also attacked and while the Americans used their guns and bombs on the Japanese, Bowditch hurled down grenades. Though slow moving, the Catalinas often flew on the deck, skimming across the water at night to surprise the enemy. One of the men who worked with him as an interpreter was Malay operative Ali bin Saleh, who had been indentured into the Australian pearling industry at Broome when he was a teenager. During the war he trained in Perth, then became a member of Z Special Unit, going on dangerous missions in the islands. He was especially useful for communicating with and interrogating locals.

While serving with the Americans, Bowditch was impressed by their massive workshops. The American habit of only drinking tea cold and occasionally putting an egg into a glass of beer surprised him. Despite all his troubles with officers and frequent fines, he was promoted to sergeant in January 1945. This was a clear indication that Bowditch, despite all his scrapes, was seen as a capable leader of men.

Several times Bowditch spoke as if he had been considered for or even participated in early selection trials for Operation Rimau (The Tiger), the ill-fated raid on Singapore shipping.

In brief statements, Bowditch indicated he had been dropped or rejected because he had trouble with his eustachian tubes, lost his sense of direction when submerged and became seasick. He implied that he and several others had been rejected. While no confirmation of his involvement in training for Rimau could be found, Jack Sue said that because of secrecy at the time, it was possible that he could have gone through selection and elimination trials.

Operation Rimau was similar to the earlier highly successful Operation Jaywick. Instead of using canoes as had been the case in Jaywick, Rimau was provided with battery powered one-man submersibles known as Sleeping Beauties (SB's) which were 12 feet (3.7 metres) long. Bowditch said they were hard to control, like trying to ride a motorbike underwater was how he described it. The operator, wearing a kind of frogman's suit with a mask and oxygen container, sat on the SB. There was a half steering wheel and a control panel. The idea was that the SB porpoised along, the rider coming to the surface to see where he was going and then diving. Once they got next to ships limpet mines were then to be attached. At the outset of training, it was made clear to all the men that if they found the submersibles hard to handle or had any other problems, nothing would be held against them for pulling out.

As an indication of the dangerous and audacious nature of the raid, the British submarine HMS *Porpoise* took the raiding party and their 15 submersibles into the attack zone, a Chinese junk was seized and the commandos loaded their gear on the vessel and sailed for Singapore; the captured Malay crew from the junk were transported to Perth aboard the submarine. A patrol vessel was encountered and its crew, except for one who survived and raised the alarm, were killed with machine guns fitted with silencers.

The Japanese eventually captured several of the raiders, who the enemy regarded as heroes because of their audacious planned attack on Singapore. In fact, the Japanese commander-in-chief, General Seishiro Itagaki, addressing the field staff of the 7th Area Army, said he felt shamed by the brave actions of the Rimau party, whom he described as heroes. For the Japanese to win the war, they had to be braver than these men. Because the captured men were regarded by the Japanese as heroes, they were beheaded in July 1945, beheading being considered a more noble death than other forms of execution. The war ended a month later.

While running to catch a train for another dangerous operation, Bowditch was stopped by a military policeman who said his jacket was not done up properly. Jim had an angry exchange with the MP and, surrounded by a ring of cheering soldiers, slugged it out with the officious man, eventually knocking him down. Bowditch was arrested by police and said a burly detective took him into a room and beat him up. Each time Bowditch fell to the floor, the tough detective supposedly said, "There's the brave Digger." Bowditch had enough sense to realise he was in serious trouble and did not fight back. After that episode, a Z Special Unit officer told Bowditch he was more valuable behind enemy lines and not to slug it out in Australia. Jim replied that he did not go looking for trouble and that the MP had chipped him over a trivial thing like a button.

The mission involved gaining pre-invasion information on Tarakan, Borneo, including the position of a well-hidden gun which had been a problem for Allied shipping. Two parties were flown in by Catalina on 24 April 1945. The plane had to touch down a long distance from the island so it would not be seen by the enemy and some hard paddling followed in folboats. One group became lost and returned empty handed. Bowditch and his offsider, Ali bin Saleh, however, got ashore. Leaving the boat with bin Saleh, who had instructions to pull out if he did not return by a certain time, Bowditch continued alone. Apart from the fact that he was on an island with 2000 fanatical Japanese, anti-tank mines were strewn about the place. Tarakan, 24 km from north to south and 16 km from east to west, was a strategic location with some of the world's highest quality oil and an airbase from which the Allies could provide support for larger operations. The Japanese knew an invasion would come soon. To prevent native slave labour from escaping their feet were mutilated.

Fortunately for Bowditch, he came upon a party of Japanese soldiers who had been out either swimming or hunting pigs, and he shadowed them. They eventually took a path which led to the gun emplacement. Stealthily following, Jim came around a bend in the path and was suddenly confronted by an armed guard. Instantly, he smashed the butt of his carbine into the startled guard's chin and cut his throat. "I could have shot him, but it would have given the game away. The butt of my carbine took half his head away. I panicked, and carved up his face, back and thighs with my knife in the hope the Japanese would think that he had been killed by a native. The guard seemed to be a young boy who looked no more than 14; he could have been a Korean. Although I killed lots of people, the mutilation of that boy stuck in my mind."

His revulsion at the grisly work he did on the guard did not stop him from completing the mission. He discovered that there were two guns, not one, hidden under a limestone cliff and was able to get within six metres of them. A map he drew pinpointed the guns. After three days he and bin Saleh withdrew from the island. Unfortunately, a radio failure prevented the invaluable information they had gathered being passed on until three days after the invasion began. The May 1945 invasion was the most ambitious coordinated operation by Australian forces in the Pacific war. During the battle, 225 Australians were killed and 669 wounded. Japanese killed were 1504. Flame throwers were used to burn the defenders out of bunkers and foxholes.

Between 24 April and 2 June 1945 Bowditch saw action in British North Borneo and took part in an enemy deception in support of the 9th Australian Division's Operation Oboe VI. This involved launching raids to mask Brunei invasion plans, particularly that of Balikpapan. As part of Operation Stallion, Prentiss, Bowditch, Carter and bin Saleh, were flown out in Catalinas to pick up intelligence from the locals. Soon after, on 6 July, Bowditch was a member of a party which parachuted into the Mahakan River lakes area of Dutch Borneo for a special operation. As the leader of a sub-party of two white men and 30 native guerillas, he organised raids against the Japanese falling back from the Balikpapan invasion, harassing them and blowing up their food and ammunition dumps. The party had many dealings with Dayaks, who lived in long houses and used blowpipes. When the people of a Dayak village thought one of their own had given information to the Japanese about Bowditch's party, they beheaded him. Proboscis monkeys, so named because of their large noses, were common in the area. They became known as "Bowditch monkeys", causing many jokes among his colleagues and local tribesmen.

A holy man, who claimed he could not be killed, attached himself to the group. This revered man raised the alarm when some Japanese barges came into view. Bowditch's friend Stan Taylor fired his Bren gun from between the legs of the holy man who just stood there pointing at the enemy. In the fierce battle which followed the holy man plunged into the river and was never seen again. As a result of this battle Taylor later received the Military Medal. One of the guerillas was a political activist who said he wanted the Dutch out of his country. Bowditch had a lot of time for him. They had long talks and became close friends.

On instruction, Bowditch was sent to reinforce another commando group at the mouth of the Kahala River, which was being heavily engaged by a Japanese patrol sent out from Moentai to destroy them. Official records said Sergeant Bowditch was mainly instrumental in killing 30 of the Japanese and pinning down the remainder until they were destroyed. On that occasion Bowditch said he got the jump on the Japanese who were in canoes and quickly killed about 15 of them with a sub-machine gun. He pursued the survivors and wiped them out in fierce battles. During that operation a plane was called in to shoot up the Japanese but began to fire on Bowditch's party. He sprang behind a coconut tree and a bullet from the plane split it wide open. He immediately jumped to his feet, grabbed a mortar and fired off a smoke shell into the area that the plane should have been strafing. The pilot realised his error and turned his fire on the enemy.

Aircraft, unfortunately, often shot up the wrong village. Bowditch went to one which had been mistakenly raked by Allied planes and found several people dead, a woman with a hole in her arm and a young boy who had been shot in the foot. The boy's foot had been split in two and turned gangrenous. In a bid to save the boy's life, Bowditch took a knife and cut off most of the foot, leaving the big toe intact. Then he called in a Catalina and had the wounded boy and woman evacuated to Balikpapan. Doctors amputated the boy's leg at the thigh, but he lived. A Dutch captain was parachuted in as the fighting died down and he caused tension in the party because of his arrogance. Bowditch had many dealings with native chiefs in Borneo and it was clear that they disliked the Dutch intensely. While he had found the continental Dutch he met on submarines in which he travelled easy to get on with, the colonial Dutch raised his hackles by being arrogant and harsh on the natives. Colonial whites, Dutch and English, were a problem, he said.

Before the commandos were taken out by flying boat, the Dutch captain insisted they dump all their ammunition and supplies where they could not be used by the locals. Bowditch alerted villagers with whom he had been working and made arrangements to dump the supplies, which included American carbines, mortars, Bren guns, pistols, hand grenades and thousands of rounds of ammunition, in a stream from which they could easily be retrieved. Said Bowditch: "I don't suppose the Australian Army leaders would be happy to know that some of our weapons were used to oust the Dutch. No doubt some Dutchmen bit the dust because of what we did." Apart from being sympathetic to their cause, Bowditch thought it would have been wrong to leave people without weapons where there were still many desperate, armed Japanese.

In Balikpapan, his dislike for the Dutch intensified when he heard that the political activist whom he had befriended had been shot by Dutch police. "I don't know why he was killed," said Bowditch, "but I suspect he probably said something against the Dutch."

Even when Bowditch was brought home to Australia and the war was over, the army insisted on delaying his demobilisation. He was made into an "escort sergeant", charged with keeping troops in order who were returning home to Tasmania by ship

By the KING'S Order the name of
Sjt J Bowditch
"Z" Special Unit
was published in the Commonwealth Gazette on
21st February, 1946,
as mentioned in a Despatch for distinguished service.
I am charged to record
His Majesty's high appreciation.

F. M. Forde

Minister of State for the Army.

Two months before his demobilisation Jim's citation for a Mention in Despatches (MID), a significant military honour, was published. Bowditch family collection.

from Melbourne. The troops making the voyage were told by an officer at the start that Sergeant Bowditch would handle any trouble makers. They were also advised not to misjudge Sergeant Bowditch because of his size as he had been in Z Special Unit. Bowditch spent a lot of time in his cabin boozing and brooding about the way the army had treated him. The tame task of escorting soldiers home made him feel bitter about being kept in uniform. Rightly, he felt he had done his bit for the war effort and each trip to Tasmania involved a bout of seasickness. He felt the army was acting in a malicious way, getting at him right to the end for bucking authority throughout his service. At war's end many commandos were offered jobs as security men on wharves and industrial sites. Bowditch would not have any of this as it sounded too much like working for the army. During the war, said Bowditch, unionists had often been portrayed to servicemen as communist traitors.

7. FREE AT LAST

At long last, he was discharged on 24 April 1946, out of uniform and living in Melbourne. Politics became one of his new interests and he made contact with members of the Australian Labor Party. Through them he met Prime Minister Ben Chifley and Minister for Post-War Reconstruction, John Dedman

For a time he was employed in the Repatriation Department as a clerk, but found it a soul-destroying job with lurks being worked all over the place. He underwent a psychiatric examination and some friends advised him beforehand that if he put on a bit of an act and indicated he was "bent", he could get a pension. Apparently he was told, as if he did not already know, that he appeared to have a highly developed antipathy to authority.

While staying in a boarding house he met and became interested in another resident, red-headed Iris Nellie Neal Hargreaves, daughter of a colonel. According to Bowditch, she had argued with her mother and moved away from home. She and Jim went out together and eventually married.

To escape the boredom of the Repatriation Department Jim went to Brisbane where he stayed in a boarding house and scanned the situations vacant looking for a job. The ex-commando then went from door to door selling Safe Way iron stands for four and sixpence (45 cents) each, his profit being a shilling on each one. In one day alone he sold 32 iron stands. Sales were helped by publicity about several house fires started by hot irons. Bowditch practised with an iron and a stand until he could toss an iron from any angle and it fell into place on the stand. It was a bit like a gun fighter becoming dexterous with his shooting iron. So proficient was he at selling iron stands that the slick operator in charge of the distribution of the stands wanted Jim to teach other salesmen.

Hearing that Burns Philp had a warehouse full of faulty floor mops that were being dumped, Bowditch went and inspected them. He discovered that due to a manufacturing fault there was not enough wire holding the mop head in place, but with a bit of twisting they could be fixed. So he became the proud and anxious owner of a large number of mops which he also offered from door to door for a substantial profit. While on the sales beat he wore his old army boots, which he found handy for kicking dogs which rushed out at him. One of his slick sales practices was to stand admiring some flower or shrub as the lady of the house opened the door. Willing to try his hand at anything, he also sold insurance and toilet chemicals.

One day Bowditch met an old army buddy in Brisbane and they headed for a pub. Later they caught a tram to go to another hotel. His friend suddenly jumped from the tram, sprinted across to a man who was standing on the footpath and king hit him. When the man fell to the ground he was kicked. Then Jim's friend ran back to the tram. When Bowditch asked him what had prompted the attack, he was told the victim had been a sadistic guard in a military prison and Jim's friend had promised to get even with him if they ever met again in civilian life.

A position was advertised for a Moreton Island lighthouse keeper who could operate a radio, do Morse code and read ships' flags. Bowditch made a successful application. Iris came up from Melbourne and joined him on the island. Life on the three-man station helped Bowditch to unwind and he did much reading. Food supplies were received every 17 days. One of the light-keepers drank rum neat saying it had cauterised a bad ulcer from which he had suffered. During his time on the island Bowditch began writing letters to the ALP on issues he felt the party should be concerned about. However, Iris became bored with the isolation and they returned to Melbourne.

An ASIO basic report compiled on Bowditch in 1950 said that after the war he had worked as a salesman on his own behalf and then for C. Deakin and Co, Brisbane, until November 1947 when he was engaged as a clerk for the "Repatriation Commission", Melbourne. From there, the report, making no mention of his time as a lighthouse keeper, said he had transferred to the Department of Works and Housing.

According to Bowditch, Iris did not know much about politics and her parents were Tories. Bowditch resumed contact with Labor people in Melbourne and was told by Minister Dedman himself that the government was planning a soldier settlement in Central Australia.

This information prompted Jim to take an animal husbandry correspondence course to achieve the long-held desire to become a farmer. Through his father-in-law's influence, he was able to obtain a job as paymaster in the Alice Springs office of the Works and Housing Department. The idea behind going to Alice was for Bowditch to get in on the ground floor of the proposed soldier settlement scheme and have a cattle station of his own. Time would show that he was not destined to be a cattleman. In any case, the soldier settler scheme for Central Australia did not eventuate.

8. NO TOWN
LIKE ALICE

Alice Springs, with a population of about 2000, was a frontier town when Jim and Iris Bowditch arrived in 1948. There was a severe housing shortage and like the rest of Australia building materials were hard to get. They were allocated a tiny residence in Parsons Street and considered themselves lucky to have such accommodation. Some residents were strong minded, even dogmatic, with a vision not only for the town but the entire Northern Territory. Many residents resented with a passion the remote administrative control from Darwin and Canberra.

A major event during that year was the opening of the ABC radio station in Alice because shortwave reception had been poor and added to the town's feeling of isolation. The cost of living was high, there being little in the way of fresh fruit and vegetables and people made do with powdered milk. About the only commodity in abundance was meat, which came from local cattle stations.

Resident in town was the wartime Australian supremo of Alice Springs, Brigadier Noel Loutit, who ran a mixed goods store. During the war, Alice had been a large military base for Australians and Americans and supplies railed to the town were transported in large convoys up the Stuart Highway to Darwin and the many camps in the Top End. There were 8500 men and 3500 trucks based in Alice. Australian troops became restless, a situation caused by boredom, a severe shortage of female company, an unfavourable comparison with the conditions enjoyed by American troops and the unlikelihood of any contact with the enemy. The men rioted through town streets, smashing some shop windows; a car was driven through the officers' mess and stones were thrown on the roof of the nursing sisters' quarters.

Officers were abused and anybody who got in their way was beaten up. Brigadier Loutit, a short man, bravely mounted a box and addressed the angry men, telling them how soldiers had endured terrible conditions in the trenches during WW1. In times of war, he told the disgruntled men, they had to go without home comforts. To a man, the mob roared out that this was "bullshit" because he had a girlfriend in town, Mona Minahan. A military policeman stood next to Loutit and said he would shoot anybody between the eyes if they attacked the officer. This foolish statement resulted in about 50 men rushing in and knocking the MP to the ground. As a result of the riot steps were taken to provide more entertainment for the troops. Captain C.J. White, an amenities officer, started a daily newspaper known as the *Mulga*, which provided news from home, race tips and details of town functions.

Alice had become the civil capital of the Northern Territory in 1942 when the Administrator, Aubrey Abbott, and his wife moved down from Darwin after the Japanese bombing. They lived in a building called The Residency. The Administrator soon found himself in conflict with Brigadier Loutit, nicknamed the "Busy Bee". Loutit treated Abbott with scorn and proudly claimed to have cut off the Administrator's chocolate frog supply from the army canteen. A request by the Administrator to have an army band play God Save the King, when he was to appear at a function, was also vetoed by Loutit. Loutit wrote regular critical reports on Abbott which were forwarded to his superiors in Darwin who looked forward to them, finding them highly entertaining. Abbott also wrote reports critical of Loutit. Late in life Loutit, living in Adelaide, told me he had written to the Governor-General during the war trying to get Abbott sacked. "He [Abbott] was an obstructionist," said Loutit. "I could not tolerate that." With obvious relish, he repeated how he had stopped Abbott's chocolate frog supply.

When the Bowditches came to Alice it was a racist town. Many Territory Aborigines, full-bloods and half-castes, had served in the war, but in peacetime they were treated as if they did not exist. Aborigines in Alice had to be out of the town area at night. Some European residents who went to Alice after the war said they did not realise that Aborigines had been banned from the town area at night; they just thought they had been "scared of the dark."

Aborigines walking down a street often stepped aside or went to the other side of the road when they saw Europeans coming.

Half-castes lived at a place called The Bungalow Reserve, with poor housing and services. This was where Aboriginal activist the late Charles Perkins lived for some time. His mother, Hettie, was employed there as a cook when the Bowditches arrived in Alice. While Aborigines were "non-people" with virtually no rights, she, surprisingly, was listed on the 1949 electoral roll as Hetty [sic] Perkins, domestic. Most were not included in the census, did not vote, could not own land, and had to apply for a certificate of exemption which allowed Aborigines to be in towns, known colloquially as 'dog tags' and which had to be carried at all times if they wanted to drink liquor. People at The Bungalow could not be outside the reserve between 8pm and 5am without written permission of a Protector, under threat of one month's imprisonment.

Just like America, where oppressed Afro-Americans took to boxing, Aborigines in Alice tied on the gloves for moments of rare glory and community applause. Boxing matches took place each Sunday night in a theatre. As part of the boxing entertainment four young Aborigines were regularly blindfolded and placed in the ring to swing wildly at each other. One of those who took an interest in the boxers and other Aboriginal athletes when he came to Alice was the nomadic writer D'Arcy Niland, husband of author Ruth Park.

Niland had been named after the tragic Australian boxer Les Darcy, who died in America. It seems Bowditch met the author, who was in a travelling boxing troupe which passed through Alice. During his time in Alice, Niland refereed bouts and wrote boxing notes for the local newspaper. According to Bowditch, Niland had also been impressed with the skills of Aboriginal athletes. Bowditch said there were many fine Aboriginal athletes in Alice in those days. One in particular could "run like the wind", and it had saddened Bowditch to see him, years later, in Katherine, a shadow of his former self, on the grog.

Apart from treating Aborigines appallingly, as did the rest of the nation, Alice was also xenophobic about some European residents, referred to as "foreigners". In that early post-war period new residents were arriving and there were visitors, some of them VIPs, from all over the world. The author Nevil Shute (Norway) passed through doing research for his book *A Town like Alice*, which was later made into a film. The philosopher and peace activist Bertrand Russell was another who came to town.

The person occupying The Residency, regarded locally as a kind of government house when the Bowditches were in Alice, was veterinary scientist Colonel Alfred Lionel Rose. He headed the Animal Industry Department and represented the Administrator in the Centre. Jim had been in town only a short time when he nearly collided with Rose in the street. At the time the colonel was wearing a turned up hat like that worn by the Light Horse Brigade; a khaki shirt on which there were some "gongs" (medals); Bombay bloomers; long socks on which there were boy scout-like tabs, something to do with a Scottish regiment with which he was associated; and from the top of his nose' there was a big hair, about six inches long, which curved back towards his forehead. Rose shouted something at Jim and reeled away. Bowditch thought it had to be one of the town's characters. When he described this individual to people he knew and asked who he was, they replied that he was the top man in town, the Administrator's representative, and that he lived in the seat of power, The Residency.

Over the years Jim got to know Rose well. He described him as a legendary figure—eccentric, haughty, irrepressible, studious, tough, at times cold and a veterinary scientist of great renown. Entirely his own person, a devoted father and a man who could not tolerate, and quickly detected "bullshit", he was admired and loved by many people in the town. The son of a minister of religion, he had served in World War I. He was a veterinary officer at Cootamundra in NSW from 1928–40; served in Light Horse regiments and Militia 1930–40 and during World War II served in armour and as a staff officer for Combined Operations in the Middle East, New Guinea and the Netherlands East Indies. His wife, Helen, died early during his time in Alice leaving him with a son and two daughters.

Bowditch recalled a major social event, a fancy dress ball, in the Commonwealth Bank staff quarters, where Rose caused an uproar. Like so many isolated centres, women were fashion conscious and dressed up for special social events. In the case of the ball the women had gone to much trouble and expense making elaborate gowns and paying a lot of attention to their hairstyles and makeup. It was attended by leading citizen, public servants, businessmen, cattlemen and their wives. Rose turned up during the evening dressed as a sheik draped in a sheet, wearing a turban. There was a loud cheer as he joined the happy throng but much to their surprise and horror, he pulled a fire extinguisher from under his sheet and sprayed the revellers. Women shrieked as the foam ruined both gowns and coiffures. Some men grabbed him and took him back to The Residency. Another time, again clad in a bedsheet, Rose appeared at a party and cried out, "Oil, oil for the lamps of China!"

Driving under the influence of liquor cost him 20 pounds in a case in which Rose represented himself in court. Charged with negligent driving after an accident with his car, he said a fly had flown into his face and distracted him. His fine was paid by "admirers".

On one occasion some important people were entertained at The Residency and Rose climbed on the roof and dropped bottles down the chimney. After a day at the races it was reported that the good colonel had again clambered on the roof of The Residency and fired random shots from a .303 rifle. Swinging from a chandelier was also claimed. A pair of women's panties was seen fluttering from the flagpole at The Residency during a vice-regal visit by Lord and Lady Slim. The Slims loved the Centre and when they came to town for a debutantes' ball, Lady Slim had a sore back. At the function a heater was placed nearby to ease the pain. The piece de resistance at the major social event was a swan made from ice on a bed of red roses, representing the Red Centre, with an electric light underneath which Lady Slim was required to switch on. When Lady Slim turned the light on the hall blacked out because a fuse blew. There were no spares in the building and people sat in the dark waiting for the lights to come back on. In the gloom, a Mrs East, offered Lord Slim some sartees which were nearby. He replied that he used to be given sartees for breakfast in India. While the embarrassing situation continued, Reg Harris, an electrician, who contributed much to community life in the town, rushed around and got the lights back on again.

In readiness for a visit by Slim's predecessor as Governor-General, the Duke of Gloucester, the hot water service at The Residency was improved. However, when the Duke turned on the hot water the whole town blacked out. For some strange reason several residents threw stones on the roof of The Residency during that visit.

The peculiar goings on at The Residency seemed never-ending, and Bowditch was involved in one memorable event involving Colonel Rose and the eminent British writer and commentator, Malcolm Muggeridge, who came to Alice as a VIP and stayed at The Residency.

Rose invited Bowditch to come to the Residency and see Muggeridge. Straight talking as ever, Rose told Bowditch that he (Jim), being "a bit of a Commie", would probably enjoy Muggeridge. Muggeridge, he told Jim, was a bit that way inclined and liked airing his views. In fact, Muggeridge was inclined to the right and had been a wartime British spy. Bowditch arrived at The Residency and began talking to Muggeridge. Rose, who had been drinking, shuffled in, grunted and studiously avoided them while reading a book by Winston Churchill. Muggeridge became enraged by Rose's behaviour, and gave him a dressing down about his bad manners. He told Rose that he would let Canberra know about the treatment he had received at The Residency. Diplomatically, Rose said, "I am reading from a work by a better man than you will ever be. I don't give a damn what you tell the Minister." Muggeridge packed his belongings and Bowditch drove him to Underdown's pub. Returning to The Residency, Bowditch proceeded to give Rose a blast and told him he could get into all kinds of official strife, but he did not care.

While Lord and Lady Slim were settling in for the night at The Residency, Rose knocked on the door and presented them with a jerry (chamber pot) saying they would probably need it during the night.

Rose headed a political group called the North Australia Party, akin to the Country Party, which was nicknamed the Nappy Party. When he became a member of the NT Legislative Council he livened up proceedings. On one occasion, he was half sitting in the chamber with a glass of rum in hand when he said, "All I can say is that the Director of Lands is a plain bastard." The Director rose and said, "I object to being called plain."

During a royal visit, Rose received a degree of national notoriety when he silenced the hubbub of the assembled loyal throng by telling them to "Shut up!" Rose was eventually removed from The Residency. After moving from the posh pad, Rose gave his address in *Who's Who* as "The Wurley", an Aboriginal bush shelter. When Rose proposed exterminating all wild buffaloes in the Territory to prevent the spread of stock diseases, Bowditch questioned the idea. This resulted in Rose berating him and asking for evidence of his veterinary science qualifications. Bowditch acknowledged that Rose was right; he probably atoned for his blunder when he wrote an editorial praising Rose on his retirement, saying the colonel deserved recognition from the government for his work in the national interest, particularly in the pastoral industry. While Rose was really more of a larrikin than Bowditch at that stage, he was fondly regarded probably because he was part of the establishment. In Bowditch's case, he increasingly challenged authority and became unpopular.

9. MAN OF ACTION

Bowditch almost took the Alice by storm, becoming involved in a wide range of activities—politics, debating, amateur theatre, cricket and union work. His activities attracted the close attention of the Australian Security and Intelligence Organisation (ASIO).

The Bowditches became "foster uncle and auntie" to some half-caste girls from the Anglican St Mary's hostel, took children home at weekends and bought them clothes. Iris worked as a comptometrist, or operator of an early type of adding machine, and helped a woman run ballet classes; she also assisted with debutante balls.

Always up early, Jim wondered at the morning glory of Alice Springs with its striking colours, crisp air and ranges. For a time, the beauty of the place mesmerised him and he was not conscious of the town's less attractive social aspects. Soon after his arrival he took to freelance writing, sending articles about the town to southern newspapers and contributed items to the local paper, the *Centralian Advocate*. An early story he wrote for the southern press was about the Aboriginal drinking problem, The article, which predicted the problem would get worse, was illustrated and showed a furtive looking white man passing a bottle of wine to an Aborigine.

The *Advocate* had not been in existence for long and strongly represented and reflected the views of the locals. The first souvenir edition—12 pages—had been published on 24 May 1947. The paper's start had led to the demise of a community publication *Dead Heart* which had run for seven months and ended with number 30. Co-editors of that publication had been Les Penhall, who in the year 2000 would be an important witness in the "Stolen Generation" court case in Darwin, Miss Buchanan and F.A. Gubbins. The proprietor and editor of the *Advocate* was a colourful person, Charles Henry "Pop" Chapman, a gnome of a man with a foghorn voice, who had mined at The Granites in the Tanami Desert in the 1930s and used to drive his Humber Snipe the 540 km into Alice with up to $30,000 worth of gold packed in powdered milk and treacle tins. A dynamic individual, he wanted to start an air beef enterprise and build a hotel at The Granites, but failed to get approval from the government, which angered him. He grew vegetables while at The Granites, had his own swimming pool and when he moved to Alice experimented with growing a variety of vegetables and fruit trees, having much success with apples. He built himself a house in Alice at Heavitree Gap called The Pearly

Gates, which also had a swimming pool; it later became the Pitchi Ritchi museum and sanctuary.

Chapman had little respect for the sitting independent federal MP for the Northern Territory, Adair Macalister "Chill" Blain. As a surveyor, Blain had done a lot of work in the NT, including at The Granites goldfield. In 1933 he headed an expedition into western Arnhem Land to the head of the Liverpool River to report on agricultural and pastoral possibilities. A veteran of both World Wars, he spent from February 1942 to August 1945 a prisoner of the Japanese in Changi, Sandakan, Kuching and Outram Road prisons. After he returned to politics, Labor attacked him in parliament claiming he had used his parliamentary gold pass to get special privileges in Japanese prison camps. The attack backfired because it was disclosed Blain had knocked out gold fillings from his teeth to bribe guards to get special concessions and treatment for sick and injured comrades.

The *Advocate* demanded to know what Blain had done for the Territory, saying he seemed to be a "silent worker". An extraordinary article in the first edition said the MHR, under parliamentary privilege, had claimed that he had been run off a mining lease at the point of a gun. The "culprit" had not owned a rifle at the time, said the paper, so it must have been an imaginary rifle, nevertheless "let bygones be bygones." It added: "But remember, the imaginary rifle is still loaded and only attention to Territory needs will assure the temper of the villain who does not hold it." This was a clear warning to the sitting member that the new paper would fire paper bullets at him if he did not work for the benefit of the Territory. It also seemed to indicate "Pop" Chapman could have had an altercation with Blain over a mining lease.

As a paymaster in a government department, Jim's work was not onerous. His boss was the resident engineer, D.D. (David Douglas) Smith, the initials also said to stand for Doctor of Divinity and Dashing and Daring. Also known as the King of Alice Springs because he headed the most important government department, Smith was married to a former Miss Tasmania beauty queen. He played a major part in surveying the route for the railway from

Oodnadatta to Alice Springs and was involved in building the wartime road from Alice to Darwin, a feat for which Americans were often erroneously given the sole credit. Like so many Centralians, Smith, at times described as a James Cagney tough guy, had strong views and a vision for the development of the Northern Territory. A member of the NT Development League, Smith in 1944 wrote a long document outlining how he thought the NT could and should be developed.

At the outset, he said it had taken a war to alert the nation to the importance of the Territory, Australia's front door. His blueprint for the advancement of the Territory included an extensive network of railway lines, arterial roads, re-afforestation, mining, fishing and pearling. On tourism, he foresaw a bright future and pointed out that in Canada it was a huge moneymaker. For the NT to develop the way he outlined, he said it would require a man with the courage of Cecil Rhodes, the entrepreneur who was said to have done more than any other to expand the British Empire. A man whose initials were taken to mean Dashing and Daring could well have been the Cecil Rhodes of the NT if given his way. Smith had the grand vision, the practical Territory experience and the eagerness to do great things. Apart from those qualifications, he wore the head attire of great adventurers and pioneers, a pith helmet. Smith became a member of the Legislative Council and strongly put his views for Territory development.

10. THE TREASONOUS NEWSPAPER

Because of his interest in politics, Bowditch soon became president of the ALP and at an early date was approached to stand for the NT seat in the House of Representatives. He declined to nominate, saying that he was just a recent "blow in" and that he felt John "Jock" Nelson, son of Harold Nelson, the Territory's first MHR, was the right person for the job. Jock had been educated at Pine Creek and Darwin. In Darwin he had worked as a newspaper boy.

After a period working as a jackeroo, Nelson became a bore-sinking contractor and agent in Alice Springs. He had been elected to the NT Legislative Council in 1947. With Bowditch playing a large part in his election campaign in the Centre, Nelson in 1949 stood for the NT seat in the House of Representatives against the incumbent, Blain.

In October 1949, Blain, in one of his last parliamentary speeches, took the opportunity to appeal to the electorate, belittle Nelson and settle a few scores with the "treacherous" communists of Darwin. Showing that he was concerned about conditions for NT government employees, he said he had spoken to "Mr Bowditch" about a justifiable increase to clerks' pay because of a 25 per cent increase in rail freight and ticket charges. Then Blain attacked Nelson and the *Northern Standard* newspaper in Darwin, which he said was run by communists. "I sympathise with this young fellow [Nelson] who has been nominated as the Australian Labor Party candidate for the forthcoming general election," said Blain. His candidature was being sponsored by the *Northern Standard*, a "treasonous paper". Blain said the Minister for the Interior knew that Nelson, in his innocence, was being used by communists. This "young man" Nelson, unfortunately, did not realise that he was being used by the communists. "That young fellow is playing with fire in allowing his candidature to be sponsored in this treasonous paper, the *Northern Standard*," Blain said.

The paper, he continued, had been communist controlled ever since the former editor, Don McKinnon, had been "kicked out" of the union executive, which was "95 per cent communists." He hastened to add that this percentage did not apply to the rank and file. Blain demanded to know how the *Standard* obtained printing machinery from the army "for a song" after the war. (The answer was simple: during the war, thearmy had taken over the newspaper building and its plant was used to print the *Army News*.) In calling for a Security Service Branch to be opened in Darwin, he told parliament that "agents of Russia" could do a great deal of harm to Port Darwin, stopping the flow of fuel to military bases. "What is going to be done about these communists astride our road to

Singapore?" he asked. Communists in Darwin, men and women, were able to "flit back and forth" by air to Singapore, Timor and Jakarta. These people were trying to win the "multitudes in Indonesia into the communist camp."

During his speech, Blain was reminded that the subject of debate was the estimates, nevertheless he continued his attack on communists. He admitted to having taken part in drawing up a list of known communists in Darwin. The list, he stated, contained 83 names, many of them on the government payroll. There were another 23 people whose names had "not been listed publicly." He claimed the government would be surprised if he named those whom he "suspected to be communists."

A sincere, likeable and honest person, Nelson did not rate well as a public speaker. To overcome this shortcoming, Bowditch, big on oratory, would write an election speech and deliver it on Jock's behalf at a public meeting, saying the worthy candidate was out bush campaigning, unable to get back in time. Admitting that his speeches got a bit flowery—one running for about two hours—Bowditch enjoyed the experience and used some of his debating and theatrical skills. Bowditch's prominent position in Alice politics brought him into contact and conflict with the indefatigable, forthright and outspoken medical man, Dr V.H. Webster, who had been elected to the first NT Legislative Council for the seat of Tennant Creek in 1947. Webster was renowned for having made the statement that every man and woman in the Territory needed to drink several bottles of beer a day to keep healthy. He also wrote a slim volume on first aid which was an invaluable aid to people living in the outback. Policemen in particular made great use of it when they were involved in situations demanding quick, and sometimes lifesaving, action. Standing as an independent (non-socialist) Labor candidate against Nelson, Webster claimed that the full force of the federal ALP Government had been being directed against him during the election campaign.

In his capacity as ALP president, Bowditch derided the claim. He said both Webster and Blain had consistently attacked the ALP with abuse and destructive criticism. "I regard Dr Webster as a political opportunist, whose aim for a long time has been primarily to hear his own bellowings reverberate through an astonished House in Canberra," Bowditch said. Years later, he said it had been a great shame that Webster did not make it into federal politics because of his determined approach and strong oratory. Webster had also made scathing comments about the running of Darwin Hospital, which caused an uproar at the time.

When Nelson won the election, Iris Bowditch became his electorate secretary. In Nelson's words, Jim "held the fort" in Alice Springs in the early days of his parliamentary life. At his first ALP meeting in Alice as MHR, with Bowditch in the chair, Nelson gave an account of parliamentary proceedings, spoke about the Korean War and the government's Communist Party Dissolution Bill. From the start of his time in Alice, Nelson said anyone with a hard luck story had a willing listener in Jim.

On the conservative side of local politics was pilot Edward "Eddie" John Connellan, founder and chairman of the outback airline Connellan Airways Ltd, later Connair Pty Ltd. Connellan was also founder and president of the Northern Territory Development League and president of the Pastoralists' Association. He also became a member of the Legislative Council. Connellan was a close friend of the strong-minded, ruthless and influential John "Black Jack" McEwen, leader of the federal Country Party, later the National Party.

In his position as secretary of the Alice Springs section of the South Australian branch of the Federated Clerks' Union (FCU), Bowditch had extensive dealings with the SA secretary, Harry Krantz, whom ASIO regarded as a communist although he stood as a Labor candidate in a South Australian election. Krantz said Bowditch took to unionism with great enthusiasm. As the union leader put it, Bowditch "imbibed it [unionism] in big mugs."

Jim also contributed items to the FCU roneoed newsletter The Clerk under the byline Doop the Snoop. Krantz explained that due to the disruptions caused by the war, the FCU had been the only union in the Territory in the early postwar years. Krantz went to Darwin in 1946 on union business. There he met author

Xavier Herbert's brother, David, and his wife. Mrs Herbert, a member of the FCU, was a nursing sister who worked and lived at the large Belsen Camp in Darwin. Her husband ran supplies in a nifty looking vessel to Aboriginal settlements.

Most things were scarce, from food to building materials, and Krantz recalled arranging for powdered milk to be sent to the Territory to feed children. Krantz was in Darwin when the huge war surplus auctions were being prepared. Apart from much sought-

Jim with Harry Krantz, South Australian Secretary of the Federated Clerks' Union (FCU) and thought by ASIO to be a Communist.

after cars, trucks and machinery, there were hundreds of thousands of shoes and about 30,000 gas masks. Buyers came from all over Australia and Krantz said rackets were worked which made a lot of money for some crooks. As union activities increased, Krantz visited Alice and Darwin from time to time and described Alice as a "docile and conservative place." Jock Nelson had always been helpful, and when Krantz went to Canberra on business he worked from Nelson's office.

Through his involvement in union affairs, Bowditch began to campaign for people who were being treated unjustly in government departments and private enterprise. In August 1949 he wrote to Krantz in Adelaide asking if Phil Muldoon, the Alice Springs head jailer, could be covered by the union because he was working under unfair and anomalous conditions. Muldoon was the second longest serving officer in the entire NT public service, having been the Alice turnkey since the establishment opened in 1938. He lived at the prison, could not be absent overnight, and was on duty seven days a week. Bowditch said he had investigated Muldoon's situation and felt that something should be done. "We all know how futile it is to fight a lone battle with the authorities," Bowditch wrote. Muldoon wrote many letters to the union and mentioned "the vicious circle in Administration in Darwin", adding: "They do not want the honest truth in Administration. You have to be a **BBBB** liar or else a Yes-man to make the grade." After 30 years' service, Muldoon was still classified as a senior constable and his salary had increased by only 48 pounds in 20 years. Krantz wrote to Muldoon and said his treatment by the Commonwealth was a scandal and that he had been forgotten by the powers that be. Muldoon said a "dirty plot" had been hatched to dispossess him of his position as the man responsible for running the prison.

In calling for action to rectify the situation, Muldoon said: "I am tired of being fed promises. Let us have some action. It is the only thing this rotten Administration appreciates. This Dictator State has been ruled with a rod of iron long enough."

Bowditch also took up the case of a woman working for a lawyer who was being paid only seven pounds a week. She had two children and lived in a hostel. As there was no award for clerks employed in private enterprise in the Territory, her employer was able to get away with paying very little. Krantz responded by saying it was a disgraceful situation and if the lawyer did not come to the party some "discreet publicity" such as a letter to *Truth* from a "disgusted employer" could be used, or perhaps the "blackmail" column, "Things I Hear." Bowditch also campaigned for the first cost-of-living allowance for women in the NT.

A controversial person who strongly influenced Bowditch's outlook on politics and union matters was the golden-voiced orator, John R. "Jack" Hughes, secretary of the NSW Federated Clerks' Union, and a president of the NSW Trades and Labour Council. Hughes had been elected to the NSW ALP executive after the defeat of Jack Lang at the 1939 Unity Conference. He was a leading figure in the left-wing group of the NSW party which took stands at variance with the official ALP line, supporting the republicans in Spain, aid for China and opposing the Chamberlain Munich agreement with Hitler. Hughes said the only war the nation should get involved in was one on poverty.

When Prime Minister Robert Menzies introduced the Communist Party Dissolution Bill in 1950, which would have enabled individuals to be declared communists and prevented from working in the government or a trade union, even when elected to office by a democratic vote, Hughes was named and said to be a member of the central committee of the Australian Communist Party. In an embarrassing error, The *Sydney Morning Herald* ran a photograph of the Deputy Commissioner of Taxation, J.W.R. Hughes, saying he was the communist union leader named by the PM.

Menzies named 53 individuals as communists; later he was forced to admit that information supplied about five had been incorrect. Bowditch met Hughes several times, once at a fiery FCU conference in Nowra, NSW, decisions from which were later declared null and void through a court ruling. At that stormy Nowra gathering Bowditch flattened a man in a fight at a social function, Present at the conference was prominent unionist Ernie Thornton of the Ironworkers Union, whom ASIO would later claim also influenced Bowditch. While Bowditch never mentioned Thornton to me, he did mention Hughes several times, describing him as a powerful speaker intent on advancing the cause and conditions of the working class. Unions, Hughes had told Bowditch, were the great vehicles to advance the cause of humanity, but they had to be diligent and tough because the establishment would use every trick to deny the average person a fair go.

Bowditch became a member of the Alice Springs Progress Association and was given the task of handling its jubilee anniversary publicity. He was also appointed to a committee to draw up proposals for better working and living conditions for all government employees. He even convened a meeting of butchers and pastoralists in a bid to have the price of beef reduced by as much as threepence a pound. ASIO entered his beef reduction action in his file. Legacy and the RSL were other involvements; he supplied the local paper with details of RSL activities, one being an approach to the British Prime Minister, Winston Churchill, seeking to have Alice included in a royal visit.

Adept with the willow, the *Advocate* newspaper praised his cricketing prowess: "Stonewall Bowditch did it again on Sunday last. What a man … The elastic arm of Bowditch was responsible for the catch of the day." Cricket had a large following and was of a high standard. The clerk of courts, Ken Bagshaw, who had played Sheffield Shield for South Australia, was such a good player it was said he would have been the next Don Bradman but for the outbreak of war. Another highly regarded player had been Ginty Garrett, a superb wicket-taker. During the war years cricket pitches had been built for the troops and the town was well supplied with playing fields.

Mine host at the Alice Springs Hotel was "Uncle" Ly Underdown, with the unflattering nickname, "The Pig", who boasted that he had once owned more biscuits than anybody else in the NT. This was because he bought a mountain of tinned biscuits in the postwar auctions which were fed to his pigs. Underdown, full given name John Rickard Lycurgus, loved cricket so much that he would, on occasions, close the pub to go and play a match. Underdown got carried away in a game and let out a loud Howzat? before realising he was the umpire. He organised regular smoke concerts for cricketers and everybody attending had to get up and entertain the gathering in some way. Two clerics used to attend the evenings and tell jokes against each other. They were Father Dixon of Santa Theresa Catholic Mission and the Reverend Fred Mackay. Father Dixon had a new car, a Ford Utility, and took Mackay out to Santa Theresa to see Aborigines making bricks. Mackay asked to drive the car, took a bend too fast, and damaged the vehicle. Dixon was upset, and said: "If it hadn't been Friday, Freddy, I would have eaten you."

Later, Underdown built a cricket pitch and nets on the roof of his pub and tried to get Don Bradman to open the facilities.

When Bradman was not available, Jock Nelson officiated. The ceremony was performed at night and got under way when Ly's mother switched on the fluorescent lights and the first ball was bowled by Jack Donnellan to Nelson, who had a bat autographed by Bradman. Ly was wicket-keeper.

At chess, Bowditch beat most players in town; one of his regular opponents was a minister of religion. And no slouch as a thespian, Jim performed in plays such as the thriller *The Shop at Sly Corner*, and, with his wife, in Oscar Wilde's *The Importance of Being Earnest*, he playing Algernon. Priestley's *They Found a Country* was another vehicle for his talent. Agatha Christie's now politically incorrect thriller *Ten Little Niggers* included Jim in the cast.

Bowditch played a substantial part in the writing of the Alice Springs Theatre Group's musical revue *Barcoo Rot*, the title for which was his idea. His experience taking part in Boy Scout *Gang Shows* in England probably helped him in this project. Other scriptwriters were Jean Tainsh and the then editor of the *Advocate*, Alan Wauchope. The well-received revue included a skit on the popular BBC radio show, *Much Binding in the Marsh*, which was called *Much Finding in the Todd* (the local river), and sent up Alice identities, including D.D. Smith and Loutit. The show's background was a radio station, and when a newscast announced that a house had been built in Alice Springs, the accommodation starved audience responded with heartfelt and deafening applause. Part of the show included a farce about the early days of pedal radio in Central Australia. An amusing sketch called *Cats* drew approving comment. (Many years later, Bowditch said he and another clerk in Alice had written a poem called *Cats* which was about sexually desirable women in Alice; people had thought it was just about felines roaming about town). Government Departments were also lampooned. The revue was so well received they set to and wrote another, but it folded after several rehearsals. Wauchope and Bowditch "clicked" from the moment they first met in the RSL. It was at Bowditch's prompting that Wauchope came to write a regular column in the *Australasian Post*, "Straight from the Heart", which ran for 10 years and attracted mail from all over Australia.

Iris, Jim in his borrowed uniform and South Australia's Governor, Sir Willoughby Norrie, after Jim's investiture with the Distinguished Conduct Medal in October 1949.

Alice Springs businessman Reg Harris said Wauchope's highly popular column did more to promote tourism and interest in Alice than the film *A Town like Alice*. Wauchope admired Bowditch who he called a "perpetual crusader". He had worked as a journalist on the *Melbourne Herald*, where he met Sir Keith Murdoch, and at the *Adelaide News*. Wauchope was a magistrate's clerk when he first arrived in Alice.

In June 1949, Jim's in-laws, Colonel and Mrs George Hargreaves, went to Alice. Colonel Hargreaves, who had investigated war surplus auction rackets, flew on to Darwin in connection with government business. ASIO ran a check on him. Iris Bowditch hosted a function in the "tastefully decorated" Rendezvous Cafe for her mother and a delicious afternoon tea was provided for 25 people.

Like a bolt from the blue, Bowditch was projected even more into the public eye when it was announced he would be awarded the Distinguished Conduct Medal for his wartime exploits. The investiture was at Government House, Adelaide, by Sir Willoughby Norrie on 4 October 1949. Bowditch wore an army cap belonging to Harry Krantz and a uniform borrowed from the Creswick Army Barracks. Despite being called "Big Jim", Krantz recalled it had been something of a problem finding items of military clothing small enough to fit him.

The Federated Clerks' Union held a dinner in Adelaide for Bowditch, his wife, and his in-laws, who came across from

Melbourne for the event. Bowditch subsequently wrote to Krantz saying the experience of mixing with unionists had been a real education for his in-laws. They now had a different attitude to "militant unionists". Colonel and Mrs Hargreaves sent Krantz a specially printed Christmas card.

One of the clerks where Bowditch worked was tall, handsome and regularly made love to the wife of a prominent citizen. This Lothario would just vanish for several hours from the office, come back exhausted, and fall asleep at his desk. On one occasion a prominent citizen armed with a pistol chased another well-known man down a street after finding him in bed with his wife. Several shots were fired, but failed to hit the weaving target. The angry husband then threw the gun at the fleet-footed fellow. Bowditch was subsequently called to give evidence for a petitioner in a divorce case. His evidence was described as having been like "what the butler saw".

Bowditch was experiencing problems in his own marriage. Unable to start a family, he underwent tests and it was shown that his sperm count was low. This led him to the erroneous belief that he could not father children.

11. NEVER TRUST NEWSPAPERS

During 1950, Bowditch became involved in the bitter national union and political struggle of the day. He went from being a clerk hailed as a war hero to a person openly branded a "commie" and was spat at during a rowdy meeting in an Adelaide theatre. The drama was sparked by the right-wing campaign to "cleanse"Australian unions of left wingers and communists. Catholic Action took a key part in the battle and "Industrial Groupers" manoeuvred to seize control of unions. The ensuing brawl led to a split in the ALP and the later formation of the Democratic Labour Party. A main target was the large Federated Clerks' Union with a scalp obtained by the right wingers being Jack Hughes of NSW who had so inspired Bowditch. In the fiercely fought election for the SA branch of the FCU, which included Jim's position as secretary of the Alice section, he supported Krantz as SA state secretary.

Bowditch found himself in the strange position of being supported by both sides in the election.

Without consulting him, the Groupers claimed him as one of theirs, probably because they felt a war hero was obviously against anyone branded a communist. Bowditch got a telephone call from an Adelaide journalist pointing out that he was being supported by both sides. Bowditch said he was in Harry Krantz's group, which resulted in a newspaper story saying that he had refused to back the right-wingers, implying that he was, in Jim's words, "a red-hot commie." Bowditch went to Adelaide for meetings with Krantz and saw the journalist who had written the report to put him right. However, he said the reporter seemed to have swallowed the "establishment's bullshit". Bowditch said he should have sued the paper.

In Adelaide, a FCU how-to-vote pamphlet, containing a message from Jim Bowditch, DCM, MID (Mentioned in Despatches), was issued which repudiated the "insulting inference" that he was in any way associated with the anti-union body seeking to "capture" the union; under the sub-heading "Jim Bowditch says", it showed how to vote in the union election. A copy went into the ASIO files along with a *Tribune* item in which Bowditch was quoted as having said that if what the clerks' union executive was doing amounted to communism, then he "would be in favour of communism." The *Advertiser* report saying that Bowditch had denied membership of the Industrial Groupers was also included in the ASIO report. Bowditch attended a noisy clerks' meeting in the Tivoli Theatre, Adelaide, to consider a call by the Groupers to remove the entire executive of the SA union. It was said to be the biggest union meeting in Adelaide, possibly Australia, with more than 600 people present. Both sides were present in force, and very vocal.

A report said about 350 people were lined up outside the theatre at 7.30 and each person's name was checked to see if they were on the union membership roll. Some people shouted: "Krantz, why don't you lift the iron curtain?" The last person was admitted at 8.30. Up on stage, Krantz introduced Bowditch as a war hero and Jim rose to speak. He had not been on his feet long before heckling and booing began. Despite the uproar, he carried on. He said he could not understand why the Catholic Church was backing moves which were designed to split the ranks of the working class, a statement which caused an explosion of jeering. Some people ran down the aisle shouting, one spitting at Bowditch across the orchestra pit. Fights and scuffles broke out. An oddly worded newspaper account of the meeting said it had been orderly, "with the exception of two bursts of uproar", one lasting for five minutes before heckling of Krantz subsided. The bid to oust the executive failed 375 votes to 272.

Soon after the meeting, Bowditch felt compelled to write a letter to the *Adelaide Advertiser* to answer various claims being made by the Groupers. However, the paper cut out 200 words, which angered him. After reading what the paper did to his letter, he wrote to the FCU: "I have decided it is much better to leave the daily press alone as one does not get very far with them, and I now hope that the matter fades out." In the letter Bowditch said, among other things, that he had referred to the right wingers as pseudo-Labor because no genuine Labor follower would attempt to disrupt a union which had made the progress the SA branch of the FCU had made in the past eight years. Furthermore, no genuine Labor follower would employ the tactic used by Groupers in state and branch elections of inferring anyone opposing them was either a "Red" or dominated by a "Red". Bowditch said the SA branch executive followed the non-political, non-sectarian rules of the union and were not "stooges" to any political party. It wished to further the interests of all clerks, whether a large portion of its members voted Liberal, Labor, independent or informal. He went on to say: "It is my personal belief that a Labor government is preferable to a Liberal for wage earners, and I vote and work for the ALP accordingly. However, I am totally opposed to union affiliation with the ALP or any other political party for many reasons, some

I have given, and certainly oppose the Industrial Group's intrusion into our union and the resulting disruption."

Bowditch called at the offices of interstate newspapers trying to explain the FCU's case to journalists. At the *Sydney Telegraph*, he said that the editor, David McNicoll, called him a "Red Ragger" and ordered security staff to show him off the premises. In a postscript to a letter he wrote to Krantz during this period, Bowditch made a Wodehousean remark: "Give those Groupers what-ho!" Bowditch and Krantz went to Darwin for the first FCU conference in the NT where Jim mixed with unionists and visited the *Northern Standard* newspaper office. In the bitterly fought FCU elections which followed, he and Krantz survived the Groupers' onslaught. During the election campaign a Catholic priest speaking from the pulpit told clerks in his Alice flock not to vote for Bowditch. On being told of this, Jim went round and debated the issue with the man. It was a typical action for Bowditch, he liked to hear what the opposition had to say on every issue and would debate the matter. Even during the vicious meeting in Adelaide and the rowdy conference in Nowra, he had surprised many on "his side" by wanting to engage the opposition in face-to-face debate, and let them have their say

While this bitter battle raged, Bowditch continued his work as a clerk in Alice. Once he was sent to Tennant Creek to report on a strange situation where the key to a safe was lost. When it was opened by an engineer the 700 pounds which should have been inside was missing. The man responsible for looking after the money admitted having spent it on drink and gambling.

12. ABORIGINAL "NEW DEALS"

As time went by, Bowditch became increasingly aware of the plight of the NT Aboriginal community. Late in 1949 an extraordinary event had taken place in Darwin which caused much discussion in Alice. There was a public protest in the northern capital against provisions of the Aboriginal Ordinance which prescribed wages at five to 10 shillings a week for gardeners and other menial workers. Aborigines marched through the street with iron bars and lengths of chain as if they were slaves. Backed by the North Australian Workers' Union, Aboriginal workers went on strike.

The Administrator, Mick Driver, directed that one of the leaders, Aboriginal Fred Waters, be removed from Darwin to Haasts Bluff Reserve in Central Australia. The act of exiling Waters received nationwide coverage and the NAWU sought a court injunction restraining the director of Native Affairs from ordering the removal. The High Court, however, ruled the director had acted lawfully and Waters was detained for six weeks in the desert reserve.

The event prompted former NT policeman Gordon Birt, then living in Adelaide, to donate one pound to the NAWU to help the Aborigines of Darwin in their fight for decent living conditions and justice. Birt wrote that as a former NT policeman he was well aware of the semi-slavery conditions native workers were subjected to and the lack of even elementary civil rights for Aborigines. He admired their courage in striking a blow for themselves. Birt went on to say he had seen many of them marched miles in chains without whimpering and he had no doubt about their courage. The NAWU, he continued, deserved praise for helping them. The authorities' latest move in exiling Fred Waters had aroused widespread indignation in Adelaide, Birt added.

At that stage Bowditch was deeply involved in many aspects of the white community's way of life. People spoke in Alice about "their blackfellers" as if they owned them; one said he dragged Aborigines behind a car with ropes; from time to time, there was talk of whipping them. One old-timer said it was possible to get "two coons" into a 44 gallon drum, the implication being that they had been shot and stuffed into a drum.

Bowditch met Aboriginal artist Albert Namatjira and admitted that at first he had not appreciated his style of painting, some people dismissing his work as being chocolate box art. However, Bowditch came to realise that Namatjira had captured the vivid colours and formations of the Centre. Several people he knew bought many

Namatjira paintings for trifling amounts in those early days. During the l950s it was announced that Namatjira, having seen the sea for the first time in Darwin, had been commissioned to paint seascapes for a women's magazine. Namatjira also appeared in a movie, *The Phantom Stockman*, starring Chips Rafferty, which was shot in Alice. A civic reception was held for Namatjira in the Sydney Town Hall and the artist was escorted from the meeting by Dame Mary Gilmore.

Jim knew Namatjira when he did not drink alcohol and remembered the concern expressed by white residents when the painter wanted to buy land to build a house in the town area. By that stage he was famous and had made a considerable amount of money. Bowditch said he believed the opposition "broke Albert's spirit", and he was forced to live at the Morris Soak "booze area" outside town. Early in his painting career he had been "ripped off" and later became a victim of racism, leading to total disenchantment, drink, and a sad, often lonely time before his death. It is interesting to note that in light of recent allegations about fake Aboriginal art, bogus Namatjira paintings were a growing problem in the l950s, some of which were sold to Americans in Adelaide in l953. The situation became so bad that Alan Wauchope wrote an article for the *Australasian Post* headed: TAKE A GOOD LOOK AT YOUR NAMATJIRA—MAYBE IT'S NOT. To protect Namatjira and other Aboriginal artists from being ripped off, the Aranda Arts Council was formed under the chairmanship of Rex Battarbee, the man who taught Namatjira to paint.

Another artist Bowditch knew and kept in touch with over the years was self-taught sculptor-conservationist William Ricketts, who claimed to be the reincarnation of an Aboriginal spirit. Ricketts had played the violin in cinemas from 1924–35 when talkies took over. Afterwards he moved to a property in the Dandenong Ranges with his mother and they led a frugal life. Inspired by the land, he began to model Aboriginal heads and animals in terracotta in his bush garden, later expanded with the help of the Victorian Government and now known as the William Ricketts Sanctuary. Through the sanctuary he campaigned for human rights, Aboriginal rights and conservation. In 1950 he spent four months with the Pitjantjatjara tribe in Central Australia, his first direct contact with Aborigines. Subsequent trips were made to the Musgrave Ranges of South Australia and four more to Central Australia resulting in the production of many sculptures of Aboriginal myths and legends. Bowditch said Ricketts, a "birdlike" man, usually included his own head somewhere in the sculptured panels. Examples of Ricketts' works were put on display in the grounds of Pitchi Ritchi.

During May 1950 a Stipendiary Magistrate, Mr John Crang, ruled that all "natives" entering "the prohibited area of Alice Springs" must have a written permit. This was part of a drive by Alice police to clear the town of "idlers". Inspector Bill McKinnon said the police action followed repeated complaints by business people and members of the public about idle Aborigines in the streets of the town. Station owners and other employers of labour were quoted as approving the moves. This action reduced "shiftless types" preying on "native workers" the *Advocate* said in a report headed: NATIVES MUST HAVE PERMITS TO ENTER TOWN. A year later there was another story headed: ALL HALFCASTES MAY ENTER ALICE SPRINGS.

Early in the 1950s, Bowditch was present when the new director of Aboriginal Affairs, Harry Christian Giese, visited Alice Springs and over two days in the courthouse addressed the NT Pastoral Lessees' Association about the proposed regulations which were to be introduced under the Wards Employment Ordinance. Also present with Giese were Territories Minister Paul Hasluck and the NT Administrator, Frank Wise, who also spoke to the gathering. Over the years to come, Bowditch clashed with Giese on many occasions, but on that first encounter he was impressed with what he told the pastoralists.

Bowditch was allowed in on certain conditions. These were that he would first submit his report for checking to Giese before it went to press, and that at times the meeting might go into closed session. Giese later told me that Bowditch scrupulously abided by the agreement and he (Giese) had a feeling of trust in him. Bowditch, he said, was a straight talking man who had a great skill in explaining complicated issues of the day in a fashion that could be understood by the average person.

These are Bowditch's recollections of what Giese said at the meeting: "It was the best speech I had ever heard on civil rights as they should have applied to Aborigines. He was obviously an angry man at the time. He had been around a number of properties and seen the conditions under which Aborigines worked and lived. Harry did not pull a punch from the beginning. He just said he was there to tell the people this period of misuse of Aborigines was finished. He delivered an incredible blast about the conditions he had seen and the pay the Aborigines received. He gave a forewarning, although it took a long time to come, that a proper award would be introduced as far as Aboriginal labour was concerned. When Giese said all workers in the pastoral industry were underpaid for the work they did there was a sort of stunned silence. No doubt nearly all those people present had heard nothing like it before. I think a lot of what he said was going in one ear and out the other. They were not prepared to accept the truth of what he was saying. During his speech he let the audience know he had been given great powers by the government and he would use them to change the treatment of Aborigines in the pastoral industry and elsewhere."

After the speech, Bowditch listened to what the pastoralists had to say. Many said they felt there was something wrong with Giese, who they said was a city man who did not know what it was like in the Territory. They spoke about the "laziness" of Aboriginal workmen and how they, the cattlemen, had to work hard to build up their properties. The fact that they fed relatives and families of stockmen had also been raised. Some cattlemen suggested calling a special meeting and writing to the government to "get rid" of Giese. It was Bowditch's understanding that considerable pressure was applied to government and Harry Giese not to interfere in the Territory cattle industry.

In 1982, Eddie Connellan, who had been president of the Central Australian Pastoral Lessees' Association, in a letter told me he did not recall Giese's address, or any reaction to the supposed speech. He continued: "One thing of which I am certain is that the

Aborigines were far better off and far happier before Harry came to the Territory. But I am not suggesting that it was his fault. It was the fault of others, who thought they were doing good."

Reflecting on that important speech by Giese, Bowditch said: "Perhaps unfairly, I have often wondered what happened to Giese and the path he finally took. What happened to the fire and vigour he showed in relation to the subject? Did he go wrong, or was it simply that he was given far too much power, because he did in fact have extraordinary control over the lives of Aborigines when it came to such matters as drink, mixing with Europeans, their social lives?

"However, there was not much control so far as their treatment by other Europeans in the outback where they were directly dependent on those who ran the properties. Not for one moment am I suggesting all property owners were racist in the worst sense of the word, although I do suggest that almost all of them were racist, at best, in the paternal sense."

The politician Jock Nelson gave a clear example of how Aboriginal policy was made on the run in the 1960s. He was appointed to a committee of five charged with the task of drawing up rushed recommendations for Aboriginal voting rights. The only other Labor member on the committee was Kim Beazley senior. At the time, a UN debate was looming on subjugated groups in various nations. Russia, in particular, was being criticised for the way it treated ethnic minorities, and Nelson said the situation in Australia was equally as bad, if not worse. The Menzies government said the report had to be ready in six weeks. Prepared in great haste, it recommended full voting rights, with voluntary enrolment, but compulsory voting once a person was on the roll. Within 48 hours of making that report, Nelson said the Minister for External Affairs, Garfield Barwick, was on a plane to New York to "make Australia look good in the UN."

Bowditch became increasingly involved in the battle for equal rights for half-castes. He gained the reputation of being one of the few white men in Alice Springs who would listen to half-castes and try to help them. Milton Liddle was one of those whom Bowditch remembered with affection. Liddle had been taken from his parents at the age of about three and put in The Bungalow with many other children; at 14 he was placed on a cattle station. When war broke out he joined the army and was sent to Adelaide as a driver. About to be sent to New Guinea to fight, it was discovered he was suffering from the eye disease, trachoma or Sandy Blight, which was prevalent among Aborigines. At some stage an Englishman had given him a dictionary, which he studied and used to check spelling in the writing of letters. Liddle wrote to the paper and said it was wrong that a person could come from overseas and after a short period become an Australian citizen, yet half-castes born in Australia, who had fought for the country, were not citizens. Bowditch arranged for Liddle to meet Territories Minister Paul Hasluck. Liddle went on to be a leading figure in Aboriginal legal aid and land rights.

Bowditch said the truly great struggle for equality and justice for black people generally was almost lost forever by concentrating on the half-castes. He freely admitted that he and others who took up the cause of the half-castes had been wrong in not also advancing, at the same time, the causes of full-bloods. In those days, he said, many half-castes had opted out of the black community and decided to identify with the whites. The half-caste community, he explained, was under awesome pressures. In the desire to be accepted by whites, many distanced themselves from their own people. The thinking at the time had been first things first, rights for half-castes. Full-bloods, as in Darwin, had more or less been regarded as too big a problem. (This same attitude prevailed when author Xavier Herbert was in the Territory in the 1920s and 1930s. In fact, Herbert had expressed the belief that full-bloods were "out of date" and the future was through half-castes.) Some half-castes who tried to become accepted by the white section of the community would later, after the reformist Whitlam Government came into power, rush to embrace their Aboriginality. Bowditch put it this way: "Fellows who would punch your head in if you called them a black, suddenly became Aborigines." While it was easy for some to sneer at this about-face it was just another manifestation of the desperation and fracturing caused by whites ever since they set foot in Australia.

ASIO noted Bowditch's increasing involvement with half-castes. Secret reports in 1952 conveyed the information that he had a large following "from the half-caste population in the Alice Springs district." A long-time Alice resident, S. Reiff, suggested that Aborigines should have separate facilities, even their own theatre where they could be shown Disney films and educational shows. This idea was criticised by Charlie Priest, a leading figure in Darwin during the so-called riots of the unemployed in the Depression, who was then living at Tennant Creek and wrote to the *Advocate* on occasions. A typical, articulate and outspoken unionist of the day, he and others inspired a composite communist character, Charlie Mack, in Xavier Herbert's novel *Capricornia*. Speaking out against Reiff's segregation proposal, Priest said the question was whether the Aborigines were to be "liquidated" or assimilated into the community. The time would come when white would be little more than a drop in a black ocean. The issue had to be resolved for the benefit of the children of today, Priest declared.

13. MEN OF INFLUENCE

Two men living in Alice had an important influence on Bowditch in the early years. The first was Englishman Francis "Frank" Whitewood, secretary of the ALP, who lived in a caravan and sent money home to his mother. Bowditch described Whitewood as his "father confessor", saying he was well-read and taught him to see values in people he otherwise would have missed. The two often sat up late at night in the caravan playing chess and discussing issues. The second was lawyer Richard "Dick" Ward, a member of the NT Legislative Council and later a Northern Territory judge, with whom Bowditch formed a strong and lasting association, both fighting for Aboriginal rights, NT political reform and other causes.

Ward's activities resulted in him being called the Clarence Darrow of the Territory. (Darrow was the American lawyer who fought legal battles for organised labour, becoming known as the champion of the oppressed and unfortunate. It was Darrow who defended the right to teach evolution in Tennessee schools.) Ward had been a contemporary of ALP leader Gough Whitlam, both having been born in the same month and same suburb. At a political meeting in Darwin years later when the similarities in their lives were pointed out by Whitlam, some wag called out, "and the same father".

About 1938 Ward became a partner in the Darwin law firm of Andrew Brough Newell. He joined the army during the war as a lance-corporal and worked as a clerk in the record section at the Larrakeyah Army Barracks in Darwin. However, he was given leave to appear in a court case on 19 February 1942, the day the Japanese first bombed Darwin, and he and others rushed out the back of the court and took shelter in a trench. One of those in the ditch was a court stenographer, Florence Wright, whom he married in 1943. Ward moved to Alice after the bombing of Darwin, set up a legal business and was drafted into the Allied Works Council.

A dedicated socialist, Ward was branded "Red Richard" in conservative Alice. A skilled orator, he was a brilliant advocate and had a firm belief in the rights of the individual. He became a leader in the Northern Territory Development League, formed to press for legislative and political reform, and in 1946 the Chifley Labor government decided to form the Northern Territory Legislative Council. Ward stood for, and was elected to, the first Legislative Council in 1947, beating Frank W. Johnson by one vote. Johnson at a later election won the seat by one vote. Ward called for Alice Springs to be made the administrative capital of the NT, a proposal backed by influential Adelaide businessmen, including Mr H.J. Bird, manager of pastoral company S. Kidman and Co. The then deputy leader of the ALP, Arthur Calwell, said he hoped the day would come when the NT would be divided into two, each part eventually becoming a state. He did not envisage this happening until the NT population had reached 250,000.

While Bowditch was secretary of the Rovers Cricket Club, Ward was patron of the Pioneer Football Club. Ward arranged for a talented Aboriginal Australian rules footballer, Henry Peckham, to play in Adelaide, where he received the best player of the year award. Ward was a man of broad interests: music, philosophy and books, of which he had a large collection, some in special bindings. He and Jim drank together, and Mrs Ward was in the amateur theatrical group in which Jim and Iris Bowditch were members. ASIO kept Whitewood, Ward and Bowditch under surveillance. Years later, an ASIO report described Bowditch and Ward as having "long histories of association with Communists and radicals."

The Cold War between the super powers caused deep divisions throughout the world, including Alice Springs. Ferocious fighting and huge casualties in Korea, and the federal government's failed attempt to outlaw the Communist Party, heightened passions, It was whispered about the town that Jock Nelson held regular meetings attended by communists in a shed on his property. Nelson told how a union activist in Alice Springs who had a large hammer and sickle emblem emblazoned on the floor of his house had been accused of subversion during WWII.

Eddie Connellan was one of those who often spoke about communists. Connellan, according to Nelson, had pulled out of the Northern Territory Development League, which he (Connellan) had founded, because he said it had been taken over by communists. Dick Ward had become a dominant figure in the organisation. The "commie" tag was trotted out often by people opposing Bowditch. It was also used as ammunition against Ward by plumber Frank Johnson during the election which saw him beat Ward by one vote. Johnson loved talking about politics, especially in relation to what happened in Australia during the Depression.

The communist jibes against Bowditch included his involvement with the Peace Council, regarded by many as a communist front, if not actively supported by "subversives", then by gullible people being manipulated by evil forces. Because of its support for peace, the World Council of Churches was also regarded with suspicion and outright hostility. A person deeply involved in the Peace Council was Marjorie Johnston, sister of Adelaide communist barrister Elliott Johnston, later a QC and a judge. When his sister planned to hold Peace Council meetings in the NT, Johnston wrote and asked Bowditch if he would help organise a venue and chair the event. As ASIO put it, "Bowditch 'came under notice' in August 1951 when he began corresponding with the SA branch of the Australian Peace Council." Bowditch, who had recently been approached and asked to become a Justice of the Peace, agreed to do so. Through his friendship with the incumbent minister, a chess player, Bowditch booked the Anglican hall for a night meeting in June 1951. A leading businessman and a Freemason both approached Bowditch and warned him against having anything to do with the Peace Council. Miss Johnston had recently returned from an international Peace Conference in Warsaw and said she saw no sign that Poland and Czechoslovakia were preparing for another world war. Warsaw, she said, would be at the forefront of any invasion and there the populace was rebuilding the city after WWII, not preparing or wanting another global conflict. The Peace Council, she added, was non-political, but willingly admitted any political creed as long as it had a genuine desire for peace. At the Alice meeting Bowditch opened proceedings by introducing Miss Johnston and said peace was a desirable state, He urged those present, about 50 by his account, to listen to what was said and to make up their own minds.

In the audience, which included his lawyer friend Dick Ward, was Darwin's Australian Security and Intelligence Organisation officer, Mr Mooney, who came down to report on the event. His secretary took notes throughout the evening. Also present was Mrs Esther Meaney, president of the Darwin Housewives' Association, who was to accompany Miss Johnston in the Territory. Mrs Meaney had been the NT delegate to the 1950 Australian Peace Congress in Melbourne. The Melbourne gathering had been attended by the Dean of Canterbury, Hewlett Johnson, dubbed the "Red Dean" because he had written favourably about Russia. His visit to Australia was criticised in the press, the *Sydney Morning Herald* saying he was "a decoy duck" for the peace movement. The Dean passed through Darwin on his way to Melbourne on that occasion and no local clergy went to meet him because of the Red bogey. However, Esther Meaney, and her husband Jack, a watersider regarded as a communist, later made a life member of the ALP, and both tireless campaigners for a better society, invited him home to Fannie Bay for a meal, his first in Australia. On his way back to England some time later, the Dean again stopped off at Darwin and was entertained by the Meaneys, once more breaking bread with the couple. To the Meaneys' son, John, the Dean seemed about "nine foot tall" and spoke in a strong, educated voice.

A short newspaper account of the Alice Peace Council meeting said Bowditch thanked the Reverend F. Rodgers Burns for allowing the Church of England hall to be used for the meeting. Mr Burns had responded by saying he had been impressed by what Miss Johnston had said, and that he was willing to support the proposed establishment of a Peace Committee in Alice. The ASIO account of the meeting gave a more detailed version. It said Johnston had arrived in Alice on 2/6/51 and she and Meaney had been looked after by Bowditch, who entertained them at his home. It said Johnston had been the only speaker at the meeting, and when people tried to ask her questions about communism and the Peace Council, Bowditch had "disallowed these". A resolution was supported which had "effectively gagged" Bowditch so that a question could be asked. According to the ASIO account, nobody would accept the position of president or secretary of a local Peace Council committee, so Bowditch and another person, a committee of two, was voted in.

As a result of his involvement with the Peace Council, Jim's appointment as a JP was either revoked or did not go ahead. The Anglican minister who allowed his hall be used for the peace meeting was transferred. Bowditch noticed that after the meeting some people tended to avoid him. While walking in the main street Bowditch saw Inspector Bill McKinnon, known as "Camel Bill" because in earlier years he had made extensive camel patrols, turn away and avoid him. Another day, he repeated the dodging act. As they used to regularly meet in the street and chat, Bowditch decided to find out exactly why he was being shunned. He called on the police officer at his home and asked for an explanation, McKinnon told him that because of the federal government campaign to have the Communist Party outlawed, it was not safe to be seen with Bowditch as people associated with communists could lose their government jobs. He said he did not want his career jeopardised by being seen with him. The inspector also told Bowditch he had also been rejected as a JP because it was thought he would not be able to swear an oath of allegiance to the Queen.

Bowditch was not concerned about being rejected as a JP. He had indicated when first approached that he would not be interested in sitting on the bench in court cases and "sending people up the river", but would be prepared to witness the signing of documents. While he did not become a JP, he did editorialise some years later that it was not right for Justices of the Peace with "known attitudes towards Aborigines" to sit on cases involving them.

ASIO noted that by August 1951 the Alice Springs Peace Council Committee had "apparently fallen through" owing to lack of interest and support by local citizens. (About 20 years after the Peace Council episode, making it about the time of the Whitlam government's election, Jock Nelson told Bowditch that ASIO had recently taken Bowditch's name from the "fellow traveller" list.)

14. MARRIAGE BREAKDOWN

On the home front, the marriage of Jim and Iris was under tension. Jim was engrossed in his many interests, attending meetings, some at The Bungalow, and travelling about on union business. ASIO claimed his wife 'prompted' him over an alleged affair with a woman, described as a 'communist stooge', a kind of femme fatale, who had been sent to Alice Springs to influence Bowditch. ASIO said that, 'from all accounts' she had been 'pulling it over' Bowditch. Furthermore, it was said this woman had stayed at the residence of

Mr and Mrs Wauchope when she first arrived in the Alice. Alan Wauchope was described in the ASIO report as being about 40, a former editor of the *Centralian Advocate* and Jock Nelson's private secretary.

According to Bowditch, his wife Iris was not really interested in politics or unions and shared her parents' belief that unionists were communists who should be avoided. Involved in so many activities, Bowditch was leading a hectic life and at times was away from home. After returning home early from one trip, he became involved in a wild fight with a red-headed man who used to drink with the Bowditchs at the racecourse, and was reportedly attentive to Iris. Considerable damage was done to the small dwelling. Iris left soon after for Melbourne. The fact that she filed for divorce was entered in the security files. Bowditch maintained that he had agreed that his departing wife should tell her parents that it was his fault that the marriage had come asunder. He came to rue this act as the payment of maintenance over the years carved into his finances. After she left he was at a loss what to do, his ego damaged. There was a woman who he described decades later as "mystical", the supposed femme fatale mentioned by ASIO, but this relationship did not continue.

To escape Alice and its problems, he took some leave and drove to Adelaide in a soft top car, where he said there was a woman whom he "admired", the peace activist Marjorie Johnston. ASIO noted the departure of the Bowditches thus: "Subject [Jim Bowditch] left Alice Springs 14/2/52 to travel overland to Adelaide in his car. He was short of money and intended trying to sell the car in Adelaide, after which he was to have gone on to Sydney. If he could not get his price for the car, he intended to get a job as a traveller or with a country newspaper in South Australia. He is said to have left his wife; she went South by plane about a week before subject left by car." ASIO kept Bowditch under observation in Adelaide. One memorandum said he was "believed" to be temporarily residing at the residence of lawyer Elliott Johnston, a member of the Communist Party of Australia State Secretariat. Bowditch's car was seen parked outside on three nights from early evening until late at night, when surveillance was discontinued. Apparently what went on in the witching hours was of no interest to the spooks.

The same report said Bowditch had been known in the Adelaide ASIO office since 1950 "when evidence was discovered that, although ostensibly an ALP supporter, he persistently supported the communist line in the FCU's affairs." The memorandum went on to say the SA Department of Works and Housing could not say whether Bowditch was still employed by the department in Alice. Beneath a blacked out section, it read: "It cannot be confirmed that this allegation is correct. Nevertheless, circumstantial evidence to date makes the allegation probably accurate."

Another secret memorandum from ASIO headquarters, with blacked out portions, said the photograph mentioned was one of James Bowditch and his wife and it appeared that this person "is probably identical with the James Bowditch on record, who recently arrived in Adelaide, per motor car." The report went on to say data from a "Q" Branch source in South Australia categorically said that Bowditch joined the CPA during his visit to Adelaide. In the same file was additional information: "On April 15th, Marjorie Vivian Johnston, C.P. of A. member and Acting Secretary of the S.A. Peace Council, said that when Bowditch was in Adelaide early this month he requested Elliott Johnston to give him a position as a permanent worker for the S.A. Peace Council. Johnston is understood to have said that he could not arrange such a position for Bowditch. Marjorie Johnston already said that during his recent visit to Adelaide from Alice Springs, Bowditch joined the Communist Party."

In his aimless and uncertain frame of mind at the time, Bowditch applied to rejoin the army and fight in Korea. In his re-enlistment application he said he was unemployed. Security vetted the application and assessed him as a risk because he was "a sympathiser." Unfavourable factors listed were the NT Security reports, his involvement with the FCU and Harry Krantz ("suspected C.P. member"), the *Tribune* item mentioned earlier and his involvement with the Peace Council. Favourable factors included that: Bowditch had "allegedly" won a DCM and been mentioned in dispatches, and he was president of the Alice Springs branch of the ALP.

The Bowditch file included a secret report, with several lines blacked out, which contained a sensational claim about why Bowditch wanted to fight in Korea: "At the end of March 1952 subject [Bowditch] said that he wanted to join the Australian Forces in Korea with a view of deserting and joining Thornton in China." Ernest Thornton, dubbed "the Red Czar" of the Federated Ironworkers' Association, had been ousted by the Industrial Groupers campaign in 1949. He was subsequently seconded by the World Federation of Trade Unions to head the Asian Liaison Bureau, based in China. The alleged intention to "desert" to China was repeated in another ASIO report. What is to be made of this assertion, not known until well after Bowditch's death so he could not be asked to respond? It is such a bizarre suggestion that it invites conjecture. One possibility, of course, is that he did make a flamboyant statement, perhaps while drinking, along the lines that he would like to desert and join Thornton in China. The fact that Thornton had taken up a post in China had received prominent coverage in the Australian press. At the time Bowditch applied to rejoin the army, he acknowledged that he had been at a low ebb, his male ego crushed by the circumstances of his wife's departure, and at a loss to know what to do.

That he was in something of a quandary is gleaned from the ASIO report which claimed he had driven from Alice to Adelaide short of money, intending to sell his car and travel to Sydney; failing to sell his car, it seems he was prepared to seek work on a country newspaper or even become a door-to-door salesman like the aimless period soon after being demobbed.

Some of those with whom he mixed in Adelaide during that period had been deeply involved in the battle with the Groupers, and it is possible Bowditch voiced the off-the-cuff colourful statement about wanting to "defect" and link up with Thornton.

The report about his supposedly seeking a job with the South Australian Peace Council clearly illustrates that at that stage in his life he was adrift, prepared to try anything. Anyone having had any close ties with Bowditch, especially journalists, could list extreme statements made by him, not necessarily while he was under the influence of alcohol. While expressing deep indignation at the actions of governments, companies or individuals, especially in cases where people or nations were being oppressed or bullied, Bowditch often said it was a situation where, "You just feel like grabbing a gun and shooting the bastards." Security men or informants overhearing such utterances could build up a file presenting Bowditch as a potential assassin, perhaps even a serial killer. During his battles with the Menzies government, Bowditch, in a rhetorical flourish, would say Cabinet members were so dense and reactionary they should be shot to advance the well-being of the nation. Why, he would ask in despair, did people let mongrels and those most hated of beings, bullies, stand over them and force them to lead miserable lives? It will be shown later that Bowditch, in print, metaphorically declared the ALP leader, Arthur Calwell, should be shot. (Of course, years later, a disturbed young man, Peter Kocan, now a poet and novelist, did try to shoot Calwell.) Furthermore, ASIO noted that Bowditch claimed to have "unnamed" friends inside the Adelaide Post Office. Did this information raise the possibility that he could tamper with the Royal Mail?

15. INSTANT EDITOR

Still uncertain of his future, his life seemingly a mess, Bowditch returned to Alice after his brief stay in Adelaide. Then it was announced he would be resigning from Works and Housing to become the full-time editor of the *Centralian Advocate*. The then owner of the paper, Ron Morcom, had asked Bowditch to take over the editorial reins; Bowditch had helped out on the editorial side during 1951 when Wauchope had been unable to continue editing the paper. As an indication of the fairly free and easy conditions in Alice, Bowditch wrote the copy for the first few issues of the newspaper under his editorship from his desk in the paymaster's office. All the copy was laboriously written in long-hand, which was then passed to the linotype operators. Because he had so much copy to write, he later developed a three-finger typing action, which increased in speed.

ASIO continued to report on his activities. On 23 May 1952, the SA regional director, notified Canberra headquarters and Darwin that Bowditch had expressed the intention to stand as the "Communist candidate" at the next federal elections. He went on to say that Bowditch was building up an association with the half-caste population in and around Alice Springs. This activity, he said, might represent the foundation of a long-range plan in connection with his political ambitions. On 17 June a field officer in Victoria, repeating the claim that Bowditch had intended joining Thornton in China, forwarded further conjecture about Bowditch's likely political moves. Bowditch, he said, was on friendly terms with and had campaigned for Jock Nelson, MHR and Frank Johnson, the Alice Springs member in the NT Legislative Council. Nelson had suggested to Bowditch that he should become his successor. Bowditch, the field officer wrote, could obtain Labor endorsement with the aid of his friend Frank Whitewood, secretary of the Alice Springs branch of the ALP. According to the report, Bowditch was "apparently" still a member of the ALP.

Working long hours each day, Bowditch wrote everything, even the social notes, which were mainly compiled from a weekend visit to the social hub, the Memorial Club. His social notes appeared in columns headed "Seen at the Club" and "Club Hub-Bub". However he emphatically denied having ever written a column in the paper called "A Cup of Tea and a Chat", by "Sue". The newspaper office had been rebuilt after a mysterious fire in 1950, but was still a primitive building. A taxi driver with a news sense used to bring visiting VIPs and people of interest to see Bowditch at the *Advocate*. These visitors were surprised at the dingy premises, especially the pokey office space in which he worked.

In a report, parts of which were blacked out, it was said that a man said to have travelled the world and had "an intense hatred for communism", had made contact with ASIO. This

Jim, Betty and her father, "Geordie" Hodgson in 1952.

man had said he thought "communism was rather thick in the Territory." He had met several communists and would like to contact the Security Service. Three men had been named by the man, James Frederick Bowditch; a reporter commonly called "Bluey"; and a travelling optometrist and optician, E.L. Rosanove. Apparently nothing was known of Bluey; Bowditch, of course, had an expanding file. In the case of Rosanove, formerly of Melbourne, he allegedly praised communism and said he had travelled through Sibera [sic] and by what he had seen there, "communism wasn't too bad."

While actively trying to enrol new members in the clerks' union, Bowditch had spoken to a young girl, Betty Hodgson, working in Loutit's store. She was the daughter of a part-Aboriginal woman, Myra Hull, and Englishman Charles Deans "Geordie" Hodgson. Her father, a strict man, had come to Australia at the age of 17 and worked as a fettler on the railway. He had married her mother, a member of the Arabana tribe, when she was 16. Betty, one of 11 surviving children, was born at Oodnadatta, outback South Australia, in 1932. To make ends meet, her father ran an SP (illegal Starting Price bookmaking) business part-time and Betty remembered him burying money in tins when they lived at Marree. Marree was a town divided into four areas: one for Afghans, another for railway workers, the third for the shops and non Aboriginal people while Aboriginal people, according to Betty, lived in rough camps outside the town. Her father could not take her mother into the pub with him because of the law.

Believing Betty to be bright, her father sent her to a Catholic boarding school, St Dominic's Priory School, North Adelaide where she spent four years being taught shorthand, typing, French, English and geography. She also learned to play the piano. Her brother, Douglas, who became a jockey and railway worker, said she was the family's "only silvertail".

Her father was transferred to Alice Springs as a clerk in the Railways office and they lived in a railway house. A regular drinker at Underdown's pub, there was a spot at the bar known as "Geordie's Corner". When Betty's parents split up, she came home from boarding school to look after the family. She found it hard to get work in Alice and for a time was employed as a shorthand typist in the Animal Industry Branch. Later she worked in the office of a transport company. Bowditch used to talk to her in Loutit's shop and began to take her out on his ex-army BSA motorbike. That the editor of the paper was riding around town with an attractive teenage half-caste on the pillion seat did not go unnoticed; tongues wagged. ASIO noted in June 1952 that Bowditch was "currently associating with a half-caste woman called Hodgson." One day Jim, with Betty on the back of the motorcycle, was involved in a collision with a car and thereafter said they should travel in a car for safety.

At times Jim and Betty went to D.D. Smith's residence and were always made to feel welcome. Betty was athletic and played basketball, hockey and tennis. In 1948 she had been a member of a team which beat Darwin in basketball. After she met Jim, Betty watched him play cricket each Sunday. He also played tennis. Betty recalled that he took her to the Memorial Club to gather his social notes for the paper. Many people converged on the club at weekends and some cattlemen came in with their wives. Claims were made that Bowditch deliberately took her to the club to confront the colour bar. Betty said this was not so as far as she knew. Jim said he liked Betty, whom he described as most attractive "some doll" and just took her with him wherever he went. However, in one recorded interview Bowditch said he did take Betty to the Memorial Club to confront the colour ban.

While there was no written rule against taking "coloureds" to the club, it was frowned on. It must be said in fairness that some prominent members of the club said they would walk out if "coloured" members of a Darwin football team on a visit to Alice were not allowed into the club. The visitors were subsequently allowed in and there was no trouble as a result. Apart from some club members frowning on the entry of "coloureds", there was also the "anti-foreigner" attitude. Italians, in particular, had a difficult time, Some Italians, who did eventually gain membership, found they were ignored and left to sit in a group on their own.

The attitude to foreigners irked Bowditch's friend Alan Wauchope, so much that he wrote a letter to the paper on the subject. In it, he said he was concerned to learn that the Memorial Club, like another club in town, had decided not to admit foreigners as members unless they first produced nationalisation papers. He considered this action as a typical insular attitude calculated to do untold harm to the government's policy of friendly assimilation of "screened foreigners". Just to make it abundantly clear what he felt, Wauchope said it was an instance of "tinpot snobbery, lack of vision, and a Pooh-Bah outlook, engendered possibly by a brief residence abroad and membership of some decadent club where rigid lines of demarcation left a knot of befuddled Colonel Blimps in splendid isolation." Furthermore, he went on to say that with the speed of modern travel and the shrinking of distances, foreigners were now our neighbours. He continued: "I have no doubt that if a distinguished 'foreigner' were to visit Alice, whether he be the inkiest of Rajah Bong, or whitest of Russian, the leaders of the Memorial Club would fall over themselves to push and to bask in his reflected glory." His letter obviously caused anger at the Memorial Club. There might even have been a threat of legal action because Wauchope later wrote that he had not been referring to the club's current committee, one member being lawyer Phil Rice, which was doing a good job.

16. FIGHTING FOR UNDERDOGS

Interesting news stories broke in Alice and Bowditch often became personally involved in them, sometimes in most unusual and spectacular ways. Early one morning, at home, Bowditch heard the strange sound of a goat's horn being blown by a large Ukranian, Feodor Cartschenko, from atop Anzac Hill. Cartshenko was a powerfully built man with a long flowing beard and vacant eyes. From discussions with the man, Bowditch surmised he had been "shell shocked" by wartime experiences. Bowditch took the religiously obsessed man home and offered to help him. Declining help, he went and camped in the Todd River, then strolled about town spreading the word of God in halting English, telling Alice imbibers that drink was bad for them. A vegetarian, he mainly lived on bread and honey. He often blew his horn and sang the *Song of David*. Children followed him and laughed when he slid down a slippery dip. However, mothers began to worry about this man who attracted children like the Pied Piper. Many people regarded him as a mental defective.

Bowditch was at the racetrack when he was told that police had arrested Cartschenko. A headlock had been applied to the large, crying man, who was then put in a car, taken to the Ghan train leaving for Adelaide, given his possessions and told never to come back to Alice Springs. Not far from Alice, he jumped from the train and began to walk in the general direction of Adelaide. The police who had run him out of town were alerted and formed a search party. The search went on for days and black trackers found signs that he had been eating wild paddy melons, which would cause severe scouring. They felt he would either be dead or very sick when found. He had abandoned a jar of honey, half a loaf of bread and a bag of peanuts.

On being told that Cartschenko would probably die before he was found, Bowditch went to pilot Eddie Connellan and discussed

11 April 1953, Feodor Cartschenko (right) with Aboriginal trackers, Jacky and Johnny who found him when he went missing. Photo by Moira Milgate.

the possibility of chartering a plane to fly over the desert to look for him. What transpired differed in the telling: Because no parachutes were available Bowditch said he raised with Connellan the possibility of leaping from the plane into a sand dune, he having read that Russians used to jump from planes into snowdrifts during WWII. Connellan's account: "Jim came to me in my office at the aerodrome in Alice Springs and asked to be flown out on a charter flight to find Feodor, then jump out with a parachute and rescue him. He said that if he could achieve this, it would make him as a journalist. I said that unfortunately we did not have a parachute, but that no doubt he would be happy to do what his friends in the Red Army did during training exercises in Siberia jump out of low flying aircraft and land on the downslope of sandhills. Jim of course at that stage was a communist. Jim agreed that if they [the Russians] could do it, he could, and I spent the rest of the interview trying to talk him out of it! End of story."

In any case, Cartschenko was found sitting in his underpants with a duffel bag containing clothes, singing religious songs. He had walked about 45 miles (72 km). Brought back to Alice, he was charged with being a mental defective. However, a local businessman, Jim Richards, told the magistrate he was prepared to take responsibility for Feodor and gave him a job in the building industry. After a while, Cartschenko moved on and Bowditch read reports that he turned up in Melbourne and then Tasmania, where he sang to waterside workers.

Some court cases in Alice Springs during Jim's time as editor involved tribal killings in which defendants were acting according to black man's law, not the imposed white man's rules. Mr Justice Martin Kriewaldt of the NT Supreme Court, a keen baseball fan, anguished over some of these cases. On one occasion, he said he went into the bush to ponder what he should do. One concerned the murder of a man who revealed details about secret rituals to women. Over the years, Bowditch had several private conversations with the judge and discussed the plight of Aborigines. Said Bowditch: "Somehow, the judge and I seemed to hit it off; strange that. We swapped ideas about what was happening to the Aboriginal people and what we thought should be done. From memory, I was convinced at the time that assimilation of the Aborigines was all that could save them, but the judge wasn't at all sure and believed, I think, that they should be able to live in their own areas with their own standards and laws. I felt he was convinced they had, as a rule, a better discipline than we have and a more heavily developed sense of true justice without the complications of muddled legal systems and law books. He had, I am sure, a great deal of respect for them as a people."

In what amounted to a front page editorial, Bowditch drew attention to a "mob riot" involving Aborigines and alcohol near the Capitol Theatre and called on the people of Alice to help police wage war against those who supplied Aborigines with drink. There were usually three types involved in this "nefarious practice", he wrote. One supplied grog "to make a quid"; another preyed on Aboriginal women; and the third, through a misguided feeling of denied rights or social injustice, gave them liquor. Bowditch said people could easily have been killed in the riot at the Capitol.

In one case an Aborigine was sentenced to two and a half years' jail for the attempted rape of a white woman. Court was told the accused had told a constable he was silly with grog at the time of the offence and wanted "to do to a white woman what white man do to black gin." Another unusual case saw a European convicted of supplying alcohol to Phar Lap. It was not the famous race horse, but a hapless Aborigine so named by his white boss.

17. OLIVE PINK

An Alice identity who took a deep interest in Aboriginal affairs and the activities of Jim Bowditch was Miss Olive Pink, widely regarded as an eccentric and one of those dreaded "do-gooders". While Miss Pink was clearly mainly interested in the plight of full-bloods, Bowditch was more concerned about half-castes. She often went to court to listen to cases involving Aborigines, and spoke to Bowditch.

During court hearings she would interrupt proceedings by calling out from the public gallery when she thought an injustice was being done. At the end of a tribal murder case Miss Pink snorted, "So much for so-called British justice." The judge heard her outburst from the public gallery and ordered her arrest. She was allowed to go once she apologised for her remark. Miss Pink was a living legend. By and large, she loathed Alice Springs and said many of its white residents were wife beaters. Sodom and Gomorrah was another epithet of hers for Alice. It is not right to call her a "do gooder", even though she was so regarded. To her way of thinking, this group, from the Prime Minister down, including Paul Hasluck,

Olive Pink and Harold Southern who, it was said,
she had hoped to marry.

who later became the Governor-General, religious organisations, various academics and leading public servants, were collectively embarked on a course of race destruction.

She had been campaigning for Aborigines since the 1930s and had a tragic and unusual background. From Tasmania, Miss Pink met her "greatest friend", Harold Southern, when they were art students in Hobart. Early in the 1900s she was in the household of the WA Governor, Sir Frederick Bedford, who had been in Tasmania. About that time the Southern family also went to Perth from Tasmania. Her friend Captain Southern was killed at Gallipoli in 1915. Each Anzac Day in Alice, Miss Pink used to honour his name.

In the 1920s she stayed with Daisy Bates, who lived near an Aboriginal settlement at Ooldea, in South Australia, close to the transcontinental railway line across the Nullarbor. Bates, an Irish journalist, had been married to Harry "Breaker" Morant, who was executed by the British Army during the Boer War. She spent 33 years working with desert tribes in South Australia and Western Australia. Bates, who regarded Aborigines as a dying race, mentioned "a jolly little artist called Miss Pink" having visited her. Daisy Bates became one of Miss Pink's great hates. The worst thing anybody could do was liken her to Bates.

Miss Pink moved to Sydney and worked in the drafting department of the NSW Railways Department. Her work was said to have involved drawings associated with the huge Sydney Harbour Bridge project. Her interest in Aborigines seems to have grown from her observations while on leave making concessional rail trips interstate. On one of these trips she went to Alice Springs and along the way painted flowers. In 1932 she delivered a speech to a meeting of the Anthropology Section of the Australian New Zealand Association for the Advancement of Science on the uses to which the Aranda and Arabana tribes of Central Australia put their indigenous flora. Vice president of the anthropology section was Professor A.P. Elkin, of Sydney University. Elkin, an influential adviser to government on Aboriginal affairs, commented favourably on her talk

During the years Bowditch was in Alice, Miss Pink issued several printed open letters on important issues which were designed to influence government policies. The letters were widely distributed to politicians, national newspapers, anthropologists, the Prime Minister and others she felt should know of her views. The letters were run off for her on a duplicator at the office of the NSW branch of the Sheet Metal Working, Agricultural Implement and Stovemaking Industrial Union of Australia. A cover note from the secretary of the union, T. Wright, assured Miss Pink that work involved in printing of the newsletters had been done in the union office and there was no cost. Wright was obviously interested in Aborigines as a postscript to a note sent to Miss Pink said: "For persons of mixed blood we need a term corresponding to Eurasian—say Euralian or Euraustian."

In a another newsletter issued on 11 May 1951, copies of which were forwarded to the Brisbane Science Congress, she firmly outlined her case against full citizen rights being handed out one by one and called for pressure to be applied on the federal government to appoint a Royal Commission to investigate the NT situation. Preferably, she said the head of the inquiry should be a Tasmanian judge and that all witnesses must be permanent residents of the NT, not outsiders or so called experts. People of part Aboriginal blood, she said, were a different problem. Commonwealth control of all the affairs of Australia's native race would be the ultimate goal. The searchlight should be focused on every aspect of the Territory situation and she listed areas of specific interest which needed close scrutiny as being wages for men and women, mission activities, appointment of staff, cattle station conditions, the operation and cost of running native wards in hospitals. In effect, she wanted everything and everybody put under the microscope. In a slight for Elkin and other anthropologists, she wrote: "Sydney University's Department of Anthropology's church-mission obsessed dictatorship over the Australian, and especially the NT full-bloods' future, and present lives (through his, Elkin's appointees or followers), has exterminating forces inherent in it, through wrong policies being advised and implemented."

Interestingly, she felt there was urgent need for male and female adult education classes, held in separate places at different times so as not to offend feelings about sex segregation, to give them skills to work out their future rather than have whites decide it for them. She said: "Let our aim be to fight for real communal development for the NT full-bloods with the tribe as the unit and a council of each tribe organising its own developmental schemes. A Commonwealth Council of the various tribes' representatives will be the ultimate goal aimed at, but not rushed."

Her next open letter came out on 13 January 1953 and consisted of six pages that attacked the Hasluck-Menzies assimilation policy, which she described as a camouflaged substitute for extermination. The new exploitation of Aborigines in Australia was now political, she said, with both Right and Left wanting to "give" full-bloods and mixed bloods "a vote", regardless of whether they could, at that stage, use it in their own interests, which in the NT they could not. Under these rights the Aborigines would be taxed while the station owners for whom they worked as slave labourers paid no tax. Aborigines could be called to serve in the army to fight for whites' interests, even for "the freedom of Koreans to decide their own future." Could, she asked, anything be more cynical and hypocritical of white Australians?

She raised the possibility of Aboriginal artist Albert Namatjira, who had been feted by sections of the white community, being used by politically-minded whites, or "mixed bloods", to betray the future of his own race in the NT. A few years before, she said, Namatjira, influenced by whites, had been prepared to take up land as a pastoral holding outside his own Aranda country. To do so, would probably have caused bitterness and untold trouble with the owning tribes-people in the area. While Aborigines resented the arrival of white pioneers they had not been able to take effective action against them. But they could, and would, resent and resist, or steal from a "black" of another tribe. Then police would be called in to support the invading "black" pastoralist. It was hypocrisy to pretend to be "raising them" by trampling on their tribal outlook on their tribal territory.

Miss Pink probably regarded much of what Bowditch did in the cause of half-castes as reprehensible. Early one morning he heard knocking at his door at home. When he opened the door, there was Miss Pink with a raised umbrella and, muttering something like, "How dare you use that phrase," brought the brolly down on his head. Bowditch was never sure what the offending phrase had been. At times Miss Pink invited Bowditch to her home for a cup of tea and some home-made scones. On those occasions she animatedly and emphatically expressed her views. He said she had mixed feelings about him because she did not approve of white men having coloured girlfriends and wives; she also did not like drinkers. While she may have regarded him as suspect, Miss Pink respected Jock Nelson, saying he was genuine and unaffected. His wife, Peg, was also held in high regard. Miss Pink abhorred the use of the expression "coloureds", repeatedly pointing out white was a colour.

For a long time Miss Pink had realised expanding pastoral activities and mining would bring an end to the nomadic lifestyle of Aborigines. Bowditch said that while she had been working in the Tanami she had tried to teach Aborigines how to establish stationary camps with vegetable and fruit gardens to supplement their bush tucker. Bowditch described her as a brave and well-meaning woman who would rather starve than accept food or help from anybody. She had kept body and soul together by growing and selling flowers and some vegetables. A special treat for her was an ice-cream and she would save her pennies for one.

While he acknowledged that she corresponded with important and powerful people in government and anthropological circles, he doubted if she had much influence on Aboriginal policy because most people regarded her as an eccentric, which was a tragedy. Furthermore, she mainly acted on her own and it was too big a task for one person.

Bowditch also referred to "Miss Pink's voodoo", which she practised at the Home Hut Native Flora Reserve, of which, she stressed, she was the honorary, unpaid curator. This place, now known as the Olive Pink Flora Reserve, had several honour avenues in which were trees named after prominent people, many of them in government and the public service, who had helped her, willingly or unwillingly. If a person after whom a tree was named subsequently offended her in some way, she would cut off or reduce the water supply to the tree. Jim said this was a form of voodoo in which, instead of sticking pins into dolls, Miss Pink cut off their water supply. He had a tree named after him, but he suspected it often had its water supply stopped. Dick Ward also had a tree named after him.

In later years, Miss Pink used to address letters to public servant Frank Dwyer, at times the Acting Administrator, with the title "Dear Shylock". Bowditch said Miss Pink really loathed Dwyer but played up to him because he was an influential person. She also named a tree after him, and Dwyer suspected she shut off his water supply from time to time. Bowditch recalled Miss Pink had a long-running battle with the fire brigade. She had once lived next to the fire station and accused the men of swearing, drinking, gambling and making excessive noise. A court case resulted from one confrontation with the firemen, and Miss Pink refused to swear on the Bible, but made an affirmation, saying she always told the truth. She claimed "language used in the underworld" had been shouted at her; the offending language was written down on paper for the magistrate to peruse. During the hearing she clashed several times with the defence lawyer, Phil Rice. She lost the case and indignantly claimed there was no justice for women in the NT.

Convinced that conditions were unsatisfactory in the Alice lockup, she asked to make an inspection of the premises. Told this was not possible, Miss Pink then started a course of action aimed at getting inside. This involved her committing a minor offence, refusing to pay a fine and then asking to be locked up. However, she was thwarted at the last minute when the officer in charge of the lockup paid the fine himself. Miss Pink often tongue-lashed D.D. Smith, even though he was sympathetic to her cause.

Late in life, Miss Pink told me that "Mr Bowditch" had come down from Darwin and visited her place with a male friend. "I think he[Bowditch] had been drinking," she said, and he had fallen into a bed of flowers. Flowers in the spot where she indicated he had landed were less luxuriant than others nearby, and this was years after the event. Obviously, she was not impressed with journalists. Alan Wauchope said Miss Pink once told him he was a disgrace to the newspaper profession.

18. NEWSPAPER WARS

Bowditch took great interest in a proposal to start a new newspaper in Darwin, the *Northern Territory News*, which would challenge the long established union paper, the lusty up-the-workers *Northern Standard*. Bowditch provided a regular column for the *Standard* called "Alice Landline". He felt the new Darwin paper was a sign of southern media interests moving into the Territory and that his own paper could be vulnerable.

The move to start the new newspaper in Darwin created some interesting bedfellows. Key figures in the project were Don Whitington and Eric White. Whitington, managing director of Australian Press Services Ltd and former chief of the Canberra bureau of the Frank Packer owned Australian Consolidated Press, had strong links with the ALP. White, head of the powerful public relations firm, Eric White and Associates, had been public relations director for the federal Liberal Party from 1944–7, bringing him into close contact with Robert Menzies. White went on to write several papers on public relations and propaganda.

Whitington, in partnership with White, had launched a weekly newsletter called *Inside Canberra* in 1948 and the Chifley Labor government had been impressed by its objectivity. The PM, Ben Chifley, may have himself originated the idea for the Darwin newspaper. Chifley was said to be obsessive about communists and regarded the *Northern Standard* as a communist publication.

The Labor government approached Whitington in 1949 and asked him to look at the possibility of starting a paper in Darwin.

Union run newspaper, the *Northern Standard*, was Darwin's only newspaper until the *NT News* arrived. *Northern Territory Times* was an earlier publication.

Dr John Burton, head of External Affairs (later Foreign Affairs) in the Chifley Government told Whitington the Labor government was worried that Darwin, as the first port of call for visitors from Europe, did not have a "reputable newspaper". Whitington told Burton neither he nor White had enough money to open a newspaper, estimated to be up to 20,000 pounds. Told that the government could help in the way of freight and advertising, Whitington went to Darwin and sounded out the local business community for funds. Initially, members of the Chinese business community indicated they would put up money. However, much more was needed. Whitington subsequently wrote that there was a communist phobia in Darwin and that he felt the idea that the *Standard* posed a threat to national security was ludicrous. Funds

The "Tin Bank", the former English, Scottish and Australian (ES&A) Bank in Smith Street, was the first home of the *Northern Territory News*.

were raised from various sources and the plant of a small Darwin job printer, John Coleman, was obtained for 1000 one pound shares in Northern Territory News Services Ltd.

Whitington asked his former boss, Frank Packer, if he would like to put money into the new paper. Packer declined to subscribe but offered the services of his head printer, George Stanbridge, to help select secondhand equipment for Darwin. An old flatbed press which was used to print labels on cardboard cartons for Arnott's biscuits was bought. It cost about 50 pounds, but took 500 pounds to move to Darwin. It printed one side only and the sheets then had to be fed back to do the other side, a laborious, time-consuming process. Two linotype machines were also bought, one coming from *Smith's Weekly*.

When the Chifley government lost office in 1949, Canberra seemed to lose interest in the Darwin newspaper proposal. But when Larry Anthony became Acting Minister for the Interior he visited Darwin, came back and called Whitington in to discuss the project. Anthony, father of later Country Party leader, Doug Anthony, discussed the problem of finding premises for the newspaper. It was subsequently arranged through government channels that the former English Scottish and Australian Bank building in Smith Street, used by the navy as a store, would be made available.

Known locally as the "Tin Bank", it was a prefabricated galvanised iron building which was said to have been shipped to Darwin from India in the 1880s. It was a rusty and dirty old building which had some bullet holes from WWII. There was a veranda on one side that had been turned into an office and staff quarters. During the Wet, the building was hemmed in by spear grass six-feet high on three sides.

Whitington had been warned that watersiders planned to dump any printing equipment for the new paper in the harbour. The printing plant was consigned to Darwin in parts disguised as plumbing equipment and other non-suspicious objects. Even before the new paper was up and running, Whitington was the subject of an attack by the *Standard* in May 1950 for "spreading lies and libels about Darwin and its citizens" in an article he wrote for the Sydney *Daily Telegraph*, Whitington, the *Standard* trumpeted, had written that communists ran Darwin and its hospital and that the *Standard* was owned by communists. The *Standard* retaliated with a satirical article by "Dick Whittington" headed: JOURNALIST TELLS ALL: SCOTCH AND SODA AND CERULEAN BLUE, a romp in the form of a diary in which an intrepid reporter books into the Hotel Darwin on a dangerous assignment in a town run by Reds. The gloves were off.

The first edition of the *NT News* was printed on 8 February, 1952 under the editorship of Mac Jeffers, a small man who became known as the "Midget Sub", a prodigious worker. That first edition ran messages of support for the paper from many political leaders. In what was obviously a poke in the eye for the union-run *Standard*, there were also many messages from the leaders of Australian unions.

An editorial said the *NT News* would "fight for North Australia." The page 3 lead in the first and many subsequent issues was headed CANBERRA DIARY, which was contributed by Don Whitington. This regular feature was later changed to BEHIND THE HEADLINES, probably because to many Territorians Canberra was a dirty word. The first edition carried an ad for

Front page of the first edition of the *NT News* carries the news of the death of King George VI and the elevation to Queen of his daughter, Elizabeth.

the annual literary competition in which Douglas Lockwood would judge short stories; one-act plays would be perused by Mrs H. Chauvel, wife of the film producer; and bushman Bill Harney would handle the verse section.

For years most of the photographs used were blocks provided by the Packer owned *Sydney Telegraph*. This explains why there were so many photos of Sydney events in the Darwin paper, a girl posing on Bondi beach had no real relevance to the Top End, nor did a bunch of Sydney musicians hamming it up for the camera.

Production of the new paper in Darwin and other events in Australia were noticed in Indonesia, resulting in a strange letter arriving addressed to both the editor of the *NT News* and Douglas Lockwood of the Melbourne Herald group of newspapers. The sender was C.A. Rebeira, FBSC, FCI, FIPS, a Ceylonese resident in Indonesia for 43 years, who described himself as a company director and adviser to many business and industrial concerns. He had read in a Jakarta newspaper about the birth of the *NT News*. While wishing the newspaper success and saying he was not anti-Australian, he warned that Australia was denying God's will that the "surplus population" of China, India, Japan and Pakistan should occupy the country. Australians, he said, had tried to wipe out Aborigines, driving them inland and hunting them like wild dogs. Now Australia and New Zealand, with so much vacant land, feared being invaded by Asia. In the NT alone there were 550,000 square miles of vacant good land, which the Asian races could turn into a bountiful area. Directing remarks to Lockwood's "mistaken idea", he referred to a newspaper article in the *Melbourne Herald* in which it was said 70 million Indonesians were "staring" at the empty land in North Australia. Rebeira declared there was no need for empty Australian land because the Indonesian Republic was now dispersing its population, which had been bottled up under the Dutch. Australia, he said, had sided with the Dutch in the dispute over Dutch New Guinea. Reports about Indonesians wanting to overrun Australia were nonsense and imaginative falsehoods.

The second edition of the *NT News* carried some disturbing information: the local brewery was up for auction under instructions from the mortgagee. With 97 years to run on its lease, the fully equipped brewery came complete with stocks of malt, hops, syrups and cordials. There was also an odd item in the same paper which had the suspicious earmarks of a quick beat-up to fill a hole. It reported that a gorilla had been sighted near Auckland, New Zealand. One person who made use of the advertising columns was Jessie Litchfield, of Roberta Library, grandmother of a later NT Chief Minister Marshall Perron.

Much was made of the fact that the *News* was owned by locals. In fact, the editorial shots were called from Sydney through Eric White and Don Whitington. A regular part of the *News* was a front page column called "True North", which usually contained bright, short items. It is thought that Whitington might have been responsible for naming the column, which ran for decades. Whitington was obviously a man with a sense of humour as he once listed his hobbies in *Who's Who* as watching birds, carousing and Australian Rules football. He had an arrangement with TAA whereby he would fly up from Sydney to Darwin and write articles for the airline's magazine and other publications. At times he visited Alice and spoke to Bowditch, the two hitting it off. Whitington advised Bowditch to move on from Alice because the place was too small for a man with his talents.

The Darwin-based managing director and shareholder in the *News*, freelance journalist Bob Freeden, drove to Alice in a black Riley during May 1952 and obviously spoke to Bowditch as there was mention of him and the car in a brief paragraph in the *Advocate*. The two became close friends. A large man, Freeden had been born in Germany, his family having fled from Nazi persecution of Jews just before the outbreak of the war. The family settled in Western Australia and Bob studied geology before taking a job with MacRobertson-Miller Airlines. In his twenties, he was made Darwin manager of MMA. Bush pilots often returned from the outback with offbeat stories. Freeden began to send these stories to newspapers in the south. Within a short time he was stringing for many newspapers outside the Herald and Weekly Times group, represented in Darwin by Lockwood. Eventually he resigned from MMA to concentrate on journalism and became involved with Eric White and Don Whitington in the *News* venture.

Freeden quickly realised that southern newspapers had a voracious appetite for exotic stories from Darwin and the Northern Territory, so he gave them what they wanted. This involved beating up some stories, even inventing them. Reports about crocodiles, buffaloes and kangaroos in the main street of Darwin were lapped up by the newspapers. Lockwood became angry when asked by his paper to provide matching stories for Freeden's creative pieces. One of Freeden's beat-ups had a crocodile marauding through Cashman's store in Darwin's main street. Lockwood would indignantly say a story was false, and his southern head office would be disappointed. However, when Lockwood was absent from Darwin, Freeden sometimes covered for him and sent stories down south. Freeden had a lisp and often told Bowditch over a glass of beer, "There is no noows in the twoof."

A true experience with a crocodile filled Freeden with fear. While doing a trip on the patrol vessel *Kuru*, Freeden went

Freelance journalist, later *NT News* Editor, Bob Freeden and an
unidentified companion at the entrance to the Rum Jungle Uranium Mine.

to Maningrida in Arnhem Land. There he asked Native Affairs
officer Jack Doolan, later Member for Victoria River in the NT
Legislative Assembly, to take him out on a night croc shooting trip.
Doolan agreed and thought he would put on a bit of a show for
Freeden. In a canoe with little freeboard and paddled by an old
Aboriginal, Charlie Mungan, they ventured into the mangroves.
Seeing what he thought was a small crocodile because its eyes were
close together, Doolan waited until they were alongside before he
fired a shot. However, it turned out to be a much larger crocodile
with small beady eyes, and it went berserk. Charlie tried to kill the
crocodile with wild swings from an axe and in the process nearly
scalped the other men. The canoe tipped and dipped and Freeden
hung on grimly. Finally, Charlie was able to kill the croc with a blow
between the eyes. Freeden was petrified and insisted on getting out
of the canoe and walking back to the camp through the mangroves,
arriving there coated in mud and badly scratched.

While the *NT News* was feeling its way, the Sydney directors
were already planning another newspaper in the Queensland
mining town of Mount Isa. Whitington was not so keen about
starting another paper, but Eric White had spoken to Mount Isa
Mines Ltd's chairman, George Fisher, and received encouragement
from him for the project.

An adventurous New Zealand journalist and author, Ross
Annabell, then became involved in the Mount Isa plans (and later

had dealings with Bowditch). After freelancing in North Queensland for 10 months from a base in Mareeba, Annabell returned to the *Mackay Mercury* and was surprised to receive a letter from Eric White and Associates in November 1952 asking him if he would like to be the editor of a new weekly newspaper in Mount Isa. They had contacted Annabell because he had applied in 1950 for the job as the first editor of the *NT News*, but had not received a reply to his letter. Then, out of the blue, some two years later, he was offered the editorship of a new newspaper to be called the *Mount Isa Mail*, on a salary of 20 pounds a week, plus two per cent commission on any advertising contracts he could sell. He accepted the position to start mid-January but, luckily, did not resign from the *Mercury* as plans for the new paper were delayed several months.

In April 1953 Annabell was flown to Sydney and in an interview with White and Whitington was confirmed as editor and given many instructions on how they wanted the paper run. They told him they had 20,000 pounds capital to start the paper and he firmly believed they had received some financial help from the mining company. Annabell was instructed to set up an office in the Isa then travel to Townsville and go by rail around western Queensland for a fortnight selling advertising space and gathering copy for the paper. The paper would be printed in Darwin at the *NT News*.

Annabell was convinced both White and Whitington had spoken to mine management who were "desperate" to have a local paper to counter the strong union influence in the town. As a result of that visit to Sydney, Annabell resigned from the *Mercury* immediately, booked a flight to Isa for late May, the aim being to have the first newspaper out on 3 July. He tried to leave the Mackay paper earlier, but the management made him work out his month's notice and he finally departed for Mount Isa on May 26. By this time, Eric White and Associates were in a "big panic" because they had heard that a journalist with access to financial backing was trying to buy the newspaper in the nearby township of Cloncurry with plans to also produce a paper for Mount Isa, beating them to the punch.

Annabell arrived in the mining centre and discovered that the temporary office which had been arranged for him was to be demolished in two weeks. Therefore his first tasks were to find a new office, engage an office girl and have a phone connected. After that he had to get cracking on stories and advertising for the first issue. The local MP, a Labor man, was suspicious about the paper. Entertainment in Isa consisted of picture theatres, pubs and a brothel, all of which did a roaring trade. Diligently doing the rounds on a motorbike, whipping up ads and copy for the new paper, Annabell was told that a Sydney company had rung a Mount Isa timber and hardware firm seeking land on which to build a newspaper office and printery. This intelligence was quickly passed on and caused further consternation at Eric White's. Then a rumour went about that the journalist said to be keen to move into Mount Isa had offered 12,000 pounds for the nearby *Cloncurry Advocate* plant and buildings.

EW & A made counter offers until it eventually succeeded in buying the rundown plant; it was later moved to Mount Isa. The plant was so primitive that the metal for the linotype machines had to be melted down each day in a wood-fired trough in the back yard. However, during the months Annabell was in the Isa he was on his own and the Cloncurry paper had not yet been bought. The first edition of the *Mail* came out on Friday, 26 June 1953, and consisted of four broadsheet pages. Prominence was given to a Sydney court case in which a man linked with plans to start up a rival paper in Mount Isa had been charged with embezzling funds from Universal Business Directories. Eric White and Associates had known of the forthcoming case and had instructed Annabell that he should mention it about town to undermine a potential competitor.

As planned, the *Mail* was printed in Darwin and flown down to Annabell for distribution. During his time in Mount Isa he led a busy life which included parties at the hospital, drinking sessions at 2 am in the pathology department with nurses and being driven home in an ambulance. Having successfully launched the Mount Isa paper, he was then directed to Darwin in September to help the *NT News* in its quest to torpedo the *Standard*. He was obviously well respected in the Isa because at a farewell party the local shire chairman got into a fight when someone shouted him down during a speech praising Ross for his efforts in starting the *Mail*.

When Annabell arrived in Darwin from Mount Isa he was allowed to live on the *News* premises in part of the veranda on the town side of the building. He had to provide his own bedding and mosquito net. To make life easier, he bought himself an electric jug and a single element stove on which to cook his breakfast and make banana fritters. It was not too bad a set-up for Darwin, which had a severe shortage of accommodation. At the time the NT News Services Ltd's director, Bob Freeden, was living in a one-room hut rented from the ABC, so Annabell did not feel so bad about his lot. However, the situation changed for the worse. Annabell was given the task of turning the paper into a bi-weekly. Because of the old, slow press it had to be run until midnight several times a week and it made sleep difficult. On top of that, an accountant sent up from Sydney was a homosexual and he lived in a room next door with a flimsy wall separating the two. The man would go drinking in pubs and bring home people, resulting in disturbing goings on behind the plywood wall.

The issue came to a head when Annabell was entertaining a nurse in his quarters. Back drunk from the pub, the man in the next room made snide remarks which could be clearly heard through the partition. Enraged, Annabell turned from a suave, mild-mannered reporter with an impressive (for those days) bachelor pad, complete with a one ring stove, into an aggressive man threatening to smash in the accountant's head. Alarmed and shocked, the nurse asked to be taken home to the hospital living quarters. Reluctantly, Annabell whipped the nurse back to hospital on his motorbike. Then he sped back to the *News* in a murderous rage and ended up hitting the man.

He described the fracas thus: "I called him out to settle the argument in good caveman fashion; but he simply stood there and insisted that he was a 'gentleman' and gentlemen didn't fight. So I let him have a mighty right smack in the kisser, but he simply stood and took it, and wouldn't fight. And, not being particularly adept in the ancient art of boxing, I had tucked in my thumb, which nearly dislocated on his ugly mug, and left me in no condition to give him a second right." The man left the *News* soon after.

Annabell had a major row with Don Whitington over a story which he did not run in the *NT News*. The story was about the

As a freelance journalist and photographer, Ross Annabell was
not averse to adventurous escapades such as crocodile and buffalo
shooting to generate his colourful stories.

Monte Bello nuclear tests off WA. Whitington had sent up a front-
page story from Sydney quoting physicist Professor Harry Messel
as saying a cloud of lethal radioactive fallout could blow across
the Top End and kill people or render them sterile. The explosion
was due the day the story would have been run in the *NT News*.
Annabell felt that if the dire predictions were true it would be too
late to warn the people of Darwin because by the time the paper hit
the street many of them could be dead or sterilised. Furthermore,
he felt the story would create panic in Darwin, resulting in a mass
evacuation down the track like the one that followed the bombing
of Darwin by the Japanese in February 1942. "Whitington was
furious, and ripped the shit out of me in his next dispatch from
Sydney," Annabell recalled.

There was one other reporter on the staff, Jim Kelly, who
mainly covered sport. Annabell wrote most of the general news,

Jim Kelly, sports reporter
for the *NT News* and
occasional astrologer.

did the layout for the paper, proofread and performed several other chores including keeping a close eye on getting the paper out on time. Lockwood and Freeden supplied him with "blacks", copies of stories they sent south. Ruth Lockwood, wife of Doug, occasionally helped out by contributing a "women's item".

In a bid to capture more readers, the *News* began running horse racing acceptances from four states, claiming to be the only capital city newspaper in Australia at the time to provide such a service for punters. It was a clear indication that gambling was a major interest in Darwin and big business. As a counter, the *Standard* began to run extensive horse racing notes from the Sydney turf expert A.B. Gray, former racing editor of *Smith's Weekly*.

During the polio outbreak which was also experienced in Alice, the *Standard* told readers the reason for the disease in Australia: the "vile, decaying system" under which people lived: capitalism. It highlighted the fly menace in Darwin and said the antiquated equipment at the hospital included an autoclave, for sterilising instruments, which had been made in 1914.

The *Standard* fulminated against Japanese being allowed back into Australia, especially Territory waters. The campaign quoted Jessie Litchfield and MHR Jock Nelson as saying it was inappropriate for Japanese to return. Japanese were described by the paper as "treacherous spies". It thundered: "We will have no more Japanese polluting the North." A series of photos showing Japanese in military uniforms doing self defence military exercises was headed: JAPS AT PLAY? Other items in the paper said Japanese had been seen taking photographs of a wharf in South Australia; JAPS AT IT AGAIN IN NEW GUINEA was the comment when a fishing boat entered the three mile territorial waters. Another unusual heading in the paper was: TUT, TUT, TOKIO! It dealt with complaints in a Japanese newspaper about limitations likely to be placed on pearlers allowed back into Australian waters and pointed out that Darwin based pearler Nicholas Paspaley (brother of Mick Paspalis) had told the *Standard* how Japanese had fished out grounds in the past. It has to be remembered that Darwin had been bombed by the Japanese and almost 300 people, including unionists working on the waterfront, had been killed, so the union paper and others were vehement in their antipathy toward the Japanese.

The subject of Aboriginal rights, especially for half-castes, was often mentioned in the *Standard*, as it was in the *News*. The North Australian Workers' Union, of course, had been involved in this cause because half-castes were members. Jack McGinness, president of the Australian Halfcastes' Progress Association, was quoted in 1953 in relation to the so-called Half-castes Bill which would give them their "freedom". He was also given space to outline plans for a hostel and other facilities in Darwin.

Professional journalists brought in to run the *Standard* were often hindered by union interference. Good stories were dropped because a key person in them was a union member who it was felt should not be portrayed unfavourably. Of course, it was open season on "capitalists". The paper trumpeted the news that it would run in serialised form the life of British trade union leader Aneurin Bevan, the Welsh coal miner who rose to be a Cabinet minister and introduced the National Health Service.

It was said that in a desperate bid to increase circulation, the *Standard* resorted to "pornography", a term used by Bowditch and others, without explanation. Presumably, this related to a contrived article under the heading "SEX" that suggested a brothel should be set up in Darwin which would reduce such crimes as young girls being "tampered with" and "peeping toms". It started by saying H.G. Wells had said one of the most disruptive forces of the 20th century had been the restless sea of dissatisfied young people. The North had "unsated youth" and in Darwin there were 3500 male adults and only 1600 females. Youth was not only unsatisfied by existing society, but their natural, quite proper sexual drives and compensating outlets were blocked by the shortage of women.

The paper warned that "thwarted energies", if not given an outlet through things like beer, swimming, fishing and so on, could lead to an explosive situation. To overcome this tropical time bomb, it was suggested that a licensed brothel like those in Townsville, Brisbane and Perth be established in Darwin to absorb "surplus, dangerous energies." The paper continued the argument by saying it should be apparent to police and administration that the stability of Darwin and district rested as much on sex as the economic factor. The situation, it said, could also be eased by bringing up more wives from down south and providing more accommodation in Darwin. The paper invited readers to respond with letters and said it would run any (printable) suggestions to overcome the problem.

The first response to this article was headed: NO BROTHELS FOR DARWIN, and was signed "Psychologist", a person said to be a well-known Darwin citizen whose identity was cloaked by a pseudonym. This mystery man said the editorial on sex had been unpalatable, that the use of H.G. Wells to start the argument for a brothel had been fallacious and that bad grammar had been used.

The paper next ran a nebulous editorial on a subject dear to the heart of Darwin—beer. In the Territory, it said, every man, woman and child swallowed a pint of beer a day, or 43 gallons a year. The response to these two editorials might not have been as desired. Enemies of the paper, including the *NT News* touting for business about town, could have and probably did brand the paper a depraved commie rag, particularly in respect to the brothel issue. Soon after the brothel and beer items, the *Standard* felt compelled to declare it was not a communist publication. The union paper which had fought so stridently for the workers over all those years was, however, doomed.

19. LOVE THY PUBLIC SERVANTS

One journalist at the *Standard* near the end of its life was the literarily inclined Bruce Muirden, who had frequent dealings with Bowditch. Muirden laboured at the paper during 1953 when it was under the control of the North Australian Workers' Union secretary, Paddy Carroll, who was not a communist. In 1950, Muirden, only 22, believing that the academics and literateurs of the country paid too little attention to Australian literature, started his own literary journal, the *Austrovert*, in Melbourne. In the first edition he explained that he had no staff and no outside financial backing. The first edition owed its existence mainly to the fact that he had saved money while working as a labourer in a NSW irrigation area. A recent undergraduate, his only literary efforts had appeared in the Melbourne University undergraduates' papers and magazines. He had also contributed copy to the Melbourne *Argus* on rural matters. Muirden went on to help the CSIRO start its rural research magazine.

A bright, different kind of literary journal, *Austrovert* saw the light of day only when Muirden saved enough money to pay for another edition. He billed Kylie Tennant as Australia's Steinbeck. Poems by Judith Wright graced its pages. When Muirden came to Darwin to work at the *Standard* his magazine was still alive, though only just. He thought the Darwin job was that of a reporter, but on arrival he was surprised to learn that he was the editor.

An ASIO man in Darwin came to the office and asked Muirden to pass on any documents he found from the old days of the paper. Muirden reported the "little chat" with the man in the newspaper. Of course, he refused to cooperate. He said the old communist stigma attached to the paper took a long time to die out. For example, he said a southern employer had him checked by ASIO when he heard he had once worked on the *Standard*. A 1953 ASIO report on Muirden noted that he met delegates to an All China Congress in Peking when they passed through Darwin. It also said that during his short term in Darwin Muirden gained a reputation for his provocative editorials, one of which had "harped on" the "arresting powers of ASIO." Nevertheless, it went on to say that Muirden, the son of Angus Muirden, co-principal at Hassett's Business College, Melbourne, also anti-communist and a lay preacher, was considered to be anti-communist.

Muirden brought a degree of erudition to the newspaper and continued his campaign to promote Australian literature and talent. He brought out the last edition of his literary magazine, Number 10, June 1953, in Darwin and it was printed by the *Standard*. Called the *Northern Austrovert*, it consisted of a mere two pages and said Muirden had been working at the *Standard* for six months. An editorial headed "THE END?" said it was probably the last edition of the publication. It was folding because Muirden said he was unable to give it sufficient time, thought and finance to make it what he wanted it to be. During its life the journal had made friends and enemies, he said. In the death-knell he recalled that critic Max Harris in his regional newsletter had bagged *Austrovert*, saying it was parrot-like and a parasitic publication with a narrow, almost circulating library concept of what is literature.

Bowditch and Muirden communicated during Muirden's time in the editorial seat at the *Standard* and Jim's contributions were prominently displayed. In his regular column for the *Standard* Bowditch expressed disenchantment with the ALP. He strongly attacked ALP leader Arthur Calwell for reported derogatory remarks about Chinese in Australia which included claims that there was a trade in teenage wives from overseas in the Darwin Chinese community. The statement had angered the Darwin Chinese, who were reported as saying that the local Chinese community was small in number and many had become related through marriage. To overcome inbreeding, it had been necessary to obtain new wives from overseas. Bowditch castigated Calwell for his comments, describing him as "the ALP big noise and general pain in the neck." He continued: "Why is it that the man receives the protection of the party and followers of the party he personally does more to discredit than anyone else? Does the fact that he is the ALP noise mean he can destroy the name of the party, insult friends and people we seek to become more friendly with?"

Bowditch spoke of "horrible" and "glaring weaknesses" in the ALP. The originator of the "tripe" against Chinese, Calwell, should be shot, he wrote. Soon after, he criticised some members of the Alice Springs branch of the ALP, which had made a "dictatorial ruling", he said, that no member of the party should have anything to say on local government issues at meetings of the Progress Association. "Why do ALP bigwigs do and say things designed to show thinking people what sort of coots they would be if in power, and yet are tolerated by the party members?" he asked. Bowditch had been an active member of the Progress Association and said he hoped ALP members who were in the association would treat the ruling with the contempt it deserved.

Muirden, like Bowditch, found fault with the ALP in an editorial bearing his name, which carried the heading: SHOULD SOCIALISTS CURSE CIVIL SERVANTS? It boiled down to the novel message for Territorians that, for socialism to succeed, the knocking of civil servants would have to cease because in a communally organised society everyone, in a sense, would be a civil servant. He strongly criticised the Darwin ALP, saying one hardly knew there was an organised political Labor organisation in the Territory. "What is to be done when socialists (and perhaps even members of the ALP) join in the popular pastime of baiting civil servants?" he asked. Unthinking general condemnation of government activity played into the hands of the present holders of social order. The ALP should help remove the stigma attached to government employment and stop blanketing the whole public service with a curse.

As could be expected, there was a lively rejoinder. In a letter to the editor, ALP secretary Aubrey Callinan, referred to "Mr Muirden's editorial swansong", which he said had displayed a lamentable lack of knowledge of both socialism and the activities of the ALP in the NT. The publication of "this kind of rubbish" by Muirden in a working-class newspaper was a surprise. It was expected in a capitalist or communist controlled press, but not in a paper claiming to be devoted to the cause of the working man. The progress of the ALP towards its ultimate goal of socialism was not helped by "armchair critics" who rarely had any appreciation of the problems involved, nor of the mechanics of social and industrial democracy. The editorial suggestion that civil servants felt themselves to be at the level of pariahs was a new low in journalism as was the suggestion that the ALP blanketed the whole civil service with a curse. Callinan said the ALP had always sought and received the cooperation of the civil service. He gave a recent instance in which an ALP deputation had met the Minister for the Interior, the Administrator and the Government Secretary and had asked for education facilities to be established at Hatches Creek and Daly River, resulting in budget allocations for the two projects. This, wrote Callinan, was cooperation, not curses. While cooperation continued, the curses would "belong in the mind of Mr Muirden."

20. BOWDITCH BUSTS THIRD DEGREE

The front page lead in the 29 October 1953 edition of the *Standard* was an Alice Springs court case in which Bowditch was a central figure. The report said it had been alleged that police Sergeant John Michael Fitzgerald had used American-style "third degree" methods when questioning half-caste Mervyn Brockhirzon about a break-in. Brockhirzon had laid a charge of assault against Fitzgerald. The case was a classic example of Bowditch reacting to "bullying".

While drinking at the Memorial Club, Bowditch often spoke to and drank with Sgt "Blackjack" Fitzgerald, who freely talked about police work; some of the things he told Bowditch were said to be "hair-raising". One night at the club, Fitzgerald, whom Bowditch judged to be under the influence of liquor, said he had pulled in Brockhirzon for questioning, and then showed him skinned knuckles, adding: "I had to play a little." On being told that, Bowditch quickly sought out the young lawyer Phil Rice, much later involved in the Azaria Chamberlain missing baby case, and with him went to the police station. There they bluffed the young officer on duty, and were shown into a cell where they found Brockhirzon battered and bleeding. Rice took a statement from the man and subsequently filed a charge of assault against Fitzgerald. In court, Brockhirzon said he had feared he was going to "cop it" from Fitzgerald. The policeman had "whaled" into him, splitting his lip, blackening an eye and cracking his dentures. The complainant denied calling Fitzgerald a rotten copper bastard who was always picking on him, or that he struck the officer. Called to the witness box, Bowditch recounted the events of the evening. Special Magistrate Bell found Fitzgerald guilty and fined him ten shillings, saying there may have been some provocation.

Before the case, Bowditch had received allegations about half-castes often being beaten up by police, but said he could not do much about it until somebody was prepared to make a statutory declaration. After a confrontation in the Memorial Club in which Mrs Fitzgerald called Bowditch a "little commie bastard", the sergeant left the police force and reportedly set himself up in Adelaide as a private investigator.

Bowditch's regular contact with Muirden at the *Standard* ended when Muirden left Darwin and went to the *Cairns Post* in North Queensland.

Staff at the *NT News* did not seem to last long because the Sydney directors of the paper were regarded as very demanding, mean and unreasonable people to deal with. On occasions, members of the staff in Darwin sent letters to each other purporting to be from Sydney saying there was a bonus enclosed for having worked under difficult and primitive conditions. Needless to say, a quick search of the envelope failed to find any cheque.

Ross Annabell, a competent and conscientious worker, was given the sack and had six weeks to work out his time. While reading the classified advertisements page proofs, he came across an ad for the free tenancy of a shack at Dinah Beach, which gave the name Gardner, c/o Lands Department, Darwin, as the contact. As he was soon to lose his accommodation at the *News*, along with his job, Annabell contacted Gardner, who proved to be a real character.

Jack Gardner, an Englishman, had been knocking about the Territory for 29 years. His father, a soldier, had been in the All India tug-o-war team. Jack had met author Xavier Herbert when he was in the Territory. He also loved reading, especially O'Henry short stories, and did some "scribbling" himself. Even though there was no rent, no key and no bond, there were some disquieting aspects to the shack deal. First, the owner of the shack was in Fannie Bay Gaol for homosexual assaults on young boys. Second, Gardner had himself recently completed 12 months in prison for cohabitating with an Aboriginal woman and supplying her with alcohol. On hearing that Gardner was soon to be released, the owner of the shack had offered him the caretaker tenancy and given him a document on Fannie Bay Gaol notepaper saying Jack was the legal occupier of the desirable piece of real estate. Desperate for accommodation and assured that the owner would not be free for a long time, Annabell agreed to move in. Gardner said he was going bush prospecting for uranium and would call in from time to time and stay for a few days. Annabell gave the shack a good clean out and scrub before he moved in. Happy in the knowledge that he would have somewhere to stay when he left the *News*, Annabell continued to work out his notice.

However, he was asked to stay on a few days longer because of the sensational Petrov spy affair, which saw the wife of a Russian diplomat who defected to Australia seek asylum at Darwin airport while being escorted out of the country by two burly guards. Annabell witnessed Mrs Petrov being taken out a side entrance to

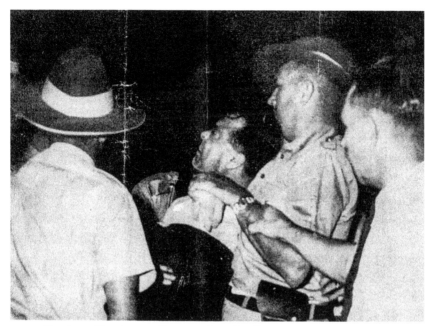

Northern Territory policeman Greg Ryall restrains one of Evdokia
Petrov's Soviet guards.

freedom while the guards pounded on the Customs door demanding
her return.

With the Petrov affair over, Annabell left and Freeden stepped
in as acting editor of the *News*. Gardner returned from a prospecting
trip with electrifying news, he and two others, Geoff Lennox and
Bill Lickiss, had made a rich uranium strike at Adelaide River and
they eventually shared $220,000. Lickiss, a surveyor draftsman
in the Lands Department, went on to become a minister in the
Queensland government. News of the find sent shares skyrocketing
and the Top End was gripped by uranium fever. Gardner added to
Annabell's own fever by hopping on the back of Ross's motorcycle
and directing him to the find, which was close to the highway near
Adelaide River.

The replacement editor at the *News* was another Kiwi, Hugh
Mabbett, who had done some gold prospecting in Queensland.
Mabbett soon quit the noisy editor's pad at the *News* for Annabell's
peaceful beachside shack, much to the annoyance of Eric White
and Associates. As a result, the *News* found Mabbett a flat near the

post office. The arrival of the wet season made the Dinah Beach shack leak, so Mabbett invited Annabell to share the waterproof flat. Once more the Sydney directors were unhappy about the ex-editor and the present incumbent sharing a residence. Mabbett, like his mate Annabell, became disenchanted working at the *News*. Packets used to arrive at the *News* from Eric White and Associates addressed to Bob Freeden containing instructions and criticism. In what was described as an "accidental opening" involving steam from a kettle, the contents of a letter sent to Freeden were perused.

The news Mabbett read hot off the press and kettle instructed Freeden to sack Mabbett and ask Annabell to come back as editor. Aware of the plans, Mabbett quickly alerted Annabell. Sure enough, while Ross was doing some freelance work at the ABC, Freeden came in and asked him if he would come back as editor. Annabell firmly declined. However, running a bit short of money, he later considered applying for a cleaner's job at the *News*, but thought it would have been demeaning for a former editor to return as the janitor.

Then Annabell was offered the editorship of the *Standard*, which he joined in late April 1954 and threw himself into the task of trying to brighten and save the paper. He came up against the usual union interference. However, he got out his first improved edition. Taking all the obstacles in his stride, he prepared an edition in his second week at the helm of which he was proud, but it did not see the light of day because the paper's last linotype machine broke down. The union directors held a meeting behind closed doors and announced there were no funds to fly up a mechanic from south or buy a new lino. The *Standard* closed. Annabell was given one month's pay. The *News* rejoiced at its rival's demise.

Soon after, Annabell, back freelancing, set out on a prospecting trip into Arnhem Land with Dr George Sleis, who a short time later was co-founder of the Sleisbeck uranium lodes. Dr Sleis, a Czechoslovak trained geologist, was reluctant to have his photograph taken and his name published. It was alleged he had worked for the Germans in the uranium industry during the war and then for the Russians. There were claims that he was on a Czech underground death list. He had come to Australia, joined the Bureau of Mineral Resources and been sent to Rum Jungle uranium mine, later joining the North Australian Uranium Company. After he received publicity for the find and his photograph was published, Sleis became agitated. He left the company, moved into the Hotel Darwin and accused people of spying on him. So unstable was he that he attacked Douglas Lockwood in the hotel and pulled his hair.

Soon after, he was involved in a bizarre episode in which he built a wall of stones across the road to his El Sharana uranium mine and then lay naked on the ground. Some shocked people from south saw him and, thinking something terrible had happened, screeched to a halt to help. He sprang up with a stick and began to dance about on the bonnet of their car. They drove off, went to the nearest town and reported the event to the police. Sleis was taken into custody. In the court application to have Sleis declared a mental defective, evidence was given about his ravings in which "Himmler"and Russians were mentioned.

Because of his involvement with the *Standard*, Annabell was smuggled into the Rum Jungle uranium mine by unionists to report on the primitive living conditions for miners.

Inspired by the uranium boom about which he wrote for southern newspapers, Annabell and others formed their own prospecting syndicate. One weekend his partners left him in a camp set up in the bush and headed back into town to resume their Monday to Friday jobs. Annabell went to a nearby hill with a geiger counter, turned it on and got a good reading. Elated, he ran down the track after his departing friends wanting to break the good news, but could not catch them. He had to wait until the weekend for them to return. During that time he danced about his "mountain of uranium" in delight and dreamed of rolling in filthy lucre. The find became known as Annamount.

21. MYSTERIOUS UFOs

Down in Alice Springs Bowditch watched each new development at the *NT News* and the uranium boom with growing interest. However, he was so busy in his own domain that he could not worry too much about faraway Darwin. Parts of the first feature film made in colour by an Australian company were shot in the Alice area by Charles Chauvel in 1953. The history making film was *Jedda* and starred 15-year-old Ngarla Kunoth who had been born at Utopia Station, north-east of Alice, and Robert Tudawali, from Melville Island, near Darwin. The story told of an Aboriginal girl brought up in a white family and her love for a tribal Aboriginal. Because of the unusual plot, Chauvel had difficulty obtaining financial backing for the movie. Bowditch later had many dealings with Tudawali, who appeared in other movies and TV series, only to fall on hard times and die tragically in Darwin. Kunoth, for a time, worked in The Residency.

Darwin people flocked to see *Jedda*, its first world premiere of a film. People lined the street and there were 1000 people inside the Star Theatre; 20 people even paddled in by canoe from Bathurst Island to see it. Some people wore evening dress, tuxedos and ballerina frocks. Kunoth wore a white ballerina length dress and matching stole. Tudawali, working as a gardener at the time, wore a white suit. In a review of the film, Darwin journalist Bill Tuckey, later one of Australia's top motoring writers, said *Jedda* would probably prove to be the best advertisement Australia has had since the discovery of the platypus. In Alice Springs the film attracted only a small crowd.

Bowditch soon became aware that gambling was rife in Alice just as it was in every other town in the Territory. A confidential report exposed the extent of SP (Starting Price) bookmaking and other gambling activities in Alice. It named businessmen and public servants involved. It said that there were two SP shops, one being financed by a butcher and run by a Department of Works and Housing clerk who also ran a book in his office and at Underdown's pub on Saturdays. Another clerk ran a book in McMahon's pub on Saturdays. According to the report, a high ranking public servant was the backer of the clerks, and another public servant ran an ins-and-outs game. Because gambling was so entrenched in the NT, any court case involving gambling convictions was avidly read. A gambling survey conducted by Bowditch found that most people in Alice favoured the establishment of legal betting shops and most agreed that gambling was common in the NT. The *Advocate* ran several gambling reports from Darwin, one headed: 15 DARWIN GAMBLING DENS RAIDED. During 1953 the *Advocate* carried an amusing report about how some people celebrated Easter in Darwin. Under the heading: POLICE POUNCE ON DARWIN GAMBLING, it told of raids on three premises which resulted in more than 400 pounds in fines and forfeitures. John Joseph Burns was fined for running a "heads and tails" game in a room adjacent to Paspalis's Billiard Saloon; Michael Paspalis was fined five pounds for permitting his premises to be used for gaming. Defence lawyer John Lyons said it was only the second time the game had been played in five or six years. The game had been staged, he said, at the request of a number of people as a way of celebrating Easter. Mick Paspalis became the richest man in Darwin and it was claimed he could even arrange tickets to Buckingham Palace garden parties. He would have many dealings with Bowditch in future years.

Because so many good news stories broke in Alice, Jim did a lot of stringing for southern newspapers and supplied stories to the ABC in Darwin. The *Melbourne Herald* representative in Darwin, Douglas Lockwood, often rang and called on him when he was in town. Lockwood made outback tours in his car which bore the low early registration number NT300. During these expeditions, often accompanied by a photographer sent from south, he gathered superb material, much of which appeared in articles and books.

Flying saucers were seen in many parts of the world and, regarding them as a joke, Bowditch decided it was time Alice had its own visitors from outer space. In February 1954 he spoke to a photographer, Trish Collier, and asked her to produce a photograph of a UFO. Using what he thought might have been a shirt collar stud, she superimposed a dramatic looking flying saucer over the MacDonnell Ranges. Bowditch ran the picture on the front page, saying it had been pushed under the door of the *Advocate* by a person who did not want to be named. This was true because he had pushed the photos under the door, and he certainly did not want to be named. The story resulted in an outbreak of UFO sightings in the Alice district, all of which he happily ran in the paper. One of the UFO stories was caused by a Canberra jet bomber which left a contrail as it flew over Alice; apart from scaring some residents, it allegedly frightened poultry as well. A dubious team of RAAF investigators visited the *Advocate* and quizzed Bowditch about the rash of UFOs in Central Australia. In fact, there were chunks of space vehicles, meteorites, scattered about the Centre. Jock Nelson had several pieces of the Henbury meteorite in a glass case at his home. Another huge meteorite, roughly in the shape of Australia, was at Mount Ruddock Station, and American collectors were keen to buy the object.

Bowditch was not alone in fabricating stories about Central Australia during 1954. Amazing stories appeared in France saying two men competing in an outback rally in Peugeot cars narrowly escaped death when attacked by "fierce natives" brandishing stone axes and spears. According to the report three planes had been sent to the area and pilots reported an estimated 100,000 savages, a previously unknown tribe, dashing about waving threateningly at them. Bowditch ran these reports under a scoffing heading.

The serious matter of politics always bubbled near the surface. In federal parliament Jock Nelson could vote only on matters affecting the Northern Territory. It was put about by his opponents that because he was Labor, further political reform in the Territory would not be brought in. Nelson stated that if he thought he was holding back political advancement he would resign. This caused deep concern in Labor circles in Alice, and Bowditch and others called on Nelson seeking an explanation when he returned from Canberra. Nelson explained that yes, he would step aside, but he would stand again and felt most Territorians would re-elect him. Prime Minister Menzies came to Alice for a special event and Bowditch questioned him. When asked if the Territory would get political reforms and a greater say in federal parliament if Nelson stepped aside, Menzies replied, "You don't expect me to answer that question."

22. WARNED ABOUT THE *NEWS*

Knowing that the *Northern Territory News* was after a new managing editor, Douglas Lockwood suggested Bowditch for the position to Bob Freeden, who at the time was general manager of the paper. Freeden telephoned Don Whitington in Sydney and suggested Jim's appointment because he was such a good news gatherer in Alice. Apart from that, Freeden had recently married a Darwin Hospital nurse, Norma Oakley, and wanted to go south. His wife had come to Darwin from Adelaide at the age of 19. On arrival, she had been warned about mixing with journalists, said to be "drunken barbarians". She had been on duty in casualty at Darwin Hospital when prospector Jack Gardner was brought in by police for an examination. On that occasion he had been fairly well dressed in khaki, an unusual condition for the bushie. She had cause to remember Gardner because he had a geiger counter with him. As he had been moved to a ward for treatment, he asked her to look after the geiger counter. This she did. Later, he was discharged and retrieved his counter, which she had stored in casualty. As Gardner had claimed to be the composer of poetry which he described as "verses for nurses", Mrs Freeden was asked if gummy Gardner had made any bedside recitations for the nursing staff. She laughed, said no, and added that he had looked very lean and in need of some "TLC".

In his book, Ross Annabell wrote that Gardner, suffering from hookworm, dosed himself with medicine used to worm dogs. A warning label on the bottle said it was not to be taken by humans. After taking a swig of dog wormer, he would follow it up with a glass of Epsom salts, which had a purging effect.

It is evident from about the end of September 1954 that Bowditch was intent on moving to Darwin sometime in the near future. From Darwin came two jubilant reporters hopeful of soon becoming tycoons, Ross Annabell and the ABC Darwin regional journalist, John Crew. Crew was making a down-the-track tour and Annabell went along for the ride. Bowditch and Crew often spoke to each other over the telephone in connection with news stories. Crew was in the prospecting syndicate with Annabell and on the way to Alice they called on mining entrepreneur Al McDonald, known as the Maori Mayor of Tennant Creek, to pick up 500 pounds from him for a down payment on the uranium find, Annamount.

McDonald, a boxer in his earlier days, had struck it rich on the Tennant Creek goldfields. The journalists called on Bowditch with champagne to celebrate their good fortune. Annabell tried to talk Bowditch out of taking on the editorship of the *NT News*. The difficulties of dealing with Eric White and Associates were detailed.

Despite having warned Jim against taking the helm at the *News*, Annabell passed on information to Betty about how to get furniture, which was scarce in Darwin. He advised her to go to house clearance auctions when people were selling to go south. On the way back to Darwin Annabell and Crew again called into Tennant Creek and picked up the cheque from McDonald. After some celebratory drinks they set off for Darwin, but sheepishly discovered they had taken the wrong turn and were actually heading back to Alice. Just before Christmas, Freeden squeezed his bulk into a bullnose Morris in Darwin and, accompanied by his wife, set off for Sydney to begin a new life with Eric White and Associates. After eight free and easy years in Darwin, during which he did not let the truth interfere with a good story, working for the PR firm would be something of a culture shock, but he went on to become a highly successful businessman with a Jaguar or two in the garage.

Also in late 1954, Jim, Betty and baby Peter went south on holidays in a Ford Anglia with a soft top. ASIO in Darwin noted their departure and notified SA and headquarters: "Bowditch departed Alice Springs on 30 December 1954 for Adelaide. He is accompanied by his half-caste de facto wife and infant and is driving a red coloured Ford Anglia roadster No. NT 533. No information as to his address whilst in Adelaide is available."

At Port Augusta, Betty left the baby with a sister and she and Jim drove to Sydney where, in February 1955, Jim met Whitington, White and Freeden. They took him to a pub and put it to him that he become the managing editor of the *NT News*. Bowditch said he would not mind the job as editor, but was not sure about handling the money side of the paper as well. They told him that because he had been a paymaster in the Department of Works and Housing he should have no difficulty handling the newspaper's accounts. Because he was concerned about taking the jobs of others Bowditch wanted to know about the existing editor and manager. He was assured that both men wanted to leave. As a result of these assurances, he said he was willing to come aboard. At the time he was getting 15 pounds ($30) a week on the *Advocate* and was being offered double that to move to Darwin.

Before leaving the group, according to Freeden, Bowditch "boasted" about his DCM. This was unusual, because he normally did not speak much about his wartime experiences. White had been "horrified", said Freeden. However, it was thought that Bowditch was so keen to get the position in Darwin, he tried to make a big impression on them by mentioning his medal. Whitington did a quick check and confirmed that Jim had been decorated for his wartime bravery. The fact that the editorship included a rent-free house in Georges Crescent, Fannie Bay, close to the sea, was probably a major attraction for Jim and Betty. At the time they were living in a one-room house which had a tin roof, no ceiling and the exterior wall was half fly wire; water pipes froze and burst in winter. The Darwin house that went with the job sounded "sumptuous". Both Whitington and Freeden wanted to appoint Jim. White, apparently having reservations, said, "All right, if you must. It's on your heads."

Whitington gave Bowditch general instructions on how he wanted the Darwin paper run. Basically, he said to play things by ear and not to get the paper branded as political. Bowditch rang Ron Morcom, by then part owner of the *Advocate*, from Sydney and told him of the situation. Morcom offered a little more money to try to keep him in Alice, but Jim really wanted the Darwin job. At the time, he said he was running out of patience with the way several things were being done on the *Advocate*. Betty had also had it with Alice, disliked the rampant racism and needed a change.

Looking back on his years as editor of the *Centralian Advocate*, Bowditch said he could have fought a lot more battles as there were many things crying out for change. Had he thrown himself into crusading more in Alice, the town would probably have killed him. The *Advocate* asked Ross Annabell to replace Bowditch, but he did not want the job. In his autobiography *Strive to be Fair*, Don Whitington covered the appointment of Bowditch to the *NT News*. He told of having urged Mick Paspalis, then the owner of the Hotel Darwin, to buy shares in the *News* so a house could be bought for Bowditch. However, Bob Freeden said this account was incorrect. The *News* owned the house before Bowditch had even been considered for the position. In the book Whitington included the early days of the *Mount Isa Mail*, but did not mention the vital part played by Ross Annabell. Whitington also wrote that he thought Canberra had over-rated the influence of communists in Darwin.

23. DARWIN SHOCK

On 11 February 1955, ASIO in Darwin alerted headquarters to the fact that Bowditch would soon be heading north to manage the *News*. It being the Wet season in the Top End, Jim, Betty and son Peter drove from Alice to Darwin. Betty recalled seeing green tree frogs in the showers and toilets as they got close to Darwin. Arriving in Darwin at night, Jim and Betty, with their baby, drove to the *News* house at 27 Georges Crescent, Fannie Bay. There they found a newspaper party in full swing. The outgoing editor, Hugh Mabbett, and the manager, Edgar Pomroy, were there with other staff members. What happened shocked Bowditch. He said Eric

Mick Paspalis's Hotel Darwin where Jim and Betty spent their first
night in Darwin. The Hot and Cold bar (foreground) became a
favourite drinking spot.

White's had "lied" to him, both Mabbett and Pomroy had either
been sacked or resigned in disgust. A "poisonous" atmosphere
pervaded the party. Bowditch had only been at the party a short
time when somebody proposed a toast to the collapse of the
newspaper. The situation was so bad Bowditch said that had he left
the gate open in Alice, he would have turned around and gone back.
He expressed his unease about taking up the job to Mabbett and
Pomroy, but they told him they had had enough and were going to
"buzz off"; Mabbett was going to Singapore to work on the *Straits
Times* and Pomroy intended applying for a job in New Guinea.

Feeling apprehensive, Jim drove Betty and the baby to the
Hotel Darwin and booked in for the night. Next morning, Jim
sorted out the accommodation. It was a situation in which the
Pomroys' things were moved out as the Bowditch possessions came
in.

Before Bowditch took over the reins at the *News*, Annabell,
working as a freelancer and still optimistic about becoming a

mining tycoon, decided to return home to NZ for a holiday. A farewell Chinese banquet was held for him, after which Annabell and friends adjourned to the *News* office. Despite the farewell, Ross lingered about town. There was another farewell party for the Pomroys, who got a card from "The Mob". An insert, purporting to be from Eric White and Don Whitington, thanked Edgar for a job well done, and said he would get a bonus cheque for 1450 pounds from the pay lady, Margaret Simpson. Mrs Pomroy and her children flew south; her husband and reporter Bill Tuckey drove overland by car. There was another farewell party for Hugh Mabbett before he left which also served as a house warming party for John Crew's "magnificent" ABC house. As a result of the party, Mabbett wrote that he had a headache all the way from Darwin to Singapore. Mabbett spent considerable time in Asia, wrote a book about Bali and was responsible for the eventual publication of another about an American couple who started a hotel from scratch at Kuta Beach in the 1930s, only recently reprinted and available in the Indonesian tourist resort. Pomroy, because of an ulcer, failed a health check for the *New Guinea Post* and instead went to the *Mackay Mercury*, where Annabell had worked. Mabbett wrote to the Pomroys from Singapore saying he hoped they were settling down and getting the "smell of EWA" (Eric White and Associates) out of their nostrils.

After all the farewell parties in Darwin, Annabell eventually mounted his trusty BSA Bantam motorbike and set out for Sydney, gathering stories along the way, to take a ship home. It was an exciting overland trip. Included in his souvenirs of the Top End was a sample of Rum Jungle uranium oxide, yellowcake, packed in the suitcase on the carrying frame over the rear wheel. The yellowcake had been given to him when he exposed the conditions at Rum Jungle, where security was supposed to be strict to prevent uranium from being stolen. Arriving in Sydney, Annabell made it through Customs with his yellowcake and took it to his parents' home in NZ. While about to write an article saying how bad Australian security was because he had "smuggled" uranium out of Rum Jungle, he received a telegram from his syndicate partners in Darwin that there was strong interest in their uranium prospect. After hiding the yellowcake in the woodshed rafters, he hot-footed it back to the Territory, hoping at long last to make his fortune. On his return to Darwin, he became aware that there was a $50,000 fine for smuggling uranium and a long gaol sentence as well.

The news about the syndicate's find was promising. Al McDonald had succeeded in getting a Sydney syndicate headed by author Frank Clune interested in Annamount. The syndicate took samples and had them analysed. Alas, Annamount's ore was low grade and the syndicate withdrew. While in Sydney, McDonald had called on newspaper proprietor Frank Packer, whom he knew from his boxing days. Packer had also been a boxer, and was glad to see McDonald. Packer ordered a journalist to write a story about McDonald highlighting "his", not Annabell's, latest rich uranium find. Despite the favourable article, McDonald could not get anybody else interested in Annamount.

Back to being a wage slave, Annabell moved into the Darwin residence rented for his ABC friend John Crew. Jack Gardner, loaded with money from his uranium bonanza, turned up in a Holden pulling a caravan and asked if he could park in the yard for a night. As usual, Gardner lingered longer. He roamed the town drinking and Bowditch ran a story about him in the *News*. Typically Gardner soon wore out his welcome at the ABC house. Ross was asked to get rid of him. Much to the relief of many, he eventually drove off to go opal mining at Coober Pedy in South Australia.

Disappointed at not striking it rich and with funds running low, Annabell again decided to quit Darwin. He borrowed 50 pounds from Bowditch and once more headed by motorbike to Sydney, collecting feature articles along the way. On arrival in Sydney he picked up his mail forwarded from Darwin and there was a "fortune" in cheques for feature articles he had written for various publications about the uranium rush and other exotic Territory subjects. There was so much money that he need not have left Darwin. However, there was no turning back, and he promptly returned the money he had borrowed from Bowditch. Annabell wrote his book, *The Uranium Hunters*, about his time in the Territory, describing his time at the *News* and the hilarious dealings with Jack Gardner.

After leaving the Territory to go opal mining, Gardner moved on to Radium Hill in South Australia. Then he travelled the world playing the stockmarket and dabbling in gemstones which he bought in one country and sold in another. Nearly 20 years after he had last seen Gardner, Annabell arrived home to find an elderly man sitting at the table, Jack Gardner. He had read Annabell's book, rang the publishers and asked for the author's address. He then flew to NZ and arrived unannounced, seemingly intent on staying for a long time. Ross's wife, Meg, was less than happy with the unexpected guest. Gardner, who regarded married men as poor, pathetic donkey-like creatures whose role in life is to carry the groceries at supermarkets, did not respond to urgings to move on. He spent most of the days and nights boozing at the local pub taking home a few bottles of beer so that he did not go thirsty during the night.

As Ross was having his ears "belted" each night by his wife, saying Jack must go, Annabell resorted to a desperate and unusual stratagem, indicative of lateral thinking. He caught a hedgehog in the garden and slipped it into Jack's bed, hoping that the unwelcome guest would come home worse for the wear, slip between the sheets and get a nasty, prickly shock. However, during his life Gardner had undoubtedly slept with many strange things and he just pushed the hedgehog out of bed. For some strange reason, possibly Gardner's animal magnetism, the animal kept on climbing back in with him, only to be booted out time and again. Exasperated, Jack picked up the hedgehog, threw it into the sitting room, and shut the door. In the morning he regaled the Annabells with his strange nocturnal encounter with the creature. Thankfully, Gardner left soon after, never to be seen again. Some days later there was a nasty smell in the Annabell household, the cuddly hedgehog had died under the couch in the sitting room.

24. THE GAMBLING OWL

The appointment of Bowditch as the managing editor of the *Northern Territory News* was officially announced in the paper on March 3 1955. With a population of about 8000, Darwin, like Alice, had a severe shortage of accommodation. Signs of the war could still be seen, including the wreck of the *Neptuna* which was exposed at low tide next to Stokes Hill Wharf. The bulk of the population was employed in the public service and the armed services.

Starting work at the *News* the same week as Bowditch was apprentice compositor Bobby Wills, who had been at the *Standard*. Because the union-run newspaper office had been formal in dealings with staff, they being addressed as Mr, Mrs or Miss, young Bobby, on being introduced to the new editor, called him Mr Bowditch. Bowditch responded by saying that nobody called him mister and that his name was Jim.

When Bowditch took over at the *News* the average circulation was 2500 and it struggled to survive. The reporting staff consisted of Jim Kelly, who had also worked on the *Standard* at one time, and a cadet, Alan Ramsey, who went on to become a senior political reporter in Canberra. Something of a terse interview took place between Bowditch and Kelly. Kelly, who walked with a kind of shuffle, had long been known as "Flannel Foot". He told Jim that he (Kelly) would look after the editorial side of the paper and that Jim could concentrate on the business side. Bowditch said that was not the way it would be as he intended doing a lot of writing for the paper. Kelly had been secretary of the Darwin branch of the Federated Clerks' Union, knew Harry Krantz and ASIO "suspected" he was a communist. In fact, it seemed anybody connected with unions or who spoke out against the government was automatically branded a communist by security.

He covered many sports, including darts, the reports on which were incredibly long. Bowditch said a good story to Kelly was a page and half of darts results. Kelly also wrote the regular creative astrology feature. While Kelly was drinking in a pub he heard a person say he had put off an outback light plane trip as the stars in the *News* had warned about plane travel. The rotund Kelly, also moonlighted for the *North Australian Monthly* magazine, under the name "Jupiter", receiving two guineas a pop for writing the stars. In the steamy reporters' room it was not unusual for Kelly, a large consumer of Temple Bar cigarettes, to remove his shirt and sit typing away with sweat coursing down his ample body.

Kelly gave a radio sports report on the ABC and was a keen supporter of the Buffalo Club. He rode a tiny motorbike with a sidecar—like a half-opened sardine can—in which his wife, Sheelagh, a renowned cook, sat knees up. They lived in an old army hut, but when Kelly's father died he inherited a considerable sum and a black Hillman sedan which he drove for years. With their new wealth, they moved into a substantial elevated house at Fannie Bay. There Kelly would walk about in the nude listening to classical music; one night, after a few drinks, he fell off the balcony. Because the music was being played fortissimo it took a long time for Sheelagh to hear his cries for help.

There was no gentle easing into the editor's job. Almost immediately Bowditch took the Territories Minister, Paul Hasluck, to task for making a contentious statement that the bombing of Darwin had been Australia's day of shame because people had run away. Hasluck made the comment during a speech at the opening of new premises for the NT Legislative Council by the Governor-General, Sir William Slim. The *News* criticised Hasluck for making the day of shame claim, and people who had been in Darwin during the bombing pointed out that there had been many heroic acts at the time. Bowditch said Hasluck's opening address had dwelt on the past and showed the government had no vision for the Territory's future.

One of those who congratulated the *News* over its stand on Hasluck was a former NAWU secretary, Jack McDonald, who had been associated with author Xavier Herbert in the 1930s. McDonald, whose son, David, was a compositor at the *News*, said the minister had come to Darwin as a guest of the people and in his "splenetic" speech had insulted his hosts by declaring that 19 February 1942 had been a day of shame because the citizens of Darwin had run away. To have said everyone panicked had been a lie, wittingly or otherwise. McDonald said he and police sergeant Sandy McNab had organised stretcher bearers among waterside workers and despite there being two rows of dead men lying on the wharf approach, these men had carried out their duties like veterans. He had seen big men cry—not with fear, but with anger. They had no weapons, only their fists. Only four planes got off the ground in the first raid, he wrote, and after that the RAAF were told it was every man for himself. Some RAAF men were later sent back from Alice Springs. McDonald said there certainly had been an exodus from Darwin, but it was led by government department heads. Most old Territorians had stayed put. The Administrator, the Police Superintendent and the Police Inspector had departed. An "outstanding exception" had been Judge Wells, who had stayed on throughout the war to protect the people of Darwin against "the tyranny" of those who were in charge of the town. If Mr Hasluck wished to find something "shameful" he should look at the Canberra records to see how much money had been paid out in compensation to civilians whose houses had been looted, not by Japanese but troops sent to defend Darwin. McDonald, who left Darwin after the 14th raid, said a pleasing feature of this tough period in Darwin was that not a single politician made a visit—not until the last shot had been fired. "Strange that they should come along now, over 10 years later, to tell us about it."

Bowditch quickly made known his views on important issues. In an editorial headed: **NEED FOR UNION UNITY**, he said for the NT to progress there had to be unity of purpose and action from all sections of the community. This being so, it was disconcerting to see that the NAWU was in the grip of a faction fight. While one group announced its intention to declare black all pearl shell collected by cheap indentured labor, the executive had issued statements to the contrary. The NAWU, he wrote, owed it to its members and to the people of the Territory, and to the "great Trade Union movement" to put its house in order.

Bowditch made the public aware of his stance on what he regarded as an important community matter, freedom of speech. In an editorial headed: FREEDOM TO SPEAK, he raised the matter of Darwin people being reluctant to air their views publicly. He pointed out that when the paper asked people if Japanese divers should be allowed back to the Territory to revive the pearling industry they had been "afraid" to comment and have their names published. This was an unhealthy situation. The editorial recalled that one of the first people elected to the Legislative Council had been a public servant who had been told that he had to resign from his job or refrain from standing as a representative of the people. A copy of this editorial went into the ASIO files. The editorial drew a letter to the editor from one Bob Steele, which said it was high time all citizens took hold of their liberties and defended themselves against the insidious influences at work in Australia, the country being run from Canberra like a police state. ASIO headquarters received a copy of the letter from its Darwin office with a note which said that since Bowditch took over running the paper he had written or edited articles "which would appear to support his well-known leftish ideas." It pointed out that Steele, "a known communist", had taken the opportunity to congratulate the editor on his editorial. In adding to the file on Bowditch, the Victorian regional office of ASIO in March composed an erroneous entry: I understand the paper at Darwin now known as *"Northern Territory News"* was previously known as "Northern Territory Standard", and was edited by one Douglas Lockwood, brother of Rupert Lockwood. It amazes me to think why the *Herald* would send Douglas Lockwood to act as their representative in London. I might add that Bowditch and Lockwood were on very friendly terms.

The clangers in this statement are: the *NT News* and the *Standard* were two different papers; Lockwood edited neither. Rupert Lockwood, Doug's brother, a communist, figured in the Petrov Royal Commission. Rupert Lockwood was said to have been a Liberal until experiences as a reporter in Europe, especially in the

Spanish Civil War, where he saw the mangled bodies of children killed by aerial bombing, turned him to communism. Douglas Lockwood definitely was not a communist. One theory behind Doug's being sent to London was that a gross error was made in the *Melbourne Herald*'s coverage of the controversial Petrov Inquiry. In referring to the "communist" Rupert Lockwood, a sub-editor changed the name to Douglas Lockwood. As a result, the *Herald* acknowledged the mistake and asked Douglas if there was anything they could do to make amends. "Send me to London", was the supposed reply.

Another theory has it that the London assignment was a reward for Lockwood's world scoop when Evdokia Petrov accepted political asylum at Darwin airport. One problem with the first theory is that the erroneous story was published on July 8 1954, and Lockwood was on a plane to London from Melbourne's Essendon airport only three weeks later, having driven south with his family, a trip that took a week in those days. And the *Herald* had to choose a replacement and get him to Darwin a week before Lockwood left so he could be briefed on the job.

ASIO also reported that Bowditch, in moving to Darwin, had taken his coloured "de facto" and their child north. ASIO made several mentions of Betty, calling her Beth in one report, and variously described her as "coloured", "half-caste" and a "quadroon". It is difficult to understand the relevance of the fact that ASIO recorded that she lost a baby in Alice. What comes through clearly in the files kept on Bowditch is that he and many others in the Northern Territory were subjected to Australia's brand of McCarthyism. Just associating with a person or expressing a democratic view against the government was enough to have you entered in a file.

Early in his editorship Bowditch was involved in a major story involving gambling in Darwin which saw him threatened with legal action by the angry Administrator. Everybody in town knew gambling was rife. Strangely, Canberra on three occasions refused assent to a NT Legislative Council approved bill which would have legalised betting shops. There were at least six illegal gaming and betting shops in town at the time, and the din from them could be plainly heard in the main thoroughfare, Smith Street. In February, one of the gambling joints, known as the "Paspalis Betting Shop", had been raided and 19 men were arrested. On the walls of the premises there were boards carrying details of southern races; two cash boxes were seized.

About a month later police visited seven betting shops one weekend, but only arrested the owner of a new one. Bowditch became suspicious about the police action. In the "True North" column there appeared an odd item saying Darwin was not the only town with SP betting trouble. At Katherine, south of Darwin, it read, only one betting shop was ALLOWED to operate, would-be competitors being shut down. How, it asked, did you become one of the chosen few? The item was written over the nom–de-plume, "Ku Cumshaw". Cumshaw is Pidgin English for a present, tip or a gratuity, the inference being that somebody was being paid. While walking down the street, Bowditch met the police officer who had led the raid on the new Darwin betting shop, Sgt Jim Mannion, often described as "an honest cop". Bowditch, who had known Mannion in Alice Springs, asked him what was going on. Mannion said he had been instructed from the highest level to raid one betting shop and ignore the others, which were commonly known to be run by one man. He told Bowditch that if he could arrange for the right questions to be asked in the court case involving the owner of the new betting shop, Roland McGuire, he would blow the whole thing wide open.

Bowditch then briefed defence lawyer John "Tiger" Lyons who, of course, asked the right questions of Mannion. Lyons claimed the evidence given showed that there was a "Tammany Hall rule" in Darwin. The prosecutor, Sgt Lou Hook, denied a blind eye had been turned to other betting premises in town. Lyons retorted that Mannion had visited seven gaming places on the one day and only one had been booked. "I don't know if that is the blind eye or completely shutting both." The *News* highlighted the fact that Mannion said he had been ordered by "a superior authority" to raid the new betting shop every time it operated. The court was told that a prospector arrested on the premises, on being taken away by police, had pointed to Paspalis's and said: "Look at them, they don't have to worry that they will go off."

The Administrator of the Northern Territory, Mr Frank Wise, who was also responsible for police, reacted strongly to the criticism of the gambling situation. Bowditch gave the issue substantial coverage in the paper and launched a campaign to legalise all betting shops. The situation attracted media coverage down south and Bowditch was asked by the *Brisbane Truth* to get a photograph of the Darwin businessman who owned the "untouched" gaming dens. Bowditch and a nervous amateur photographer went to a betting shop, but somebody became suspicious, called for the boss, "Mick", and they ran out of the premises. Only a blurred photograph was obtained of their quarry, Mick Paspalis. Later, Paspalis discussed the episode with Bowditch, who explained his stance on betting shops. He and Paspalis became good friends. Oddly enough, when Wise, a former WA Labor Premier, first went to Darwin as the Liberal Government appointed Administrator in 1951, he was likened to a race horse. A no-nonsense man who disliked red tape, he got things done. A *People* magazine article written about him in 1952 said Territorians grudgingly admitted that his "preliminary gallops" showed unusual form. In racing parlance, he was seen as a steady miler rather than a flashy five-furlong sprinter.

However, the Administrator accused the media of sensationalism and issued a long defensive document. In it he said that some years previously as a politician he had carried out research into SP betting Australia-wide so he could introduce a bill in parliament to control gambling. His investigation had given him a thorough insight into the gambling industry, especially the activities of off-course betting and the part newspapers and other agencies played in providing information for SP bookies. He pointed out that in some instances newspapers received large sums of money from SP bookies to provide racing information. Gambling was such a big thing in Australia, he said, the Flying Doctor Service, in some remote centres was tremendously busy on Friday afternoons and Saturday mornings, receiving telegrams for dispatch to SP bookmakers.

Good humouredly, Wise pointed out that if British Prime Minister Winston Churchill appeared at 10 Downing Street wearing a bandage, he would not get as much attention in the press as would a horse called Raconteur if it suddenly sported a bandage or a different sort of shoe. And if Prime Minister Menzies were to get a scratch it would not be mentioned by the press. However, if some "equine fancy" were scratched there would be a stop press. Wise said one of his responsibilities was to keep vicious things within due bounds and to use the law to do so with due regard to public welfare. Much of the agitation over the betting shop issue was from interested parties and expressions of opinions, some under privilege, clouded but did not clarify the issue. Years previously, he said, Darwin had a regular two-up game every Saturday. Pi-que joints and other games were played all night in some places, but it did not have them now. There was no street corner betting or betting in public houses. He said that as far as he was concerned, until the Government had a good look at all the implications of the subject of legalising off-course betting, those who broke the law would be made aware of the fact that they were acting illegally. Knowing that it was impossible to abolish gambling, he said he had no feelings at all in the matter. However, what he did deplore was the "sensation" being made out of the incident.

Wise's statement was run on the front page next to a Commonwealth Savings Bank ad that carried the message 'A Wise Bird Takes No Chances'. It showed a young bird in helmet, goggles and parachute out on a limb with a safety net underneath. Many readers took this to mean Bowditch was lampooning Wise and it infuriated the Administrator; he rang Bowditch and threatened to sue. According to Bowditch, the placing of the Administrator's statement next to the bank ad had been coincidental. Much of the populace, however, regarded it as an audacious jibe at the Administrator.

Drastic action followed the case. Within two weeks, Sgt Mannion was "banished" to the mining town of Tennant Creek, north of Alice, In Bowditch's words, Sgt Mannion had been "heartbroken". Despite the *News* editorialising against the move, a

The bravery of Sgt. Mannion

From DOUGLAS LOCKWOOD

DARWIN, Tues.—Sergeant (First Class) James Joseph Mannion has walked into fire, swum crocodile-infested rivers and faced a killer's bullets without flinching.

But in Darwin today this Northern Territory policeman quailed before his greatest ordeal — the congratulations of colleagues and townsfolk on his award by the Queen of the George Medal.

The citation said: "For outstanding bravery."

Mannion said: "I'm a bit embarrassed." — and went back to his desk work at NT police headquarters here.

But it hasn't always been files and paper work for big Jim Mannion, whom Territorians regard as one of their best policemen.

A killer's shots

● There was the day in June, 1952, when he exchanged shots in Katherine with a man who is now in gaol for murder.

● There was the day in December, 1956, when Tennant Creek's main store, owned by A.P. Campbell and Co., was destroyed by fire and explosion.

One man was killed and others were burnt so badly that they were in hospital for months.

Petrol drums and gas cylinders were exploding and the whole of the building was furiously ablaze when Mannion arrived.

He walked calmly into the gathering inferno to make sure that no injured person was trapped.

"We will never forget him for that," Tennant Creek resident Ken McIntyre said at the time.

Neither has Australia. For it was Mannion's bravery in this fire which got him the George Medal.

● There was the day local people say, when Mannion, in top gear against SP betting, couldn't resist the impulse to tap a bookie's weary "cockatoo" on the shoulder from behind and tell him:

"Wake up. The cops are coming."

Mannion is a strict policeman who enforces the law to the full.

He has stopped SP betting and after-hours hotel trading in more than one Territory town. The people might have been expected to resent that in a heat which encourages enormous thirsts and in isolation which prevents legalised betting.

But they didn't re-sent Mannion. "Because," they say, "he is always scrupulously fair."

Mannion has been 22 years in the force. He served with the 2nd 27th Battalion in the Middle East and New Guinea, and at the war's end went back to the remote country police stations along the borders of Arnhem Land, where his police work with native trackers often kept him away from home for weeks at a time.

"I wish I could get back out there right now and escape this embarrassment," says Mannion.

Doug Lockwood's story about the awarding of the George Medal for bravery to Bowditch confidante, Sergeant Jim Mannion.

line taken up by Jock Nelson in federal parliament, it was claimed the move had been planned before the gambling case.

When Mannion went to Tennant Creek he became involved in a devastating fire which killed one person, seriously injured four and 30 others needed treatment. The fire was in Campbell's garage and store; Mannion fought his way into the exploding building to check if anybody was trapped. A TAA plane was diverted to Tennant Creek to pick up the injured. For his bravery Mannion became the first person in the NT to receive the George Medal. Despite having been banished to Tennant, Mannion rose to the rank of inspector, returned to Darwin and was highly regarded by the community.

In the cavernous factory at the *News* the team included linotype operator Arthur Wright, a walking encyclopedia of knowledge about Darwin, especially its boisterous early union days and the many characters and pioneer aviators who had passed through the town. He had travelled with a Queensland boxing troupe in his younger days, was working at the *Northern Standard* when the Japanese attacked and was the brother of lawyer Dick Ward's first wife.

Although a staunch unionist, Arthur was aggrieved by a union dispute which resulted in his father committing suicide after being sent to Coventry. The tragic event involved a union ban placed on a hotel over a matter supposedly involving the use of Aborigines as cheap labour. His father, a winch operator on the wharf, was seen going into the Club Hotel during the ban for an after-work drink, and was ostracised by fellow unionists. He became so distressed by his treatment that he put a stick of dynamite in his mouth and lit the fuse.

If asked for information about a person, Arthur Wright would first recall their full names, where they came from down south or overseas, and many anecdotes about their time in the Territory. A great believer in fitness, he walked long distances. His wife, Pat, also worked in the *News*, proofreading, feeding sheets into the press and bookbinding. She also operated the guillotine, and Bowditch got her to cut up paper for him on occasions. He would place the paper beneath the large guillotine, then get Pat to activate the machine, she having a ticket to do so. Before so doing, she would go through all the required safety checks, including asking Bowditch where his hands were, before she pressed the cutting button, he invariably replied that his hands were in a safe place, on her bum. After she cut the paper, Pat would join in the fun and instruct him to replace his hands in the original safe place.

After 10 months in Darwin, Bowditch wrote to former *Northern Standard* editor Bruce Muirden in Cairns asking him if he would be interested in the position as editor of the *Mount Isa Mail*. In the letter Bowditch said that when he was editor of the *Advocate* and Bruce was on the *Standard*, he (Jim) had hoped for the demise of the *NT News*, which was an alleged threat to the *Advocate*. The *News* was supposed to have been tied up with big southern combines. This was not true, Bowditch told Muirden. The *News* was a struggling organisation backed by a small number of shareholders, most of whom lived in Darwin. There was no connection with southern papers, except to provide a news cover for which they were paid in the usual way.

He told Muirden that he and Betty now had two boys, one aged two, the other six months. He wrote: "We plan, repeat plan, to leave the family at this size. As you know, Darwin is a most expensive place to live in and we find that even with our small family and a pretty good salary, the going is not so good." They later had two more children, daughters Ngaire and Sharon. Bowditch told Muirden he would probably be taking over the direction of the Mount Isa paper from Darwin. And so it was. Apart from being responsible for the running of the *NT News*, each three months Bowditch drove to Mount Isa as general manager of that paper and sorted out business problems. It was a journey of 1100 miles each way and took 27 hours of driving. Betty accompanied him on several such trips. Muirden did not go to Mount Isa. Instead, he worked on country newspapers at Bathurst, Mildura and Deniliquin and in 1960 joined the *Adelaide News* as features editor and cable editor, then spent two years in London with AAP.

Life was never easy on the *NT News*, with its worn-out equipment and tight cash flow. A press arrived from Perth on the back of a truck and the driver demanded 800 pounds before he would unload. Bowditch told the man, to be perfectly frank, he needed 90 days to pay. With that, the driver said he would take the press back to Perth. A quick check of banks failed to secure the money, so Bowditch called on Mick Paspalis, who had the accountant Norman Young in his office. Paspalis asked Young what he thought about the request for the money. According to Bowditch, Young said not after the way the newspaper had treated Mick over the gambling episode. Enjoying the situation, Paspalis

Mick Paspalis in front of one of his many properties, the Fannie Bay
Hotel. He came to Jim's financial aid at a difficult time and they
became friends.

laughed and baited Bowditch for about a quarter of an hour. Then
he signed a cheque for the amount, saying he wanted eight per
cent interest, to be paid back in a year. There was no contract, just
a hand shake. "I don't know what I would have done if he hadn't
given me the money," said Bowditch. "It was such a hassle keeping
the place going."

The very existence of the paper was placed in jeopardy
because of an unusual event. NAWU vigilance officer "Wild Bill"
Donnelly, another person of interest to ASIO, called at the office
and asked Bowditch to come outside. He said he did not want the
paper to run a court case involving a watersider, a family man, who
had been charged with pilfering. Donnelly claimed the man had
been set up. Bowditch said he could not keep the story out of the
paper, that everybody received the same treatment in the *News* and
there could not be any exception to that rule. Donnelly accused
Bowditch of being anti-working class. Becoming angry, Bowditch
said Donnelly would not complain at all if a bank manager, a clerk
or some other person was written up in the paper. Donnelly said
that if the story appeared in the paper not one bale of newsprint
would cross the wharf for the *NT News*.

The story was run and Bowditch wrote an editorial upholding
freedom of the press in which he revealed the *News* had been
threatened with a ban. True to his word, Donnelly put a stop to
unloading newsprint for the paper. At the time Bowditch said the

paper was "insolvent" and the ban cost the *News* a lot of extra money. The paper had a bank overdraft of 17,000 pounds and revenue was about the same amount. The cost of having newsprint brought in by sea was about half that of overland freight. The freight on newsprint by road in those days was 68 pounds a ton. Roads were poor and prone to being cut by Wet season rain, so a lot of newsprint had to be held in store. The *News* was placed in a tight spot when supplies of paper in store began to run low. Coincidentally, Betty needed meat for dinner, so Jim called at the Koolpinyah butcher's on the way home. When he saw the butcher wrapping the meat in clean white paper he had an idea, and asked, "How much of that paper have you got?" Bowditch bought up all the butchers' paper in town to keep the paper going until more supplies could be brought in by air and road from south. The ban remained for 18 months before it was lifted. Bowditch believed it was lifted because the watersiders realised the paper fought for the working class.

Donnelly was a hard-working crusader himself. Born in 1917, the year of the Russian Revolution, he had a bust of Lenin on his bookcase. Before Bowditch came to Darwin, Donnelly campaigned for better wages and conditions for men employed in the pearling industry; he also spoke out against the indentured labour system which was soon to attract the attention of Bowditch. Donnelly was the subject of a humorous episode when he intervened in a dispute on a ship in Darwin. Below deck, he was trying to hammer out a solution to the trouble when the ship sailed without him noticing.

When somebody told him to look out "the window", Donnelly glanced out the porthole and realised the vessel was under way. He and some crewmen went to the captain and asked him to turn the ship around and make a kissing approach to the wharf so that Donnelly could jump off. The captain refused. Donnelly, the captain said, had caused the company a lot of trouble in the past and, as far as the skipper was concerned, the first landfall would be Broome in Western Australia. Furthermore, he told Donnelly to get below and come on deck next morning with a brush and a pot of paint to cover up rust. A heated exchange ensued and finally the captain reluctantly returned to Stokes Hill wharf where Donnelly slipped ashore, right in front of reporter Jim Kelly, who had been tipped off about Donnelly having been shanghaied. A story appeared in the newspaper under the heading: THE RETURN OF THE NOT SO VIGILANT VIGILANCE OFFICER.

Donnelly worked long hours looking after the welfare of watersiders, often neglecting his own social life, and was apt to quote Thomas Jefferson, Abe Lincoln and the Declaration of Human Rights. Like Bowditch, he had met and been impressed by the oratory of Jack Hughes of the NSW Federated Clerks' Union.

25. CRUSADING EDITOR

As word spread about town that the editor of the *NT News* was a fighter for the underdog, a steady stream of people came to the office seeking help. A considerable number were women with children who found it hard to pay rent or bills and, in some cases, faced eviction. Of the "many scores" of people threatened with eviction who asked for help, Jim said he had about a 70–80 per cent success rate. Most of the eviction threats involved women with children who had been deserted by husbands or men who could not cope with domestic life. Women in such situations, he said, "really copped it." While it was rare for women to walk out on kids, Bowditch observed men often avoided their family commitments. On being approached by a woman facing eviction or unable to pay a pressing bill, he would stop what he was working on and immediately try to solve the problem. He did not pass the woman to a reporter; he handled the matter himself. Once he had the facts, he was on the phone. Probably because of what he had seen his mother go through at the hands of bailiffs, he detested the idea of families being pressured or "bullied" in any way, a situation which immediately raised his hackles. To save a woman from being evicted he would try various courses of action, negotiation, pleading, cajoling and even threatening. "You are not going to look very nice in the paper if we say you are throwing a woman with five kids out on the street."

Terrible things might have been done to some of the houses but Bowditch could not just stand by and see people "buried". His attitude, he admitted, could have been "psychopathic" due to what had happened to his mother. Many times he pulled money from his pocket or raided the office kitty for an advance and gave it to somebody who was "doing it tough" a common expression of his. He repeatedly called on Dick Ward to help people facing eviction and the lawyer did not charge a fee in most cases. Ward played a major part in the setting up of the NT Housing Commission and was at the ceremony marking the handover of the first house to a tenant.

Because Bowditch was basically an easy touch, he went guarantor for many people in the purchase of second-hand cars. It was jokingly said that Bowditch had "the biggest fleet of bombs in Darwin." A man came to him with a sad story about his father being near death in Asia, and how he could not afford the airfare home. Bowditch provided money for the fare so the man could speed to his father's bedside. Instead of heading for Asia, the man quickly departed down south. The dying father story had been a fabrication. Some women thought the editor of the *NT News* was a wonderful man. An English battler, Lew Stewart, of the Housewives' Association, who worked tirelessly to improve the lot of pensioners and for the formation of a housing commission, often praised the campaigns of "that Jimmy Bowditch" and caterer "Auntie" Billie Nicholls, later Mrs Pitcheneder, involved in many fund-raising functions, plied the editor with cakes and sandwiches. As gratitude for his help in fund-raising, each year she threw a birthday party for the entire *News* staff. A large bustling woman with great energy, she was in a distressed state when she once called at the *News* office. She sat close to Jim and confided that some women had been saying hurtful things about her. With that, she burst into tears and placed her head on Jim's shoulder; Bowditch responded by patting her on the back and soothingly murmured, "There, there." A staff member happened to look through the opening to the editor's dive and was greeted by the sight of little Big Jim engulfed by the

Man of mystery,
Carl Atkinson.
Often called on for
physical work at the
NT News, here seen
holding a highly
venomous box
jellyfish,

sobbing woman. The supply of sandwiches and buns became so great Bowditch had to politely tell her to desist.

When social writer Joy Collins fell down stairs and lay there injured, she cried out, "Get Jimmy Bowditch!" The cry was repeated when a coconut tree fell on her car. A woman having a row with a stroppy plumber rang Bowditch and asked him to come to the rescue. He drove to her house and found she, having soundly abused the recalcitrant plumber, had been pushed into a trench; the enraged departing plumber had then belted a tap with a large hammer so that it would never work again. From these examples it is evident that the rescue and soothing of damsels in distress was another facet of his unusual editorship.

Under Bowditch's editorship the *NT News* circulation rose to 4000 but it was plagued by frequent trouble with plant. A local diver, marine salvage expert and larger-than-life character Carl Atkinson was called in to do repairs on the press and other equipment. A powerful man, he would lift large pieces of machinery which normally took several men to handle. Once he had been called to the *Northern Standard* office to help get a tipsy man trapped by the arm in a printing press. On that occasion he used a crowbar with such dexterity the machine was not damaged. The injured man was taken to hospital but he was reluctant to be treated by a bearded doctor saying that he (the doctor) might have nits in his whiskers.

Atkinson, who lived on the waterfront in a collection of huts at Doctor's Gully, was said to have beaten up Australian film star Errol Flynn in New Guinea. In many ways Atkinson was a mystery man and he helped the legend along. Bowditch said Atkinson had been "dirty" about having been arrested as an enemy alien during WWII, but had soon been released. It was suggested that he had been born in Melbourne in 1913, son of Enoch Atkinson. However, it was also suggested he had been known as Carl von Mueller, and his name had later been changed to Atkinson. Whatever the true story, he led an adventurous life. In Sydney he was said to have lived at bohemian Kings Cross, been a private eye, introduced waterskiing to Australia, worked for the marine firm of Messengers and did diving work in Sydney harbour.

Other claims to fame were that he was the arm wrestling champion of Alice Springs, that he destroyed mines which were still floating about Darwin harbour when he first went there in 1945 and that he took Sir Charles Lloyd Jones crocodile shooting, the businessman returning to Sydney in a Rolls Royce. When Atkinson drove to the Darwin post office with a female passenger in a distinctive vehicle, he was surrounded by some drunken sailors. They told him to get out of the car and leered at his passenger. Two sat on the bonnet, Carl told them to piss off, and they foolishly ignored his directive; one even tried to tweak his nose. In a graceful action, Atkinson flung open the heavy door of the car with so much force that it broke the kneecap of one sailor. He then grabbed the two on the bonnet and dealt with them in quick time.

Japanese salvage crews used a floating crane brought from Japan to recover the wartime wreckage of sunken ships.

He also had his own home-made recompression chamber and saved the lives of many pearl divers who suffered the bends. Pets he had in Darwin were a snake, Sammy, and a croc, Cuthbert. Among his more unusual possessions were the wartime wrecks in Darwin Harbour. Some standover men came up from south intent on taking control of the wrecks, rumoured to have valuables in safes, from Atkinson. When they arrived in town they made inquiries about how to find Atkinson, and he was tipped off. When the toughs arrived at Doctor's Gully they were bailed up at the end of a shotgun by a man who worked for Atkinson. Atkinson then bashed the daylights out of the hoods. They tottered away and left their car which was flooded by the incoming tide.

A Japanese company, Fujita Salvage, with 120 men, came to Darwin towing a large floating crane and began to remove the wrecks. One ship, the tanker *British Motorist*, was raised, righted and used as a mother ship for the salvage operations. The Japanese would raise large portions of metal, transport it to the shallows and then an army of workers, all squatting, would chip the rust away.

The Japanese cook, Tsutomu Watanabe, bought a pedigree collie dog, named it Fuji, and won a prize in the North Australian Canine Association's Championships. The Japanese liked the animal so much they had documents prepared to enable them to take it back to Japan with them when they finished salvage work.

A dispute arose over the ownership of the USS *Peary* and the government put the ship up for sale. This infuriated Atkinson, who issued a writ to stop the salvage operations. The head of the company, Mr Fujita, and his young interpreter went to court. Bowditch was present in the Hotel Darwin when Atkinson discussed payment for the wrecks with Fujita and his increasingly nervous interpreter. While admitting he was a "little racist" when it came to Japanese because of his war experiences, Bowditch said he liked Fujita. Fujita foolishly said he would not pay Carl for the *Peary* as he would get it for nothing from the government.

Suspecting he was being diddled, Atkinson jumped up in a rage and roared. Fujita took to his heels, ran down the corridor and out into the street, with Atkinson in pursuit. Later, Atkinson came back, laughing. Fujita also cautiously re-entered the hotel and negotiations resumed. Bowditch borrowed a typewriter from the hotel reception office and in a cubicle designed for taking telephone calls typed up an agreement for an amount said to have been 12,000 pounds. The carriage on the typewriter kept hitting the partition and the result did not look like a slick legal document. Nevertheless, Atkinson gave Bowditch a "sling" for his services. Bowditch felt not all the wrecks should have been removed. One at least should have been left as a reminder to Australia of what had happened during the war.

The hut in which Atkinson lived had a mango tree growing through the bedroom. It was claimed that whenever Atkinson made love to a woman he swung from the tree and beat his chest like Tarzan. In any case, many people were envious of him, his speedboat and the "harem" of nurses he used to entertain.

Bowditch was told about a puzzling event involving Atkinson who was seen in protective gear up a power pole near Doctor's Gully late at night.

He asked Atkinson for an explanation. According to Atkinson, he had climbed the pole when a girl he was parked with in a car became worried about the fate of a cat chased up there by a dog. Bowditch said it was a dubious explanation; he proffered the theory that it was more likely that Atkinson had been running an illegal power supply down to Doctor's Gully.

26. TAKEN TO THE CLEANERS

One of the more unusual challenges Bowditch faced as editor was coping with a procession of strange office cleaners. The most notorious of these was without doubt the English remittance man Donald Charles Duncan. Myopic, thirsty and better class, he was known as Dapper Donald, a strange title considering he was often found in a crumpled and dishevelled state by Her Majesty's constabulary. Drunken Duncan was another nickname. He had a list of convictions for drunkenness in Australia going back to the '30s in Western Australia. When Darwin Stipendiary Magistrate Stuart Dodds asked Duncan why he had come to Australia, he said his father had called him in and said the town already had a village idiot, so he had better go to the antipodes. Duncan got the job at the *News* by audacity. He called on the editor one day, looked about his messy office and, in a pukka accent, said: "You need a cleaner, old chap." Apart from being the cleaner at the *News*, Duncan also took the morning and afternoon tea orders and pedalled off on a bike, pipe in mouth, to nearby shops. Often he came to evening parties at the *News* and, after imbibing the fluid which results in Dutch courage, would give a damsel a continental pinch on the derriere. This habit of pinching ladies resulted in his being locked in a wardrobe one night. Office staff the next morning heard odd noises coming from the wardrobe, cautiously opened the door and out slumped a very limp Dapper Don.

Naturally, Donald put the bite on Jim for a loan from time to time. Dapper Donald was an ardent and critical reader of the newspaper. He would peruse each edition from cover to cover and pick out spelling errors and misuse of grammar. Then he would march in to Bowditch's office and tell him he would have to do something to prevent butchering the Queen's English. These lectures from the head of the sanitation department were delivered late in the day when the editor was keen to get up the road for a drink, and often resulted in Dapper Donald being politely told to bugger off. One of his many court appearances was notable for the fact that he wore two left-foot sandals. Duncan had been educated at one of England's great public schools and came from a well-to-do family.

In 1960, when I went to Portuguese Timor for the *News* aboard the MV *Malita*, which ran supplies to an American drilling team searching for oil in that colony, Duncan got the urge to do a similar trip. He wondered if the skipper of the supply boat might take him on as cook. Duncan was told to go to the wharf and speak to the skipper, Bert Cummins. Soon after, filled above the Plimsoll line, Duncan made his way to the wharf at night and fell into the harbour. He kicked off his clothes, floated on his back and called for help. All night he drifted backwards and forwards with the tide.

Early in the morning, a young girl, on the wharf with her father who was fishing, happened to look over the side and saw Duncan floating by. She raised the alarm, and later said she knew he was not just swimming because he did not have any clothes on, except for a sock. Hauled out, Duncan was taken to hospital and became the centre of media attention, having survived a night drifting about in "crocodile and shark infested" waters. He was photographed sitting up in bed with his pipe and three young girls who had been on the wharf. He was quoted as saying he survived the ordeal because he had been taught at school that whenever you got into a difficult situation you should relax and not panic. The story got nationwide coverage; an Adelaide paper ran an editorial saying Mr Duncan was an inspiration to the youth of the country with his advice that you should not panic in a difficult situation.

Thus one of Darwin's most prominent drunks was held up as a shining example to the nation's youth. Duncan had the story mounted and pointed at it with pride, laughing in his distinctive fashion as he did so. He was delighted when a gold cigarette case and lighter were sent to him from his family in England. Proudly, he showed them about at the *News* and that night went to the Workers' Club, got drunk, was arrested and when he sobered up found the items were missing. For several years Dapper Donald had a room in a boarding house run by Mrs Julie Papandonakis, who felt sorry for him, even though he used to help himself to the salami and cheese she kept in a downstairs fridge. A vivacious woman with a well-built husband, Tony, who was in the excavation business, Mrs Papandonakis had a long association with Bowditch and the *NT News*. Several of the *News* staff boarded at her house, including me.

When she yelled, "Righto, you boys!" you knew that you were in trouble with the landlady. She gave Bowditch a tongue-lashing over an item he wrote in the *News*. In the early days when she and her husband were battling, Tony had a compressor but could not afford a truck to tow it to job sites, relying on a friend to do so. At times, he and a workmate would carry jackhammers and other equipment, which could be stolen if left overnight on an excavation site. One morning, Bowditch saw them trudging along with the equipment and wrote a paragraph for "True North" which went something like this: "No wonder the Greeks have so much money, they are so mean they carry their jackhammers to a job rather than use a truck." On reading this, Julie flew into a rage, drove to the *News* and got stuck into Bowditch. When she explained the situation, he apologised. But what had upset her most was that her husband was described as Greek when he had only recently become naturalised and was proud to be Australian. During the time Dapper Donald lived at her place, Bowditch would regularly ring up and ask if the missing cleaner was there. Invariably, she replied that he was sleeping it off after a bender. Her mother often told her to get rid of "that drunk", and despite reading the riot act to Duncan from time to time about his drinking, she could not bring herself to throw him out on the street. Duncan repeatedly told staff at the *News* that Julie was a "good sport" and he always knew his room at her place was waiting for him when he got out of Fannie Bay. When Duncan was drying out in Fannie Bay Gaol his place at the *News* was often filled by another thirsty cleaner. He was a tall Irishman who got about in thongs, his shirt unbuttoned and a wild look in his eyes. Police picked him up at night sitting naked on the footpath outside the Catholic girls' hostel, his clothes folded neatly beside him. When asked what he was doing there, he told the police he liked fresh air. He and his clothing were bundled into the paddy wagon.

For a short time there was an ex-naval man with bloodshot eyes who joined the list of *News* cleaners. His peculiarity was using the pot in which metal slugs from the linotype machines were melted down to cook his meals. Staff would arrive at work to find a piece of tin across the pot with remnants of sausage. Apart from having an unusual frying pan and imbibing heavily, he also liked gambling; he was fired after it was discovered he had been using the *News* phone early on Saturday mornings to ring up all over Australia to get the latest good oil on nags. It was said that he eventually died from lead poisoning caused by cooking his snags on the *News* metal melting pot.

At long last, it looked as if the *News* had a sober, reliable cleaner, Ted Maloney, who took up residence on the premises in a room at the back of the paper, along with his cockatoo and two dogs. Drinking, he said, was for fools, admitting he had once been a heavy drinker, but had seen the light and given it up years previously. Coming across members of the staff drinking on the premises at night, a frequent occurrence, he would shake his head and scornfully tell them what fools they were. Maloney, who claimed to be "Red Ted Maloney", a notorious Melbourne knuckle man, had a fish trap in the shape of a V meeting in a box where the fish were trapped. The catch had to be emptied at low tide and he was spiked in the hand by the barb of a stingray's tail. The pain from such stings is said to be excruciating, and for a long time after the victim supposedly feels agonising pain with each tidal change.

Poor Red Ted once more turned to grog to try to ease the pain. In the grip of booze, he would ring Bowditch at home and threaten to bash him. During these calls, often late at night or early in the morning, he would remind Bowditch that he was the notorious Melbourne pug. Jim just laughed off the threats and on arrival at work would find Ted snoring, his pets nearby, unable to carry out his threat to do violence upon the person of the editor. However, Bowditch was himself suffering from a hangover when he took an early morning call from Red Ted, once more threatening to bash him when he arrived at the office. Bowditch responded by saying he was coming to the office straight away. Bowditch sped to the office, strode into Ted's room and said in view of the fact that the cleaner often boasted to be a mean fighter, let's see just how good you are. The cleaner broke down and admitted he was not Red Ted, merely a relative. Maloney departed soon after and set up a rough camp near the back of the racecourse. He died after a fall from a cliff and Bowditch paid for his burial.

Once more, Dapper Donald found himself gainfully employed as cleaner and protector of the Queen's English at the *News*. "It's not good enough, old chap," he would say. He also remonstrated with stone hands (compositors) in the factory who threw paper galley proofs on the floor. They responded by telling Dapper Don in no uncertain terms that they were giving him work and to pull his head in or stick it somewhere else. Taking himself on a holiday by ship to Perth, Dapper Don was killed when a car driven by a friendly lady on a scenic tour ran off the road at a port of call on his way back. Bowditch was contacted in the capacity as next of kin and asked for burial instructions. The West Australian police were shocked when Bowditch asked if Dapper Don could be cremated in the bush and his ashes sent to Darwin for forwarding to his relatives, whom Jim had contacted in England.

The possibility of placing the body in a box marked natural history specimen and flying it to Perth for cremation was also canvassed. Dapper Don, however, was eventually buried in WA. Bowditch understood that a plaque commemorating him was placed in his family's church. Police came and took away all

Duncan's possessions from his room at the Papandonakis boarding house. Bowditch told Julie that Duncan's relatives would probably send her something as a reward for having been so good to him, but nothing eventuated.

A bleary-eyed individual who claimed to be an experienced photographer approached Bowditch for a job, and while the *NT News* had no capacity to make pictorial blocks at the time, Jim said he would keep him in mind if there was an opening in the future. The man drifted about town and appeared in court in a case involving a well-known prostitute who appeared in pornographic snaps taken by the photographer. She told the magistrate the nude photos had been taken so that in her dotage she could see what she looked like in younger days. Showing her one photograph, the magistrate asked if it had been taken for the day when she could no longer bend over backwards.

27. THE POXY VICAR!

Next to the *News* building on the harbour side was the Church of England Christ Church and the incumbent was the Reverend Father Arthur Gwynne-Jones, a pontifical-voiced Englishman, with short legs but a large, long body. Also known as the Liquor Vicar and the Shikker Vicar, he loved food and alcohol in all of their devilishly seductive forms. He and Bowditch had a most unusual relationship. Bowditch first met the cleric at the navy's HMAS *Melville* Chiefs and Petty Officers' Mess, strategically located in Smith Street just across the road from the house of worship and the newspaper, where both men regularly adjourned to bend the arm. Perched on a stool and viewed from the back, Bowditch said Gwynne-Jones resembled two pears sitting one atop the other. He had a large body and a similarly proportioned head with a peaked crown; his bulging jowls extended to his almost non-existent neck. All up, he weighed about 18 stone (120 kg). At the time he was telling off-colour jokes to the sailors. In a colourful turn of phrase, Bowditch described him as a man who preached like a saint, drank as if the world was about to run dry and swore like a saddle-sore stockman. The clergyman was said to have come to Darwin from Quorn, South Australia, in 1955 where he had been known by the nickname "Hector the Rector", a thirsty chap. In Darwin he soon established a reputation as a legendary imbiber. Barmaids would refuse him service and he would bellow at them, his face crimson, "I am the vicar!" apparently expecting them to be overcome by awe. Seasoned Darwin barmaids could handle any situation, and firmly told him to go home. The vicar also frequented the Darwin Club where, on becoming tired and emotional, he imposed on some poor member of his flock to drive him home. One of the non-church attending adherents turned into a reluctant good samaritan by the vicar was Les Penhall, who had been in Alice during Bowditch's time. When the vicar slumped down into Penhall's Morris Minor, the springs sagged and it took on a lean.

A Darwin church leader often referred to the new Church of England head in Bowditch's presence as the "clerical error". Bowditch claimed authorship of the title "Shikker Vicar". The vicar invited Bowditch to the vicarage for a drink and a chat; his refrigerator was well stocked on such occasions. While he had catholic tastes when it came to liquor, gin proved to be more than mothers' ruin, it got the vicar into much trouble. At social functions he instructed waiters to supply him with three parts gin and one of squash. The waiters would say, "Your squash, vicar." The demon squash led to an embarrassing situation. Bowditch drove the vicar, who was in full regalia, to the official blessing and party to mark the opening of the swimming pool at the Rum Jungle uranium mine community centre at Batchelor. Somehow, the ebullient vicar, who had been drinking squash, fell into the pool, with a great splash.

Like a giant wet walrus, he was dragged from the pool, laughed about his swan dive, apologised to ladies who had been drenched and called for another squash. When people at the party heard that Bowditch and the vicar had come down together from Darwin they cracked jokes about the odd couple. Gwynne-Jones responded by saying Bowditch had been good company, and had behaved like a "little angel". Outraged members of his flock petitioned church authorities to transfer him elsewhere.

The cleric often walked by the *News* office and called out to or had a chat with Jim. Their relationship turned nasty when he ordered some job printing. Because the print job was not regarded as urgent and it was a major task just getting the newspaper out, it was put aside. The vicar often dropped in and asked for his printing. Time and again, he was told that it was just about ready. Annoyed, one day he came into the office and began to abuse the girl at the counter. Bowditch threw the vicar, swearing like a drunken sailor, out of the office. The man of the crumpled cloth then wrote a letter of complaint to the directors down south and said the *News* was a nest of communists. This claim was probably due to the fact that one of the staff in the factory in which it was torrid to work said the place was like a Siberian prison camp, and draped a red flag on a stick out the window, which nobody bothered to remove. Another possible cause of concern for Sydney would have been the member of staff who annoyed Bowditch by cutting out hammers and sickles and Nazi swastikas, all in red, and pasting them to the wall. When they were removed under instructions from Bowditch, the man would set to and snip replacements. The vicar also complained that parties in the *News* staff quarters on the verandah facing the church, even though there was a vacant allotment in between, disrupted his Sunday morning services. In answer to a complaint, police went to one party at the *News* on a Sunday and ended up having a drink with the boys. At the church, an elderly lady played the harmonium, a keyboard instrument in which notes are produced by air blown through reeds. To supply the wind she had to pump furiously with her feet. Amused members of the flock said it seemed there was a race between the hard-working organist and the vicar to come to the end of a hymn. Because of his odd body shape, the vicar had difficulty keeping his pants up. One day he narrowly escaped dropping his trews in front of the congregation as he shuffled from the aisle to the preaching desk. During one evensong, he became annoyed by the loud bingo call from the nearby Chiefs and Petty Officers' Mess, so he lifted his skirts, ran down the aisle to the front of the church and bellowed at the navy establishment to cut the noise.

The woman who cleaned the vicarage was often paid with the small change from the church collection plate. An exceedingly erratic driver, the vicar was involved in an accident at the Botanical Gardens, but it was hushed up. On receipt of a strange telephone call from the cleric asking him to come and see him, Bowditch went to the vicarage. When he arrived the hospitable vicar turned on some drinks. It became evident that the cleric was leading up to something. Finally, the startling reason for the invitation was revealed. He told Jim that he had a personal problem, and seeing that he, Bowditch, was a man of the world, he might be able to help him. Much to Jim's surprise, the vicar then took out his penis and pointed to what looked like several sores. Did Bowditch have any idea what it might be? In typical Bowditch fashion, Jim laughed and said: "You dirty old bugger, you've got the pox, vicar." This had momentarily stunned him, but Bowditch quickly added that he was only joking, that it was obviously a growth. He advised him to see a doctor. Bowditch said he had been surprised to think that Gwynne-Jones had been so embarrassed he had not consulted a doctor. The vicar took Jim's advice, saw a doctor and reported back that it had been a fungal growth due to his sweaty crotch.

Bowditch also had a long association with the Anglican Church warden, Peter Spillett, a civic-minded public servant who was a member of the first Darwin Town Council, elected after the war in 1957 with dire predictions that it would collapse. Spillett said Bowditch and Jim Kelly had given the council good and fair coverage in the paper and helped it to survive. The newspaper treatment had raised the image of the council in the public's eye and "kept it honest." By 1959 Darwin was declared a city without a town hall, no workforce, no money.

Despite all the problems, the council built an Olympic swimming pool open to all races.

As the warden of Christ Church, Spillett had the painful task of writing to church authorities to have the vicar removed. When the church refused to extend the minister's incumbency, he left and got a job as a clerk at the Works and Housing Department, living in a hostel. A joke spread around town that it was hoped he would not make a clerical error in his new job. He and Bowditch clashed in competitive fashion in the impromptu speech section at the North Australian Eisteddfod. The subject was a room of your own. The ex-vicar, with a booming voice which sounded like Prime Minister Menzies, won.

When Gwynne-Jones decided to quit Darwin and return home to England a series of farewell parties were held for him in various hotels. During one drinking session he was asked what he would do back in cold England after so long in Australia. He replied that he would be staying with his sister and brother-in-law who had a centrally heated house. Slapping his forehead, he said, "God, I hope the brother-in-law drinks!" He told the jovial gathering that when he boarded the plane to leave Darwin he expected a Scottish piper would play a lament. After his departure, word came back that the vicar had moved on to Spain and was teaching the sons of the rich how to speak English. It tickled Jim's sense of the absurd to think that there were Spaniards being taught to speak like Bob Menzies. Bottoms up, no doubt, would have been an important English expression he taught his students. His invaluable recipe for squash could also have been passed on to the Spaniards.

On one memorable occasion Bowditch took part in a church group's debating night and livened up the evening by saying that to some people sex and grog were as important, if not more so, than religion. The audience gave him an "appreciative clap" for his entertaining, if unusual, speech. Debating, he felt, should be a regular part of all schooling as it helped people to marshal facts, present cases and be confident.

28. WHIPABLE WILLEY

Keith Willey,
renowned for smart
page layouts and
cheeky headlines.

In 1957 Bowditch was able to induce a bright reporter, Keith Willey, who had been editor of the *Advocate* in Alice, to come north to Darwin as news and chief sub editor. Willey had been the Queensland under-18 breaststroke champion and was in line for the state Olympic squad until his work prevented regular training. At one stage Willey had been the court reporter in the Adelaide office of the Melbourne *Truth*. When he joined the Adelaide office reporter Peter Blake was the SA representative for the Sydney *Daily Mirror* and the pair got on well, sharing a flat at Henley Beach. With wide experience in reporting and subbing in several states, including on the Melbourne *Age*, Willey did much to raise the standard of the *NT News*, using bright page layouts and snappy headings. Bowditch acknowledged that Willey taught him how to do newspaper layouts, the *Centralian Advocate* layouts having been "terrible".

Alliteration was one of Willey's skills. For example, he wrote catchy headings such as BRAYBROOK BATTERED BLUDGEON BANDITS, which was about the manager of the Buffalo Club thumping two hold-up men. NT HOOP HIT HOPS, SAY COPS, centred on a jockey who drank too much. DONGED BY FONG CLAIMS OYSTER KING, was the heading on another zany story. This involved Englishman Eric Grosvenor Lewis, owner of a fishing boat, who brought bags of rock oysters to the *News* and talked with Bowditch. Lewis, who normally wore a singlet, shorts and sandals, objected to being thrown out of the Vic Hotel and brought an assault charge against mine host, Richard Fong Lim. During the unusual hearing Lewis said Fong Lim had told him he was barred and to get out of the pub. However, the mollusc vendor said he did not know the meaning of the word barred and thought it related to the noise made by sheep, "Baa." He attested Fong Lim had told him to put down his glass of beer and then hit him, hence the newspaper heading.

The charge against Fong Lim was dismissed and Lewis was ordered to pay court costs. The Fong Lims were said to be "dirty" on Bowditch, believing he had induced the Oyster King to take the court action. Normally the relationship between the newspaper and the Vic Hotel was exceptionally good. Acting under orders from his father, Richard Fong Lim went to Hong Kong on occasions to look for a wife. While he was away the *News* staff drinking in the Vic would express mock sympathy for "Poor Richard" having to entertain the girls of Hong Kong. On his return, his mission unfulfilled, the *News* boys continued the chiacking. Willey said it must have been an onerous task for Richard to take a "casting couch" to Hong Kong. As it turned out, he married an Australian girl. Richard's brother, Alec, full of fun, who agreed that Richard was stressed out by entertaining the female population of the British colony, served in the hotel and went on to become the first Australian born Chinese lord mayor of an Australian city, though Harry Chan, also an Australian-born Chinese, was mayor from 1966 to 1969. Alec also had six daughters, one of whom, Lorelei, became a reporter on the *News* and another, Katrina, subsequently also became lord mayor of Darwin.

The Oyster King featured in another court case when he donged a cook. On that occasion Lewis complained expletively about the tucker served in the Humpty Doo rice farm canteen. In the fight which broke out the head cook, who defended himself with a rolling pin, received two black eyes. Journalist Doug Lockwood attended the subsequent court case and pointed out that the only thing not on the extensive breakfast menu at Humpty Doo had been Rice Bubbles, which was surprising. The battered cook appeared in court wearing sunglasses and sporting a swollen nose.

Willey's writings about the Territory won him three consecutive Walkley Awards for journalism, a record. He also wrote several books about the north. When Willey arrived in Darwin with his wife and daughter, Joanna, they experienced the accommodation shortage. The fact that public servants had cheap accommodation and other perks annoyed Willey. The Willeys once lived in one of several old army huts at Nightcliff which had a communal toilet. A roster for toilet cleaning was in view. Naturally, all the dunny cleaners were women, one being "the Greek lady"—apparently nobody could spell her name. An undertaker made coffins in one of the huts and Keith had a rum with him from time to time.

Boyish looking, Willey wore glasses, still enjoyed a daily swim and a drop or two. He played rugby league for the Brothers side and when a hypnotist called at the *News* Keith got the man to put him under in an effort to become a better player. His hair unruly because of swimming and his long socks rolled down to his ankles, Keith never looked a picture of sartorial elegance, not that anybody else on the staff would rate a mention in *Tailor and Cutter*.

Willey's wife, Lee applied for a job as a typist in a government department. In her application she gave as referees the names of James Frederick Bowditch and Jack Haritos. The practice in those days was to run a security check on all applicants. Naturally, Bowditch was known "the subject of frequent correspondence with Headquarters over the past few years." In the case of Jack Haritos, the ASIO report said he was "probably one of the Haritos brothers" referred to in the summary of information held by Headquarters re the vessel *Gladys Mary*. This vessel, it stated, appeared to have been involved in smuggling operations in the past.

The Haritos brothers were well known and highly respected in Darwin. They were fishermen, crocodile shooters and there was a Haritos store in which Lee Willey worked for a time. The Haritos brothers took the Duke of Edinburgh crocodile shooting when he visited Darwin. Lee Willey was approved for employment in government. She went bush for a weekend at Stapleton Station where the colourful and tough Winnie Bright, sister of Esther Meaney, lived. Winnie used to ride into Katherine with guns on her hips and on seeing a Japanese Betty Bomber shot down during WWII had helped her father collect documents and other items from the wreckage. At the end of the weekend Bright came back to Darwin with Lee, and Keith was found slumbering on the lounge, an empty rum bottle nearby, the house less than tidy. Winnie told Keith that if he were her husband and she came home and found him sprawled out with a rum bottle she would take the whip to him. Keith said he was sure she was serious when she said it.

Willey was also a stringer for southern newspapers and magazines and knew a good story when he saw one. He derived maximum mileage out of offbeat stories both in Darwin and down south. For example, suggestions that Darwin barmaids were less than perfect and that Darwin men were sloppy dressers and should wear suits were milked for all they were worth. Keith wrote a long piece of doggerel in defence of barmaids. An obituary he penned about an alcoholic Darwin bank dog which died and was much missed in pubs was a classic.

Letters to the editor supposedly written by people down south, especially from a person in a suburb of Melbourne, saying that Territorians were weird or lacking in social graces sounded suspiciously like the work of one K.G. Willey. They sparked the desired, colourful response from locals. Often he came across interesting yarns in pubs at night and took notes on pieces of newspaper, beer coasters or anything else that he could find. He would come to work next morning and decipher his notes, putting the bits and pieces together like a jigsaw puzzle. He often sat in the Vic just gazing into the depths of his glass of beer as if musing on the meaning of life; at times he would recite snatches of *The Rubaiyat of Omar Khyayyam*.

There was an anxious time when Willey thought he had discovered gemstones. During a trip to the Daly River he found red tinged stones in the wash and thought, hoped, they could be valuable. He sent his wife to Adelaide with samples of the stones and paced the *News* office impatiently waiting for Lee to ring. He confided to colleagues that he had found these red looking stones which when held to the sun could easily be rubies. "God, woman, ring!" Keith said, gesturing at the office phone. Alas, a jeweller told Lee the find was carnelian, a semi-precious gemstone, an entire bagful not worth much.

Due to his interest in swimming, Willey campaigned to have the town's dilapidated saltwater pool at Lameroo Beach repaired. In a report he wrote about Lameroo there were two photos of him, one showing him holding his nose because of the stench. Willey also thought up and became the editor of a quarterly publication, the *Territorian*, official organ of the Cattlemen's Association of North Australia and the NT Game Shooters' Association, which was printed and published by the *NT News* every two months.

Lawyer Dick Ward gave Willey the diary of a swashbuckling rogue, "Ginger" Palmer, who was found hanging by his belt in the Darwin lockup. There were conflicting stories about Palmer's origins. Some said he was Australian. Another account maintained he had been a ship's carpenter in the Royal Navy and had served at Gallipoli, but did not go ashore. In the Territory he was often in trouble with police and at one stage was ordered out of the Territory, retreating to Thursday Island. The diaries told how Palmer once stole a 45ft ketch from Cairns, set his accomplices adrift, sailed to the Dutch East Indies where he dodged Dutch authorities, killed many people, some with axes, and sired several children before being captured and brought back to Australia. He changed his name and returned to the Territory. An Aboriginal woman saved him from drowning when he was attacked by a crocodile. As a reward, he subsequently left her on sandbank to die, but she was rescued by other Aborigines. A detective told me that Palmer was "an evil old bastard." Near the end of his life, he lived in a camp at Shoal Bay with his Aboriginal wife. He slept on the frame of an iron bed without a mattress and reeked of rum. In the mangroves nearby was a large dugout canoe. Willey turned Palmer's diary into a chapter in the book *Naked Island & Other South Sea Tales*.

29. ENTER THE AUTHOR

Sydney or the bush? Out of the blue, in 1958, a job advertised in Darwin in the Australian Journalists' Association's (AJA, now part of the Media Entertainment and Arts Alliance or MEAA) newspaper, coincidentally called The Journalist attracted my attention. At the time I was working as a cadet reporter on Sydney's *Sun* covering courts, police rounds, the stock market call, even recording the New South Wales lottery numbers as they came out of the barrel and phoning them through to a copytaker back at the newspaper.

My newspaper career had unexpectedly started as a copyboy at the *Sun*. At the time I was attending the prestigious Fort Street High, whose name according to the school song was supposed to ring round the world. I was working as a lolly boy ("peanuts, lollies and chocs!") at night in Parramatta theatres and later, on weekends, at Halvorsen's Boatyard, Bobbin Head, one of my claims to fame there being that I cleaned out the oily bilge of a yacht which became the mother boat in a Sydney to Hobart yacht race. Along the way, I managed to do some cross country running and a bit of boxing at the North Sydney Police and Citizens' Youth Club.

An aunt of mine knew the *Sun*'s artist, illustrator and caricaturist Tony Rafty who, during WWII, had entertained troops in a military hospital in Darwin by drawing cartoons on the walls. He later became close to President Soekarno of Indonesia during the struggle for freedom from the Dutch, and got to know Jim Bowditch through the Australian Journalists'

A 1957 view from the Water Tower behind the Vic Hotel showing what would become Brown's Mart, the old Tin Bank, home of the *NT News*, and the Town Hall, later to become Darwin's first museum. Courtesy NT Archives, Les Dyson, PH0030-0010.

The newly arrived author is introduced to two Darwin staples, beer and exotic wildlife.

Club in Sydney. Tony arranged for me to be interviewed for a job as a copyboy and I found myself employed. As a copyboy I experienced a wide range of duties from sending subbed (edited) newspaper copy down the chute to be converted into metal, to handling photographs that flooded into the *PIX Magazine* library, distributing material of interest to various magazines, picking up packets of syndicated material from overseas from various city agencies. So by the time the Darwin job was advertised for a third year cadet at the fabulous amount of 18 pounds ($36) a week, I was ready to trot.

Interviewed in Sydney by a PR man named Bob Freeden, mentioned in this book, I received a letter confirming my appointment to the position and stating that accommodation would be provided, "primitive as it is." Fellow *Sun* workmates made wild and some ribald comments about what the lodgings would be in far away Darwin.

Upon arrival in Darwin, I was met by the editor of the *Northern Territory News*, quietly spoken Jim Bowditch, who was to have a big impact on my life. He took me to the Victoria Hotel where, after jumping over a chunder puddle near the entrance, I was booked in for my first night in the Top End, the Vic at that time having a number of rooms for guests. The next day I was shown around the premises, known as The old Tin Bank and the promised primitive accommodation, a walled off part of the verandah next to the factory, where a press often cranked away loudly at night. There were push-out windows, speargrass grew up against the building, there were strange rustlings and animal cries in the undergrowth at night.

It was decided that I, being a gentleman of the press, would not have to endure this situation for long and an arrangement was made for me to be lodged in a house occupied by a Fannie Bay Gaol prison guard and his wife, who let out several rooms, there being a grave shortage of accommodation in Darwin.

One of the earliest assignments I was given at the *News* involved writing up a fashion parade from the MC's notes at the Seaview Hotel, Nightcliff a far cry from the Sydney Stock Exchange

Wedding of the author and Judy Simon. Left: Jim gave the bride away
and, right: arranged for a guard of honour of paper boys with rolled-up
NT News papers. A young girl presents Judy with a bouquet.

Bulls and Bears. Several other short term accommodation places
followed. As fate would have it, the severe accommodation shortage
in Darwin resulted in my meeting my wife to be, New Zealander
and former nurse, Judith Merlyn Stacey, who lobbed in town intent,
like so many Kiwis, on voyaging to the "Mother Country", England.
Another Kiwi nurse she had worked with in Auckland had travelled
to Darwin and told her to drop in as it was an interesting place with
plenty of work.

The fiancee of a linotype operator at the *NT News* was
living in a place with the colourful name of The Crazy Cottage
at the back of a Greek dress shop in Smith Street, which could
accommodate six girls. While I was writing up a court case, the
lino operator announced there was a new girl, a Kiwi, at The
Crazy Cottage where he took me in his car after work. Employed
as a clerical assistant, Judy worked in the accounts branch of NT
Administration. We married in Darwin in May 1959. Big Jim
gave the bride away, her parents being unable to travel from New
Zealand, and even organised paper boys and girls to form an arch
of rolled-up newspapers for the newlyweds. The reception was held
at the Bowditch residence.

In 1962, with two daughters, Lizbeth and Sara, and a Darwin
bitsa, named Rangi after a famous Maori Guide, we moved to

Cairns, North Queensland, where I worked on the *Cairns Post*. It was less boisterous than the *Northern Territory News*. The newsroom prominently displayed a list of DEAR DEPARTED naming the many reporters who had worked there over the years, with comments. BANG left no doubt that the reporter named had been fired. One reporter had a whole fusillade of BANGS after his name and a suggestion that he had been a victim of heat exhaustion, his excuse to management for having over-indulged in booze and collapsed, requiring hospitalisation

A young reporter on the *Post*, Colin Dangaard, subsequently went to New Zealand and worked on the *Rotorua Post*, based in Taupo. When he decided to move on he asked me if I would like to work for the *Rotorua Post*. Why not? So off to New Zealand we went with Rangi the dog, the daughters, and a son Peter, acquired in Cairns. On the Rotorua paper was reporter/author Ross Annabell who knew Darwin and Jim Bowditch well. Ross and I shared a prospecting dish and many yarns about the Territory. While enjoying my time on the *Rotorua Post*, I started a column called "Yesteryear", which dug up details behind old photographs and ephemera, encouraged by local historian and author, Don Stafford, who owned a volcanic attraction named Tikitere and had written a book on the Te Arawa, a Maori group who trace their ancestry to the original migration canoe.

Offered a job on Auckland's *Sunday News*, NZ's first Sunday newspaper, I moved to Auckland with a presentation Maori club given to me as a farewell present by the wonderful *Rotorua Post* team. An admitted failure of mine in Auckland was tracking down the identity of an annoying person who used to paint in large red letters, "The phantom piddler was here." An Auckland University student I interviewed with a certain gleam in his eye seemed to indicate he knew the identity of the piddler, but wouldn't tell.

Pausing long enough to acquire another NZ souvenir, second son, Craig, we blasted off in 1967 for Sydney again, where I resumed working for *The Sun* on "Hotline", a consumer affairs column which sorted out wide ranging problems for readers before Ombudsmen existed.

Ross Annabell at Mount Tarawera, New Zealand, on a fossicking
trip with the author.

I subsequently worked for both the *Sun Herald* and the *Sydney
Morning Herald* where topics covered included the Poseidon share
boom and Melbourne abortion law reformer, Dr. Bertram Wainer.
I started a so-called "luxury round" covering book and art auctions,
gem dealers and mining ventures. Becoming a general reporter for
the *SMH*, I covered a lively Town Hall meeting with Germaine
Greer, university student protests demanding public bars be opened
to women and calls for penal reform.

In 1972 Darwin called once more and I took up the post as
Press Officer in the Department of the Northern Territory, once
more meeting up with Jim and Betty Bowditch. My job included

editing the Northern Territory's award-winning monthly business newsletter while moonlighting as a writer of satire for several local publications.

In the following years I became Press Officer for the Northern Territory Leader of the Opposition, Jon Isaacs, and later worked in the Adelaide office of ALP Senator Nick Bolkus. In Adelaide Judy and I started two shops Invicta Antiques and Den of Antiquity, as well as a mail-order book business. Along the way, the "Little Darwin" blog was born, covering books, art, satire, politics, photographs, ephemera and oddities. So-called retirement resulted in a relocation to Magnetic Island, Queensland.

30. EXTRAORDINARY NEWS

The years from 1955 to 1962 were action packed for Bowditch and Darwin. Extraordinary story after extraordinary story broke which involved him doing things which no other editor in Australia would contemplate. During that period the paper changed ownership twice and he began working for the rising media mogul Rupert Murdoch.

As an example of the exceptional news stories which kept surfacing in Darwin, in 1957 Doug Lockwood won the *London Evening News* award for the World's Strangest Story. This was about a 12 year old orphan boy who had climbed into the wheel nacelle of a Dutch DC3 aircaft just before it took off from Koepang, West Timor, on a flight to Darwin. When the plane landed in Darwin the unconscious, injured boy, Bas Wie, was found hanging in the struts. He became known as the Koepang Kid. After strong representations by Darwin people, he was allowed to stay in Australia and lived with the NT Administrator, Mick Driver, and his family. Wie became a respected Darwin resident, had much contact with Bowditch over the years, and in 2001 was helping alcoholics to dry out. He died in 2016.

New Hot and Cold bar at Mick Paspalis's Hotel Darwin featuring
the Rigby cartoon. Photo: National Film and Sound Archive.

Always skating on thin ice financially and despite the fact
that it was a well read and lively publication under Bowditch's
leadership, the *News* lurched on, However, the southern directors
began to discuss unloading the paper. At one stage, in what can only
be regarded as an act of desperation, they even suggested offering
the paper to the Catholic Church. Then a secret deal was done with
Swan Brewery whereby they bought the *NT News* and the *Mount Isa
Mail*. There was a brewery war on at the time and Swan wanted
to capture the Territory market against fierce competition from
Carlton & United. Bowditch said he believed Eric White played the
two breweries off against each other until Swan bought the paper
to thwart its competitor.

Bob Freeden, who kept a watching brief on the paper from Eric
White's office in Sydney and Bowditch went to Swan headquarters
on two occasions to receive "riding instructions". The brewery was
furious when a lighthearted item appeared in the paper about an
Aborigine called Banana who had been picked up for drunkenness
was referred to in print as "Pickled Banana". What really upset the

brewery bosses was that Banana's condition was linked to a party held to mark the opening of a new hotel in Darwin. In the newly opened air conditioned bar, the Hot and Cold, at the Hotel Darwin, owned by Mick Paspalis, there appeared a mural by the then popular cartoonist, Paul Rigby, showing a Pommie businessman in bowler hat and suit arriving at Darwin airport with a slinky blonde dressed in black on his arm. Subsequent scenes highlighted the adventures of the blonde—dressed in a bikini, waterskiing behind a stingray, examining a snorting buffalo and being leered at by blokes in shorts, singlets and thongs. In the end, the businessman, sans blonde, was shown boarding the plane with a case of beer on his shoulder bearing the message WING YOUR WAY WITH SFA.

Rock 'n' roll caused a culture shock in Darwin. Doug Lockwood complained to Darwin Council about the noise which came from the nearby Town Hall. His children had been unable to sleep because teenagers rocked and rolled until 4 am, screaming and stamping in a frenzy of "half-witted abandon". Councillor Ted D'Ambrosio was reported as saying Mr Lockwood had forgotten that he had once been young and that they used to dance the Black Bottom and the Charleston.

There was an odd theft in Darwin in 1958 when three hundredweight (150 kg) of uranium was stolen from the showground. Authorities were quoted as saying it was the first recorded theft in the world of uranium and that thieves would probably try to smuggle it out of the country for sale "in the islands". The mysterious islands where the uranium might be sold were not named. It being the Cold War, presumably the customers for the uranium were Russians.

Bowditch went to the Supreme Court in Darwin for the Albert Namatjira appeal to Mr Justice Martin Kriewaldt against his sentence for supplying liquor in Alice Springs and sat with and spoke to the artist outside the court. An editorial Bowditch wrote in the *News* on October 10 1958, about the imprisonment of Namatjira, was included in Professor F.K. Crowley's *Modern Australia in Documents*, Volume II, 1939–1970.

During 1958 NT MHR, Jock Nelson made two important announcements. He said that in the event of a federal Labor government being elected it would set up a NT Development Commission similar to the Snowy Mountains Authority and the possibility of building an atomic energy power plant in Arnhem Land would also be examined. As early as 1955 the director of the Atomic Energy Division of the Chase Manhattan Bank, Dr L.R. Hafstad, a former director of the US Atomic Energy Commission, had said Darwin could be among the first places in Australia to put atomic power into large scale use for industrial and domestic electricity.

Lockwood won a Walkley Award for journalism in 1958 for his report about Aboriginal girl Ruth Daylight, who had been taken from the bush humpy in which she lived at Hall's Creek, WA, with her mother, dressed up in white finery and presented to the Queen Mother at Yarralumla, then sent back to her humble life in a humpy.

There was an arrangement between Lockwood and Bowditch whereby they gave each other a copy of press telegrams they sent to the papers they serviced down south. This meant that on straight news stories they were not scooped. Ruth Lockwood said there were times when Bowditch would "sneak along the side of the house " in the early hours of the morning, wake Doug, whose bed was alongside the louvres, and mutter details of a story he had just heard, often thrusting a copy of something he had lodged at the post office through the louvres. On such occasions the whole family woke up.

A surprise arrival in Darwin was Group Captain Peter Townsend, the dashing RAF officer who had wanted to marry Princess Margaret, but had been prevented from doing so because he was divorced. He was travelling with teenage Belgian heiress Miss Clare-Luce Jamagne and denied he would marry her. Of course, he did. Onlookers said Princess Margaret was better looking than the Belgian and one woman, probably a staunch monarchist, declared the girl was suffering from teenage acne.

When news came through that the busty blonde English star Sabrina was to pass through Darwin by air, Lockwood and I sped to the airport with a tape measure. The idea was that the tape would be run about the vital part of her vital statistics, reputedly insured for 100,000 pounds. A photographer would record the event for posterity. Alas, the tape measure remained unused because the tip about Sabrina was wrong. It was Sabrina's mother who stepped out of the plane, not her famous daughter. Still, mum was a jovial, also statuesque lady who said she was sorry to have disappointed the panting press.

31. KILL THE EDITOR

While Bowditch was held in high regard by many, there were some who resented and even hated him. In typical fashion, he became enraged when he was reliably told that a storekeeper often sold grog and methylated spirits to Aborigines on the sly at inflated prices. He drove to the store and confronted the owner with the allegations. The upshot of the heated conversation was that three friends of the storekeeper gave Bowditch a severe beating. Rather than complain to the police, he retreated and licked his wounds.

A white South African who refused to eat with Aborigines at a government experimental farm threatened to bash Bowditch when questioned by him. The irate man left the farm after reports in the *News*. He then got a job in a Darwin butchery. In an odd twist to the story, unionists "rang the tin on him" and he was declared "black"; he soon left the Territory.

Without doubt, the most bizarre episode concerning Bowditch during his editorship was the time he woke up in his car parked at a secluded spot with the engine running and found a hose from the exhaust pumping poisonous fumes inside. There was conjecture that he had been knocked out or drugged, driven to a quiet spot and an attempt made to murder him, making out it was suicide. The odd event took place when Bowditch was investigating a tip that a brothel that practised racial discrimination was operating in the suburb of Nightcliff.

A Brisbane madam was running the house in Progress Drive. She bought beds, furniture and carpets from local suppliers and made it known that she would make sure they received special attention from her girls should they wish to visit the premises. Bowditch went to Nightcliff to investigate and began asking questions. During the investigations, he did not come home one night and about the middle of the next day he turned up in a groggy and weak state.

He told his wife that he woke up in his car, with the engine running and a hose leading inside from the exhaust. He had no idea what had happened or how the car came to be at the spot. Somebody, he said, had obviously been trying to kill him. A suspect was a person connected with the brothel who was said to be a "nasty piece of work." Bowditch made no complaint to the police, but the place was raided and closed down.

If attempts to murder Bowditch failed, he came close to ending his own life several times. About 1965, following discussions with Murdoch and others, it was decided to appoint a managing director to the *NT News* which, as a result, required a change in Jim's title, he being the managing editor. Bowditch said he was content to be the editor with control of all matters editorial. The managing director, Rod Lever, came to Darwin and a function was arranged for him to meet members of the business community at the Hotel Darwin. Murdoch's right hand man, Ken May, was there and some solid drinking took place. Bowditch drove away from the function in the office VW, crashed into a telegraph pole, brought down power lines and blacked out his suburb of Fannie Bay. His head went through the windscreen and badly smashed his nose. He remembered being questioned by police at the scene, but an ambulance man told them they should not quiz a man with his injuries.

Bowditch subsequently told police he swerved to miss a dog. Betty, after hearing that Jim was not seriously injured, refused to go to the hospital to see him because she knew the accident would have been due to heavy drinking, and she was annoyed. Daughter Ngaire went to see her father and cried when she saw his battered nose which had to be rebuilt. Several ribs had also been broken. He quickly assured his daughter that he had hurt nobody but himself. To repair the damage to his nose, he had to wear a helmet-like device. It had a long attachment which fitted over his nose and he said it made him look like a "Martian". *News* compositor Bobby Wills said he thought Bowditch looked more like the comic hero Hawk Man with his beak-shaped nose.

Still sore and sorry, Bowditch attended the *NT News* Christmas party in the Green Room at the Hotel Darwin. His odd appearance afforded much merriment. Each time he ventured into a pub there was an outbreak of raucous laughter. Whenever there was a power blackout in Darwin, people would say Bowditch had hit another pole.

Only his grey hair saved Bowditch from a beating by an angry musician at the Victoria Hotel. Bowditch had been to squash practice and dropped into the Vic for a snort. There was a band playing in the beer garden, its amplifiers blaring so loudly that Bowditch could not hear himself speak. On two occasions he got up to go to the toilet and on returning pulled out the electric plug used by the band. After the second disconnection, an angry bandsman, addressing him as "old man", told Bowditch it was only his grey hair that saved him from having his head punched in. Having just unofficially launched the Darwin Noise Abatement Society, Bowditch eventually sat down and resumed drinking with compositor Bobby Wills, who had dropped in from the cowboy night at the Star theatre during interval. In light-hearted banter, Wills disputed the claim that local boxer Dave Napier could be billed as the NT heavyweight champion when he had never fought a title bout. Bowditch ended the learned discussion by bopping Wills on the head with his squash racquet.

Down south, Bowditch became known as "Mr Darwin", the wild, crusading editor who had his finger on the pulse of North Australia. This, he said, was responsible for projecting a larger than life image. He explained the situation thus: "The reputation I had down south was distorted. A lot of journos who came up from south really expected to see a man about seven foot tall, covered in red hair and muscle, rushing around beating up cops. The truth of the matter was that the cops used to rush around beating me up. I had many clashes with cops, but I never won one. They are bigger, faster, younger, and stronger. Certainly, I probably brought the majority of it [trouble] on myself."

An English female writer presented a different view of Bowditch in a book. She described him as a slight, anxious man deeply concerned about the welfare of Darwin and the economy of the Territory.

Despite the encounters with the police and frequent equipment breakdowns, Bowditch said his first 10 years on the paper were ones of enjoyment.

There is no doubt that Bowditch enjoyed writing editorials. He drew much of his inspiration for them from the British Labour newspaper the *Daily Mirror*, which used to arrive in its weekly overseas edition bound-in volume with its distinctive yellow covers. Several times in Darwin during talks with Labor leader Gough Whitlam, Bowditch raised the need for the ALP to have its own national newspaper like the British paper. It was his firm belief that for the ALP to get its unfettered message across and educate the community about the need for social changes, it was highly desirable for the party to have its own paper. If the British labour movement could run a successful mass circulation newspaper, then why not Australia?

Usually, Jim started his working day knowing exactly what he intended to write about in the editorial. However, the editorial was normally the last thing he wrote. He explained his approach to the job: "As editor, you are thinking about how you are going to fill the paper and meet a deadline. I think it is a very satisfying business and an exhausting one. Because of its demands, we all make mistakes, sometimes bad ones. I write best when my back is to the wall and under great pressure. I can crystallise things under pressure, the same as a soldier. Under pressure, I wrote a lot of readable editorials, some of which caused certain things to happen."

Of the many editorials he wrote during his time, he nominated a piece written as a result of the assassination of Martin Luther King as his favourite. It read:

BIG JIM

There are some men who by the example of their lives and an almost indefinable greatness of character reach the hearts of people in the furthermost corner of the earth.

When such a man dies violently, shock and sadness touch millions who have never seen him, never been within thousands of miles of him.

John F. Kennedy was such a man, Martin Luther King another.

The news of Dr King's death today has swept the world, as much as his own country.

Tears will have been shed for him in every land and massive rage felt against the cowardly assassin responsible for cutting down a man who steadfastly preached and practised the code of non-violence.

It would be trite to extol his virtues here.

His massive strength, depth of wisdom and unfaltering kindness and gentleness have long been accepted by the world, and recognised with the Nobel Peace Prize.

It is reported that America trembles now, fearing the murderer's bullet may trigger such passionate hatred among the nation's Negroes that near civil war will result.

This newspaper believes, and hopes, that such was the power and influence of Dr King that only madmen and complete fools would desecrate his memory by reacting in a way so utterly foreign to the doctrine he lived by, and asked all to follow.

We believe that if the millions now mourning, in their mounting anger, are reminded quickly and properly of Martin Luther King's aims, his terrible death could become a weapon to further his teachings, rather than an excuse for his violent enemies to open the way to racial holocaust.

Violent reaction would mean that all his work and efforts had failed and his death been in vain.

It may be as well for those who see his death, and America's shocking racial upheaval generally, as a sign that nothing is right with that land, to remember that these are the tribulations of a democracy. They are part of the price we pay for "freedoms", not possible in countries where dictatorships are the order.

Martin Luther King believed in freedoms ... for all people—white as well as those who shared his ebony skin colour—and for whom he devoted his whole life.

His death should not be used as an opportunity to attack the country he loved, the freedom he extolled and the code of non-violence be constantly preached.

On the broader question of the role of a newspaper, Bowditch said he used his papers to educate the community about important issues. In Alice he had taken up the advancement of half-castes, especially in relation to voting and citizenship. While legislation was good to an extent, in matters of discrimination there had to be community education to overcome ingrained attitudes. Through his newspapers he tried to break down the widespread discrimination against and attitude to Aboriginal people.

Although the *News* ran many humorous stories during his editorship, Bowditch did not see a newspaper as a form of entertainment. This was made evident in an exchange he had with adventurous Kiwi journalist Bob Hobman, who worked sporadically at the *News* from 1967 to 1974, and went on to organise epic raft and outrigger canoe voyages from Indonesia to destinations such as Madagascar and Darwin.

One night Bowditch asked Hobman what he, deep down, thought about newspapers. Hobman said he regarded newspapers just as entertainment for the masses. This honest answer did not please Bowditch. In Hobman's words, emotionally expressed in the year 2001, he said: "He [Jim] never quite trusted me after that, even though I loved him then and love him still."

Hobman said he had worked for only two great editors in Australia who clung to their ideals, charisma and magical story-telling techniques, Zell Rabin, mentioned elsewhere, and Jim Bowditch. He deplored modern Darwin and lamented the situation where many people remembered Bowditch only as a drunken "little Pommie" who achieved nothing.

All of what Bowditch had battled for during his time as editor of the *NT News* had been swept aside by modern, crowded

Darwin. Recalling the Bowditch era, Hobman said it had been a "mad time". "You couldn't get away with any of it in these sanitised days." Hobman spoke of the occasions when the editor, after consumption of liquor, adopted the famous "wombat crouch" and threatened people, including members of his own newspaper staff. Hobman observed that a person so challenged only had to wait a short time and the editor would collapse, mumbling, on the lawn.

Another journalist who thought he might have been the only staffer not challenged to a fight by Bowditch is Dennis "Doggie" Booth, sports editor at the *NT News* under Bowditch, who revealed a soft side to Jim. While Bowditch was regarded as tough and took strong stands against people and organisations, Booth noted several occasions which showed he was a gentle person. One involved the loss of a kitten where Bowditch had used masterful language to write a touching story. Booth had worked with great newspaper men in Australia and Hong Kong, including Rohan Rivett, editor of the *Adelaide News*, and said Bowditch was the best. Once Bowditch was convinced a reporter knew what he was doing and was sure of his facts, he would let him have his head. Booth also pointed out that Bowditch did not just blindly support unions. If he thought an individual unionist or a union was wrong, he would give them a blast, often in a strong verbal face-to-face confrontation.

In turn, if unionists felt Bowditch or the *News* was wrong, they also forthrightly told him so. Brian Manning gave an example of this. He became annoyed with the *News* during a time of high unemployment when the newly formed NT Trades and Labour Council supposedly "seized" the vacant old town hall which was to be demolished for an entertainment centre and the Beaufort Hotel (which didn't happen for several years, mainly because of cyclone Tracy).

In the hall, they set up the Unemployed Workers' Relief Centre. Rather than the building having been seized, Manning said councillor and former mayor Ken Waters had "slipped" him the keys and issued instructions for the hall to be supplied with toilet paper and other requisites. Despite his great wealth, Manning said Waters, founder of the Liberal Party in Darwin, and father of John

Waters, QC, an ALP stalwart, had been sympathetic to the plight of the unemployed and had an enlightened attitude on many issues. At the time, Manning said unemployed people had been camping on Lameroo Beach, much to the consternation of the council.

In the centre, food donated by local businesses was cooked in the kitchen on a roster. Rules determined by those using the premises included no drugs, no drunks. Prospective employers called in the mornings to pick up workers for various jobs. Those who got work chipped in money to buy food. A meeting was held each night to discuss issues. To put pressure on the federal government, each morning the unemployed, carrying placards, would march to the employment office demanding work. A young unemployed student carried a sign: BILLY [McMAHON] CAN YOU KEEP SONIA ON $10 A WEEK? This was a reference to the PM and his wife. The student, went on to become a professor at Yale University in America.

The *News* ran a report in which the centre was described as "a soup kitchen". Manning gave Bowditch a blast for so describing what went on there. It had done irreparable damage, there having been a knee-jerk reaction by "extreme right wing arseholes." He explained that the unemployed helped themselves, were highly organised and the town hall was a social hub which gave the men shelter, hope and dignity and showed organised unemployed people could achieve much if given half a chance.

However, some members of the council and the community had taken fright at the centre being called a soup kitchen. Nearby residents claimed real estate values dropped, The Darwin Council reacted unfavourably and admonished Ken Waters for handing over the keys to the hall without full council approval. Police eventually raided the town hall and evicted the unemployed, who had to be carried out. Doors and windows were barricaded to prevent the unemployed regaining entry.

Years later, Manning was delighted to hear that one of those who had strongly objected to the workers' relief centre, living in the Philippines and running a "sleazy bar", had lost $US40,000 to a crooked banker who did a moonlight flit.

Manning also knew how to invoke the name of Bowditch to right wrongs. A man of action not put off by obstructionists, official dithering and red tape, Manning did not pussyfoot around. He went to the aid of a band of Muluk Muluk people who were "just dumped" and left to fend for themselves by their European employers at the beginning of each Wet.

They were engaged in buffalo shooting for the pet food trade. In all, about 35 men, women and children were camped around a tiny hut at the 13-mile, near the highway, with very little money. Manning discovered that they had been charged for things during the shooting season which should have been supplied by the employer. As a result, after six months' work, they had almost no money, or were even in debt. Furious at this, Manning, in company with the group's spokesmen, Major Bangun and Leo Jackaboy, went to the Welfare Department seeking assistance for them.

At the counter, Manning was attended to by a person who did not seem very responsive to the plight of the group. This fellow told Manning they would have to move to the Bagot compound to be housed and fed. Both the Aboriginal men shook their head and said they would not go to Bagot because residents there would "humbug our women." Told this, the officer insisted they would have to go to Bagot. Manning responded: "Look, it's nearly Christmas. These people have nothing to tide them over until they go back to work after the Wet." Still, the officer was adamant—Bagot. Annoyed by the "bullshit", Manning replied: "Oh, well, I'm going to take this mob to camp outside Harry Giese's [he being the head of the department] house on Christmas Day and invite Jim Bowditch to come along and get a story."

This got an instant response. The young officer said to "hang on a minute", and disappeared out the back of the office. About five minutes later, a more senior officer, Ted Egan, later appointed Administrator of the NT in 2003, came to the counter. After the story was recounted, Egan arranged for Manning and the two Aborigines to go to Bagot with a truck and load up drums of flour, cases of powdered milk, cartons of bully beef, cereals, baby food and even some drums of prunes. The Muluk Muluk people today have a permanent camp at Knuckey Lagoon.

A typical day at the office for Bowditch in the old Tin Bank days would begin with him arriving, usually at speed, in the open area on the town side of the *News* which was used as a parking lot. The surrounds were like a jungle. Frill necked lizards used to cavort there in the grass. A lizard was photographed, frill extended, its tail across a car tyre track. To this picture was added a balloon in white ink: Yeeow! He ran over me bloody tail!, and hung in the office.

A female staff member ran screaming from the toilet after a lizard scampered in with her. Possums roamed the building at night; feral cats howled in the long grass; hairy caterpillars appeared in their thousands, followed by flocks of parrots which feasted on them. Linotype operator Timmy Forday had a close encounter with a 12-foot python when he was using the washing machine at the rear of the building, He happened to look up and saw the large snake rocking from side to side, apparently mesmerised by the backwards and forwards agitation of the machine. Forday raised the alarm and workmates came running. Armed with a spear gun, compositor Brian McKnight let fly and broke a fibro panel. The poor snake was later found dead in the grass.

Carrying a portable typewriter, a small but bulging briefcase and juggling the mail picked up from the post office, Bowditch would stride purposefully into the office through a glass door which opened out from the reporters' room. (Finding the door locked one night and he without a key, Bowditch knocked a small hole in a glass panel to get at the inside lock.) Out would come a packet of cigarettes; a cadet reporter who started with the *NT News* in the 1960s said his first task each day was to buy two packets of Rothman's for the editor.

During the time Keith Willey was news editor he would give Bowditch a rundown on what was happening on the news front. It was not unusual for the briefings to contain details of some colourful overnight event in town, often in a pub.

There was no special treatment for Bowditch when he appeared in court. True to his word, when convicted for driving under the influence of liquor in 1960, there was a front page report headed: NEWS CHIEF UP FOR DRINK DRIVE, which spilled over to fill all of page four. Magistrate Stuart Dodds said the three-day hearing had been long and traversed many fields "from the dramatic evidence of an editor with a catch in his voice, to the banality of a wife doing her best to help her husband when he was in difficulties."

Bowditch was represented by Dick Ward and the court was told the defendant, after nearly running a car off the road, had hit a parked vehicle. He had gone up to the driver of the vehicle he hit and said, "Sorry, old chap, are you hurt?" Bowditch had also offered to fight the driver of the car he nearly ran off the road. That driver had called him an idiot and a drunk. While not exactly explaining how he came to be on the accident scene, it was said that watersider Bill Donnelly had applied sticking plaster to a cut on Jim's nose. A policeman, whose evidence was accepted by the magistrate, said Bowditch staggered, his head lolled from side to side and he appeared to be drunk. At the police station, it was claimed, Bowditch was heard talking to himself and was seen trying to light a bent cigarette with matches that had no heads. A public servant told the court he had offered to drive Bowditch home before the accident as he had seemed disturbed because of an argument with a photographer from the south, and business worries. A doctor who examined Bowditch an hour after the accident said he did not appear to be drunk. *News* readers were told the editor of the paper had been fined 40 pounds and disqualified from driving for two months.

Many events in Darwin seemed to take on extraordinary twists like no other place in Australia. For example, a novel story was the refurbishing and reopening of the Chinese temple, which had been closed and looted during the war. An important event for the Chinese community and the town itself, the temple was opened with great ceremony and locked up at night. However, at night mysterious drumming was heard from within. The gods were asked what was wrong and the joss sticks answered that they were like flowers behind a screen. This was interpreted to mean they did not want the doors closed at night, so they were left open and the drumming immediately stopped. A thief then entered and repeatedly took the contents of the donations box. Green dye helped capture the culprit.

A kind of perambulatory journalism operated in the 1950s and 1960s. Simply by walking from the *NT News* you could talk to or give a wave of recognition to clergymen, a fight promoter, union activists, leading public servants, police officers, "John the Log" (a man said to have been arrested unable to start a getaway car for bank robbers in London), businessmen, bankers, entrepreneurs, characters galore and publicans.

On the town side of the *News* was the Crown Law Office in the old Brown's Mart stone building where lawyers such as John Gallop, later a judge, worked. Another Crown Law officer was the gentlemanly George Dickinson who strolled about town at a sedate pace. Dickinson, who liked to discuss politics and current affairs, had a wry sense of humour. He told how the Pidgin English for the moon in New Guinea was "kerosene belong Jesus Christ."

After WWII, Dickinson, with a great interest in and knowledge of the Japanese, had attended the Manus Island war crimes hearings as an observer. Having worked for the *Sydney Morning Herald* and being in charge of its court reporting section when *SMH* reports were regarded as gospel, he was interested in newspapers. He would enthusiastically talk about proprietors such as Sir Warwick Fairfax of the *SMH*, Frank Packer of the *Telegraph* and Ezra Norton of the *Truth*.

Dickinson wrote an illustrated report on kadaitcha murder cases in the Northern Territory which appeared in *South Pacific*, the magazine of the Australian School of Pacific Administration. So-called Aboriginal "hit men", the kadaitcha wear emu feather boots to hide their tracks to carry out secret killings. He also wrote articles for *Walkabout*.

Bowditch's frequent involvement in unusual news events and escapades often drew whimsical and understated comment from Dickinson. "I see Mr Bowditch has been active again," he would say to me, a mischievous twinkle in his eye.

Cells behind the old police station in Bennett St, occasional home to
Bowditch, Dapper Don and others.

At the Bennett Street police station was a bear-sized policeman,
Sergeant Greg Ryall, the man who put a headlock on one of the
Russian guards escorting Mrs Petrov. Photographs of him choking
the Russian were flashed about the world. On the wall behind his
desk was a well-worn baton which had been issued to Ryall in his
younger days. When I suggested that Ryall must have massaged
many a skull with the baton, the officer emphatically said that when
he was young he had not needed a baton to subdue anyone.

At the rear of the police station were cells which from time
to time accommodated the editor of the *News* and its celebrated
cleaner, Dapper Donald Duncan. When a conservative secretary at
the *News* was arrested for driving under the influence, he asked that
Bowditch be contacted to bail him out.

The police rang Bowditch at home and he laughed when told
that the man had been arrested. He drove to Bennett Street and
told the officer on duty at the counter the reason for his attendance.

When the officer said the prisoner was sitting in a nearby office
waiting for him, Bowditch reacted. He demanded to know why the

company secretary was receiving special privileges. Bowditch said that whenever he was arrested he was lodged in the cells. To the consternation of the arrested man, Bowditch refused to bail him and told the officer to throw him into the cells. With that, he walked out of the police station. Not long afterwards, he re-entered the station, laughing, and bailed the anxious man.

Walking back from the courts to the *News* via Smith Street, the main drag, the roving reporter usually called at the Burns Philp office to get the latest shipping information. Then he continued past Italian and Greek taxi drivers who whistled at the girls; betting shops; clubs; the Star Theatre with its open air front stalls; Cashman's Newsagency which seemed to be busy all the time; and the Bank of NSW and the Commonwealth Bank which had both been damaged during the war.

32. THE GREAT WHITE HUNTER

Bowditch received frequent visits from skilled and genial PR man Allan Stewart, who had been involved in the Humpty Doo rice project near Darwin. American investors and the Australian government hoped Humpty Doo would become "the food bowl of Asia", an expression no longer heard in modern Australia. While nightclubbing with clients down south, Stewart was asked to help with the troubled Territory rice project. Reports that magpie geese were eating the rice frightened off investors. The armed services had been called in and used Bren guns, carbide guns, sonic screamers, shotguns and low flying aircraft to try to frighten the geese away. An old warhorse himself, Stewart had a varied background. In Sydney he unsuccessfully contested two elections against Labor candidates, In one election he gave the firebrand Eddie Ward of East Sydney a close run and used a tailor's dummy wearing a threadbare suit to show how much soldiers were appreciated. He also failed to gain Liberal pre-selection on another occasion by making rude comments about politicians with an unflattering description of a Liberal as being a person with two feet firmly planted in the air.

At one stage he managed country shows for Australian radio and revue artists such as Willie Fennell, George Foster, Don Baker and Kitty Bluett. He was even involved in the publishing of an arithmetic book for children. In PR fashion, Stewart, a great raconteur, often did things with a flourish and would order a waiter to take a bottle of champers with his best wishes to somebody he spotted in a Darwin nightspot. He and Bowditch had a long association until the end of their lives.

After his services were no longer required at Humpty Doo, Stewart underwent a major career change when he billed himself as the Great White Hunter and set up the Nourlangie Safari Camp, 120 miles (200 km) southeast of Darwin. The area teemed with waterfowl, buffalo, crocodiles and barramundi. An old timber camp provided the safari facilities, but was rough and ready. It was a classic case of under capitalisation. The potential, however, was enormous and Stewart set about using his undoubted PR skills and connections to promote the venture and the NT.

Bowditch, of course, gave Nourlangie good coverage in the *NT News* to help Stewart along. Through his contacts in Sydney, Stewart brought up two photographers, Ray Jamieson and Ernie McQuillan, to take publicity photographs of Nourlangie. They were at the camp in June 1959 when a flying saucer, described by a New Zealander, Coral Mason, as "a red blob going up and down in the sky", was sighted.

Stirling Moss, the British racing car ace and his wife went to Nourlangie. Bowditch had to tell Moss about the death of a close racing friend in England.

From America came safari experts making films on big game hunting around the world. Stewart flew south about once a week to appear on the *Westinghouse Hour of Sport* and did much to promote the Territory.

Stories which came out of Nourlangie were many. A rich American big game hunter who had a huge trophy room back home came to Darwin with his special guns to shoot at

Allan Stewart and offsider, Nym at the entrance to Nourlangie
Safari Camp.

Nourlangie. Due to poor eyesight, he had thick lenses and looked a dangerous man to be wielding high powered rifles. At Nourlangie, he went to a primitive outdoor dunny and when he pulled the chain no water flowed from the cistern perched above his head. Hearing the clang, clang of the chain, Stewart quickly called to one of his staff to get a bucket of water. A ladder was thrown up against the toilet, the staffer clambered up with the bucket and poured some water in the cistern and quite a bit of it directly on the Yank. The drenched hunter emerged with water running down his glasses.

In another unfortunate mishap, the American nearly choked himself on the clothesline while walking about at night. On a crocodile shooting trip with the American, things proceeded at a slow pace. Several times while they were driving along Stewart remembered vital things which had not been loaded on the truck at the start. On each occasion Stewart pulled up under some shade and his Aboriginal offsider, Nym, was sent loping back to camp to pick up the missing gear.

Tucker on the trip was a hunk of beef and some damper carried in a grubby hessian bag.

Two Melbourne men who had witnessed the misadventures of the American big game hunter at Nourlangie told of their experiences, over drinks, in the Hotel Darwin and laughed so much they had tears running down their faces. They said it had been such a hilarious experience that they had not minded the fact that their smelly towels had not been changed during their time in the camp.

Nourlangie had enormous potential, but had an obvious cash flow problem. It became known that the White Hunter was hitch-hiking between Darwin and southern capitals to appear on shows and in some court cases. Stewart and his partner began stuffing baby crocodiles and selling them to tourists. One day, Stewart, wearing his usual broad-brimmed hat, limped into the public bar at the Hotel Darwin. Some reporters from the *NT News* were there and called Allan over for a drink. Knowing Stewart was experiencing tough times, Bowditch went to pay for the drinks. Stewart insisted that he pay for the shout himself, and pulled out a big roll of notes. Peeling off one of the bills, he threw it on the bar and said: "Thank Christ for baby crocodiles." Stuffed crocs, he explained, were about his only source of income.

Due to a "thirsty" lawyer failing to seek an adjournment in a case of domestic litigation, Stewart was surprised to find himself arrested for contempt of court and lodged in the Bennett Street lockup before being transferred to Fannie Bay Gaol for 30 days. Word got out that the White Hunter was in the slammer at Bennett Street. Mates in the nearby Vic Hotel gathered under his cell window, passed in cigarettes and serenaded him with The Fannie Bay Blues. The Vic Hotel did the catering for prisoners and publican Richard Fong Lim sent in a bottle of beer hidden under a napkin with a meal for Stewart.

When it was discovered that due to a survey error the Nourlangie camp was five miles inside the Woolwonga Aboriginal Reserve, it was closed down by the authorities. However, with Bowditch's help, a protest meeting was held in Darwin and the

Administrator set up an Appeals Board (the first in the Territory's history), to hear Stewart's case. Stewart represented himself at the hearing and the lease was restored.

In 1972 Stewart unsuccessfully stood as an independent for the NT federal seat against the sitting member, Sam Calder, known as "Silent Sam". Stewart said the NT needed a more vociferous and experienced voice. During his campaign he addressed the Women's Electoral Lobby and set out his platform. Australia, he said, could support a population of 60 million. In an attempt to capture the "donkey vote" in that election he had his name changed by deed poll to Alexander Allan-Stewart so his hyphenated name would be at the top of the ballot paper. Even though he did not get elected, he appeared on TV in the *Tommy Hanlon Show* and was presented with the White Hunter of the Week Award.

Ngaire Bowditch says Jim, an animal lover, advised Stewart that rather than promoting hunting, he should swap guns for cameras and offer photographic opportunities, a suggestion Stewart accepted and of which Jim was proud. Now known as Burrungkuy, Nourlangie was absorbed into the Kakadu National Park when it was created in 1979.

33. DARWIN'S HOUDINI

Bowditch was mentioned nationwide in connection with the manhunt for "Darwin Houdini", Arsenue Calma, who escaped from prison several times. His monotonous escapes led to an inquiry into the running of Fannie Bay Gaol, which resulted in bizarre revelations about things that went on in the tin-walled calaboose. These included the fact that female prisoners entertained male inmates and some warders and ingredients for home brew could be bought in the gaol. Calma escaped twice in 1955. On July 12 1956, while serving four months for breaking, entering and stealing, he was placed in solitary confinement. The next day, his cell was found to be empty. He had scaled the wall in his cell to a narrow window 12 feet above the floor, and squeezed through bars feet first. At one stage he was hanging jammed against the bars by his ears and painfully tore himself loose. Each time he escaped the community was warned that he could be dangerous.

In those days prisoners serving long sentences were sent south. In Melbourne's Pentridge prison, Calma had met a Catholic priest who helped him develop commercial art skills. In one escape he simply ran straight up the prison wall and did a back flip over the barbed wire at the top. After each escape he hung around Darwin and was often seen from time to time. Frustrated police chased him all over the place. He was arrested with another man, but managed to talk his way free. During his time on the run he did many daring and audacious things such as joining the drinkers in an RAAF mess and wrote a letter to the Assistant Administrator, Reg Marsh, offering to give himself up if he could serve out his time in Darwin as he was "engaged to an inmate."

Bowditch took a close interest in the man after about his third escape from custody. Despite a large manhunt, he remained at large. Police nearly caught him several times. Calma let it be known he had been up a tree listening to police describe in colourful language what they would do to him when they caught him. On one occasion he was in a hut at Stuart Park when six armed police surrounded the building. He jumped into a wardrobe and peeped out the keyhole. Suddenly he darted out of the wardrobe and escaped in a hail of bullets. Police claimed they fired into the air but Calma subsequently said he had been hit on the foot.

Bowditch, who went out to the hut, also claimed the police fired at Calma. One officer had even told Bowditch to sniff his recently fired pistol and said the escapee would soon be captured or shot. Bowditch wrote a piece critical of the way police used firearms in built-up areas. Severe restrictions were then placed on the use of firearms in the town.

Bowditch felt that Calma was more likely to be shot dead than captured alive and discussed the manhunt with relatives and friends of the fleeing man. Relatives said Calma's personality had changed after he had been knocked down in a pub brawl in Pine Creek and badly kicked and beaten about the head by several men.

They told Bowditch Calma had been taken to hospital and had never been the same since, being involved in violent events, including the stabbing of the best man at a wedding. Convinced that Calma needed psychiatric treatment, Bowditch spoke to a man in the Workers' Club who knew Calma. Eventually he got a message saying Calma would like to meet him. Arrangements were made for Jim to pick up a man about midnight at Stuart Park and he would then be taken to the escapee. Apprehensive about what he might encounter, Bowditch put his service revolver, a rusty .38 Smith and Wesson, in a coat. When his contact drove up, Bowditch slid in alongside the driver and threw his coat in the back. However, the gun hit the door handle and made a loud noise. The driver picked up the coat and took out the gun. He then accused Bowditch of a double cross. After some quick talking, an apology and a handshake they were on their way to the rendezvous. Just to show he was not planning anything untoward, Bowditch threw the gun into long grass next to the road and could not find it when he went back later hoping to recover it. Calma was hiding in a stormwater drain in scrub in a gully behind the Haritos store. A voice asked, "Who's that?" When told it was Jim Bowditch, a torch came to life. There was Calma, no shoes, no shirt, thin and wiry. They shook hands and spoke for about an hour. Calma laughed and joked about the police chase. Calma "raved on a bit" about his sentence. Bowditch tried to get through to him the futility of being on the run. He urged him to come and see his old friend, the lawyer Dick Ward.

Calma said he would like a day to think about the proposition and to come back at the same time the next evening. Before slipping away into the darkness, he asked Bowditch not to mention what had happened that night. During the next day Jim wanted to discuss the situation with Ward, but did not want to put him in a difficult position. He went back to the rendezvous point on his own that night and waited for an hour before Calma turned up. Calma was a bit uneasy, and they smoked and talked. Finally, Calma said "Let's go. I'll do what you want." It was about 2 am when they arrived at the Ward residence. The lawyer opened the door and said, "You must want to see me." Bowditch told Ward that he had Calma with him. They drank some beer and Ward undertook to represent Calma. Ward rang Fannie Bay Gaol and said he was bringing in the escapee. They drove to the prison and officers surrounded the car. Calma caused Ward to smile when he said, "If you want to speak to me, speak to my mouthpiece." Calma then shook hands with Ward and Bowditch and was taken inside the prison. Southern newspapers spoke of Bowditch contacting the "Darwin underworld" to arrange a secret rendezvous with the wanted man.

Despite evidence submitted about the change in Calma's personality after the beating, the court did not take much notice of what was said. He served out the remainder of his sentence a model prisoner. When he was released he visited Bowditch, and thanked him for his help.

34. THE *SEA FOX* SAGA

Strangely, without any advance Hollywood-type publicity, a large luxury yacht, the *Sea Fox*, sailed into Darwin in June 1959 bound for Sydney. The exotic crew included a chain-smoking chimpanzee, who was supposed to have been Jimmy the Chimp in a Tarzan movie. Skipper of the vessel, which had sailed down from Singapore, was B-grade movie star John Calvert, billed as America's greatest magician. It was not the first time Calvert had been to Australia, having had star billing in *Fantasy*, a 1950 magic show, in Sydney. He used to pilot his own DC3, the *Mystic Lady*, about America putting on magic performances which included lots of leggy female assistants.

Also aboard the yacht was "Mrs Calvert", a young Filipino singer named Pilita. During the voyage to Darwin the poor caged chimpanzee had been let out for a bit of exercise. He had gone

The yacht *Sea Fox* berthed at Stokes Hill wharf and Jimmy the
Chimp, cigarette in mouth, caged and in disgrace.

berserk, chased crew about the vessel with some locking themselves in their cabins while others jumped overboard. Jimmy had then climbed a mast and refused to come down. Brave Captain Calvert, supposedly a Golden Gloves boxing champion, according to his scrapbooks, stood at the bottom of the mast and ordered Jimmy to come down. Jimmy mutinied, ignored instructions from the captain, and just hung there in the rigging. Not to be outsmarted by a chimp, Calvert produced a bunch of bananas and Jimmy began to salivate. Just as Adam was brought undone by an apple in the Garden of Eden, Jimmy succumbed to the seductive bananas.

Down the mast he came and just when he was about to grab the fruit, Calvert took to him with a belaying pin. Strangely, Calvert reportedly hugged the stunned chimp like a baby for a time before the groggy animal was dragged back to the confines of his cage. When he arrived in Darwin the chimp morosely peered out from his cage and tried to set fire to the rigging with cigarettes given to him to smoke.

One of those to board the yacht soon after it arrived in Darwin was Carl Atkinson of Doctors Gully, who gave the vessel a thorough going over; no doubt he gave the female crew members some close attention as well. Once the word got about town that there was a yacht with a monkey and a film star in port people flocked to the wharf.

The *Sea Fox* had been in port only a short time when two young crewmen arrived, naked, at Bennett Street Police Station. They told an amazing story. One of them claimed that Calvert had warned him to keep away from Pilita and threatened to cut off his "nuts" if he did not obey orders. The nuts he referred to were not the ones consumed by chimpanzees. The man, wearing only shorts, had made a pass at Pilita, and Calvert pulled out a knife, apparently intent on nut removal. The police were told the actor had grabbed the crewman by his shorts, whereupon he quickly slipped out of them, ran along the deck and jumped into the sea. A friend of his, also wearing only shorts, had jumped overboard with him, and in the process lost his trews. The two men were taken back to the yacht by the bemused police and after diplomatic negotiations Calvert allowed them back on board.

Calvert called into the *News* office and spoke to Bowditch from time to time.

Despite the exotic aura created by the Hollywood star and the luxury yacht, it was obvious that Calvert was not flush with money. After receiving a bill for some laundry, Calvert winced and said he might marry a washerwoman. To improve his financial position, he decided to put on a magician's show in Darwin. To promote the event, he announced he would drive blindfolded down the main street. When the police heard about this they were dubious. Calvert subsequently went to police headquarters and spoke to Inspector Jim Mannion and Chief Inspector Clive Graham. At first he did a few sleight of hand tricks with coins and got them amused. Then he asked Clive Graham for the time. The inspector looked at his wrist, could not find his watch, so looked at his other wrist again no watch. Calvert had slipped it off without him knowing. After that, Calvert had the police eating out of his hand. He assured them that he had done the blindfolded driving stunt in many places and would not run down any pedestrians or collide with cars.

True to his word, with Mannion watching and filming the event with his movie camera, Calvert drove down Smith Street watched by a big crowd. At the town hall his magic show, which included a display of mental telepathy and hypnotism, attracted a medium crowd. At one stage Bowditch and I were invited up on stage and participated in the performance. Calvert picked up Bowditch "like a feather" with one hand. The entire *Sea Fox* crew, even the one threatened with removal of a vital part of his anatomy, worked as stage hands and wore elaborate costumes. Pilita, of course, drew a lot of attention and in a levitation demonstration Calvert caused her to rise about five feet into the air. One of Calvert's acts was a "Dr Jekyll and Mr Hyde" performance which had a gory scene in which a person's head was cut off, causing a terrified member of the audience to run from the hall.

Not long after the stage performance, the *Sea Fox*, much to the sorrow of Darwin because it had brought a touch of Hollywood to town, set off for Sydney. However, off Arnhem Land, the yacht reported it was taking water and likely to sink. Calvert made things difficult by not being able to give his exact position. News reports went overseas about a yacht carrying an American film star, his wife and Tarzan's monkey sinking off the Australian coast.

In America, a woman took particular interest in the news and wanted to know exactly who this "Mrs Calvert" was on the yacht as she was Mrs Calvert. Furthermore, she said her son, John Andrew Calvert, only 13 months old, was fretting for his daddy. She also revealed that something similar had happened to the yacht before when it had been damaged by a cyclonic storm. On that occasion she had left the yacht while it was repaired and returned to America to give birth to John Calvert Jnr. The yacht then had been called *Thespian*, not *Sea Fox*.

The story grew more interesting by the hour. An RAAF Lincoln bomber flew out from Darwin to look for the *Sea Fox* and me aboard for the *NT News*. The yacht was found on the second day of the search, but did not seem very low in the water. When the plane dropped a container with a bilge bump inside there was much embarrassment. A new cylindrical container had been used to house the pump and when the parachute opened the vital bit of equipment shot through the bottom into the sea. The same thing happened when supplies were dropped. Calvert came on the radio and screamed for another pump to save the yacht. In a bright idea, he suggested a pump from the Darwin sewerage system.

The bomber circled the yacht and guided in other RAAF aircraft from Townsville. Throughout the event Calvert took movie pictures of the crew manually pumping and ordered them to work faster to make it look more dramatic. Back in Darwin, Bowditch was kept busy supplying a running account of the saga. Eventually a naval tug, HMAS *Emu*, was sent out and took the *Sea Fox* in tow, heading for the Methodist mission at Elcho Island. Bowditch and Lockwood flew to the island.

News of the impending arrival of the yacht with a monkey aboard created great interest on the island. Aborigines living inland rushed to the mission centre hoping to see the monkey and called the yacht, the "Monkey Ship". When the yacht finally got to the island it was taken into the shallows and beached, shored up with timbers. However, the tide swept the supports away and the yacht washed over on its side and stove in some planks, causing flooding of the interior. Calvert collapsed.

The wealthy refrigerator philanthropist, Sir Edward Hallstrom had offered the Chimp a place in Sydney's Taronga Zoo if it survived and came to Darwin to personally organise the travel arrangements. It is reported the chimp took an instant liking to the industrialist and gave him a hug.

Flown back to Darwin, Calvert was confronted by some ex-crew who said they had had very little to eat, mainly potato soup, on the voyage from Asia to Darwin. Calvert retorted that the soup had been so thick a spoon would stand up in it. They also claimed that Calvert had been surprised to sail into Darwin because he thought he was somewhere near Geraldton in Western Australia.

Carl Atkinson went to Elcho Island to patch up the yacht and return it to Darwin. Calvert and his circus flew off to Sydney to perform his magician's show for Harry Wren, the showbiz entrepreneur. Soon after, Bowditch put on a fine stage performance himself, winning the impromptu speech section at the North Australian Eisteddfod. He also received the Walkley Award for Journalism for his coverage of the *Sea Fox* saga. Years later, in a rage, he would throw the award against his lounge room wall much to Betty's disgust.

Down south Pilita became a popular TV singer and signed recording contracts. As the months went by she and Calvert were involved in many hi-jinks. Pilita said she had been married to a Spanish "beast" who had mistreated her, caused her to work hard and took all her money. Calvert made the headlines when he barged into a room and accused a consular official of "kidnapping" Pilita. The consular man denied the charge and said they were just good friends.

Another newspaper report said Pilita was brandishing a large ring and engaged to marry Calvert, his wife having divorced him. Calvert announced that he was planning dramatic one-hour films called *The Sea Fox*. Footage he had taken during the drama off Arnhem Land was to be used in the series. Also, he claimed the mock-up of the nuclear submarine which Stanley Kramer had used in the movie *On the Beach*, shot in Melbourne, had been bought and would also be used as a set.

However, a dispute developed over the proposed *Sea Fox* series and Calvert performed another vanishing act. He left the country, making a brief stopover in Darwin to inspect the *Sea Fox* at Doctor's Gully. The yacht inspection took place at night and after looking at the battered yacht Calvert told a reporter he ought to issue a writ against "this guy Atkinson." Atkinson had not been present when Calvert went to Doctor's Gully because he was at the movies and there was no warning of the visit. When told what Calvert had said about him, Atkinson replied: "If I knew he was coming, I would have hit him with a writ." By this time Calvert was out of the country and a Tasmanian film company claimed he had taken some valuable film which belonged to them.

Atkinson researched the history of the yacht and discovered she had been built in 1917 and was 79ft long, not 120ft, as Calvert said. The yacht was in such bad shape in 1962 that harbour authorities told Atkinson that if he could not refloat the vessel she would have to be removed from the foreshore. Once more the *Sea Fox* took to the waves, but she was a sorry, battered sight. An Adelaide businessman said he intended restoring the yacht and sailing her in the Sydney–Hobart race but despite these intentions, the yacht rotted away.

35. OF MICE, MEN AND GARBAGE

A Darwin news story that attracted much national and international attention involved the great Darwin Council garbage strike in September 1959, which resulted in Bowditch and Mayor John "Tiger" Lyons trading more than verbal blows. It started when the garbage men went on strike seeking better pay and conditions. Lawyer Lyons had been briefed by Bowditch in the gambling case which led to Sergeant Mannion's transfer to Tennant Creek. He was often followed to court by his dog which even sneaked in under the bar table at times. During call-overs of the court list, Lyons often took adjournment dates down on a packet of cigarettes. And when he finished the contents of the packet, he threw it and the important notes on it away. From time to time, he would tell the exasperated magistrate that he had no note at all in his appointments book about various cases. The mayor opposed the call for better pay and conditions for the garbos and dug in his heels. Bowditch supported their cause. In an unusual move, a roster was drawn up and the councillors themselves manned the garbage cart. Mayor Lyons was photographed in shorts emptying bins into a truck. The idea of a mayor collecting garbage caught the imagination of news editors all over the world. A cartoon in an English newspaper showed councillors in top hats and frock coats emptying smelly bins into Rolls-Royces.

The *NT News* supported the strikers and, after Lyons said one of his dissenting councillors might have been "caught short", wrote that decorum and democracy had gone out the door at council meetings presided over by Tiger. This infuriated Lyons; the next day Bowditch received a telephone call more or less ordering him to come to the mayor's home. Bowditch said that if the mayor had something to say, he could come to the *News* office. A follow up call said that the mayor would be holding a press conference and that Doug Lockwood would be there. In view of that, Bowditch went to the mayor's house. As Bowditch entered, the mayor said, "Here's the little cunt now." Lockwood excused himself and left.

An extraordinary event followed. On command from the glowering mayor, the town clerk, dressed in wig and gown, rose and read a 4000-word statement defending the mayor and councillors and demanding an apology from Bowditch. The unusual tirade ended: "The cat is out of the bag. You should know that a large ginger cat [Lyons had whispy ginger hair] is prepared to take on all comers, including little pink mice [referring to "commo" Jim].

During the diatribe, Jim uttered a few guffaws and smirked. When the serious-looking town clerk finished, Lyons invited Jim to discuss the matter further over a few drinks. On reflection this proved to be a foolish gesture. After a few too many drinks, the editor and the mayor exchanged heated words. The mayor said he should flatten Bowditch. The response by Bowditch poured fuel on the fire. He told Lyons he was not going to fight him because he (Lyons) would probably die of a heart attack. The mayor was so furious, he pulled off his shirt and they went out on the lawn and began to wrestle. Both fell into Mrs Lyons's prized rose bushes and were scratched. The episode was the talk of the town the next day and the mayor's long statement was run in full in the *News*. The garbos eventually won their battle, with the help of a scratched little pink mouse.

36. GLADYS AND MICK

Bowditch's widespread reputation in the Northern Territory as a man who would help anybody in trouble saw him deeply involved in an unusual battle involving two "little people": rawboned white drover Mick Daly, 36, of Top Springs, NT, and slight Aboriginal girl Gladys Namagu, 22, of Hall's Creek, WA. Daly, a burly six-footer, illiterate, had formed a relationship with Namagu, who had been born a spastic and allegedly sterilised by her tribe so as not to have children. She travelled with Mick as his droving team moved stock about the north. He was arrested and appeared in the Katherine court for cohabitating with Namagu, who in the Territory was regarded as a ward under the protection of the Director of Welfare, Harry Giese.

In court Daly declared his love for Gladys and said he wanted to marry her. Mr Dodds, SM adjourned the case and asked for a Welfare Department report. The report did not consider Daly a suitable person to marry Namagu and he was convicted and placed on a 12 months' good behaviour bond. He still maintained he wanted to marry Gladys. A police officer advised Daly to contact the editor of the Darwin newspaper, Jim Bowditch, as he helped people in trouble. The Welfare Department moved Gladys to the Warrabri settlement near Tennant Creek.

Daly rang Bowditch and explained his plight. This set the wheels in motion. Bowditch checked his story and wrote a report in the paper. As often happened, Bowditch consulted his lawyer friend Dick Ward, who became a major player in the saga. On Daly's behalf, Ward made an official application for permission to marry Gladys. Giese refused, without meeting Daly, and said he relied on reports from field officers. The fact that Daly could hardly read or write, drank a lot and was a drover, no doubt coloured Giese's attitude. Bowditch said the reports had probably been "totally unfavourable." On the other hand, Gladys and Mick got along very well. There were few, if any, white women who would put up with his way of life. Gladys had led a tough life in Western Australia and her body carried scars. Despite her emaciated, battered and twisted body, she had eyes which were alive with life.

As the case gained momentum and questions were asked in federal parliament and the NT Legislative Council, Namagu was brought to Darwin and sent to Bagot settlement. At first, journalist Doug Lockwoood had not agreed with Bowditch's stand on the matter. Lockwood felt Giese had been correct in refusing permission for Daly to marry Namagu as he was a "rough egg."

Bowditch invited Lockwood to go with him to Bagot and check on the departmental claim that she could not marry Mick because she was already tribally married to a man in WA. Namagu said over and over that she wanted to marry Mick. It was suggested by a senior government officer that she was simply saying what the questioners wanted when she said that she wished to marry Mick. She admitted living with a man in her tribe for a while but said she could not be tribally married because she was unable to have children. Tribal elders had operated on her to prevent her having children. Bowditch said that as a result of that questioning of Gladys, Lockwood had been convinced that she wanted to marry the drover. The way officials had acted at the questioning, refusing to accept her answers, angered Bowditch so much that he went away fuming.

Daly was in town at the time and anxious to see Gladys. Bowditch devised a daring plan. Early the next day, he got reporter

Keith Willey to drive him to Bagot, which was "off limits" to all whites except those with passes or employed there. Before he clambered over the fence, he told Willey to ring the police station if he did not see him in an hour's time. Willey laughed. Bowditch entered the compound and Aborigines directed him to Gladys. He then "kidnapped" her, told her to come to his place and she would see Mick. She gladly gathered her meagre belongings and followed. They climbed over the fence to the waiting getaway car. Taken to the Bowditch house, she and Mick sat and hugged under a banana tree. Bowditch then dashed off and obtained a permit for five shillings to employ an Aborigine, Namagu, before the hue and cry began.

Ward carried on the legal battle and got many letters from Giese refusing to budge. The letters were legalistic. Ward suggested that Bowditch should run the letters to reveal the cold official line. Bowditch thought this was a brilliant idea. In fairness, he rang Giese and told him what was about to happen and asked him for a comment. What transpired went something like this: Giese said he would have to get legal advice about the paper intending to run his letters and rang off; he rang back and said he was claiming copyright to the letters and refused permission for them to be published; Bowditch rang off and contacted Ward for advice, telling him that Harry was claiming copyright; after listening to Ward, Bowditch began to laugh and rang off; then Bowditch rang Giese and told him that, acting on legal advice, the paper was still going to run the letters because it was thought that his (Giese's) letters had no commercial value and copyright did not apply; end of conversation.

Bowditch then gleefully narrated the episode to office staff. Of course, the letters were run and readers were told that Giese's claim to copyright had been rejected. In an editorial, Bowditch asked: "Can it be that the Welfare Department considers men who sleep with Aboriginal women are not the right type to marry them? If that principle was applied generally, a great many marriages between whites would never take place."

In the Legislative Council, where Ward was the leader of the minority elected members, the Daly-Namagu case was strongly

"Red Richard" Dick Ward, Lawyer and MLC represented "pro
bono" many of those whose causes Jim Bowditch espoused.
Courtesy NT Archives 0046/0003.

aired. In a no confidence motion launched by Ward against Giese
(who was a nominated member of the Legco), the lawyer delivered
a brilliant speech without notes for one hour. A *Hansard* reporter
said Ward had been a pleasure to record, being concise and using
perfect English. Ward, he said, could hold his own in the British
parliament. During debate a letter from Daly to Bowditch was read
which gave an insight into the mind of the man the authorities
would not let marry Gladys. With an Eva Downs, 22/9/59 dateline,
it read:

> Dear Jim, I just got your letter yesterday & I was verry pleased
> to hear from you that Gladys is well, I miss her verry much
> too & I hope I can get married to her after I am finished
> with these bullocks, we will be at Anthony's Lagoon dip next
> Friday and it will be nearly the end of november before we are
> finished. I hope Gladys dos'nt change her mind in that time

because I love her verry much & I'm sure that I wont chang my mind about her. I would like Gladys to stay with you Jim. I think she would be more happier & in good company with you people. Your wife and Zenie (this was Zena, Betty's sister) treat her verry well & I appreaciate it.

You might be gone away for your hollyday before I can get back therefor you may have to send Gladys over to the Bathurst Isd [Island] later on if necessary. How is Gladys getting on with Sister Augustens lessons. I'd love her to learn about religion & allso to read and write a little. If she likes her lessons & gets intrest in it she will learn a bit but if they don't like it there verry hard to teach so you tell her that I would like her to learn all she can that Sister tries to teach her.

Well Jim I will be looking forward to your letter aggain I think the best place to addres the next one letter Brunet Downs. Im not sure if that spelt right you had better look at the map.

Gladys told me on the phone she went swimming. I enjoyed that little chat with her, how did she like the circus. Tell her we seen the elephants when we were going to Katherine in the Taxi we were patting them on the Trunk. I gave Johnny Wyndham 10 for Gladys & I sent £4 for Gladys last letter did you get them.

If you get a chance you want to take Gladys out fishing I can garentee she is a verry good fisherman. Well Jim I will say Cheerio for now & I hope to hear from you soon please let me know how things are progressing, allso exstend my thanks to Dick Ward I'm very grateful for his help, only for him Gladys would be in W.A. eating dry bread & beef & sleeping in the ashers with dogs and blackfellows.

Give my regards to Betty and Zena & the children. I hope you are all well. Sending a few bob for Glady.

The Member for Elsey, Harold "Tiger" Brennan, asked Giese if this was the letter of an insincere man. Brennan said he had accompanied Ward to Giese's office and the Director of Welfare had not wanted to see Daly or Gladys. When Giese had been asked if he would like to ask Gladys any question he had none to

Gladys Namagu at the *NT News* office. The hole in the door behind
her is from when Jim lost his keys and 'broke in' to get to work.

ask. Members could see from the letter that Daly was "absolutely
honest" and sincere in his affection for his girl. He went on to say
he did not know if the nominated government representatives,
who always had the balance of power in the Council, had been
instructed which way to vote. But if Daly's letter did not change
their views then they would fall low in Brennan's estimation.

While Gladys was living at the Bowditch house she suddenly
became rotund about the stomach region and Jim feared that she
was pregnant. She was induced to undergo a medical examination
and it was discovered that she had developed a layer of fat, no
doubt due to the changed diet and better life she was living. In
particular, she loved powdered milk, and eagerly mixed up jugs of

milk and drank them quickly, using a tin of powdered milk a day. At times she came to the *News* office with Betty Bowditch, usually wearing a hat, and stood about, shyly listening. When she spoke she had a high pitched voice. Keith Willey who had helped Bowditch "kidnap" Gladys from Bagot, usually received a big smile and a hello from her.

Daly came to Darwin after some droving and made a bee-line for the Bowditch house hoping to find his love there. Bowditch had cause to go home and found Mick and Gladys sitting under the banana trees, drinking—and it was not powdered milk. Knowing that Mick could be charged with supplying liquor to an Aborigine, Jim hastily bundled them inside. As Gladys had lived a rough life which Mick had aptly described as being in the ashes with dogs, living in a house was a real experience.

Daly declared that if approval were given for him to marry they would wed in the Catholic Church. As the church recognised tribal marriage and Gladys was said to be tribally married to a man in WA, Darwin's Catholic head, Bishop J.P. O'Loughlin, said he could not approve of their marriage. However, he eventually set up a committee consisting of two missionaries, two Welfare Department officers and Catholic lawyer "Tiger" Lyons, Bowditch's wrestling partner, to investigate the case. The man said to be Namagu's tribal husband was brought to Darwin from WA and questioned by the bishop's committee. He said that while he and Gladys had lived together for some time, they were not tribally married because she was childless. Bishop O'Loughlin announced there was no impediment to Daly and Namagu being married in a Catholic church. The *NT News* headlined: GLADYS TO WED.

The breakthrough came while the Bowditches were south on holidays and Gladys was living with Dick Ward and his wife. A meeting was arranged between Giese, Mick and Gladys, with Dick Ward and an expert on the Aborigines, Bill Harney, present. Under questioning from Harney, Gladys revealed that her alleged tribal husband, Arthur, was her "uncle" under tribal law. Harney told Giese that meant Gladys and Arthur could not marry. Giese gave his OK for her to marry Mick.

Cupid was busy at the time. Jim and Betty married in Sydney and Mick and Gladys wed in the Darwin Catholic Cathedral. At the Darwin wedding reporter Keith Willey, standing in for Bowditch, was best man, Dick Ward gave her away. Gladys wore a plain wedding dress and a hat with white shoes. She carried a bouquet of artificial flowers. Mick, decked out in brand new gear, carried a 10-gallon cowboy hat. The wedding ceremony was performed by Father Copas who went on to become a bishop in New Guinea. Harry Giese and his wife attended the wedding and congratulated the couple. The reception was held in the Ward house.

When the Daly–Namagu marriage ended after seven years some people went to Bowditch with a "we told you so attitude." He responded by saying many white marriages did not last so long. Bowditch said that Harry Giese remained a good friend to Gladys after the marriage break up. Gladys formed a relationship with a white pensioner who loved her dearly, but at times she caused him great distress when she succumbed to wanderlust. At times, beside himself with worry, the man would call on union fix-it man Brian Manning and ask him to speak to Gladys and get her to come home.

37. ENTER RUPERT MURDOCH

As a young boy wearing knickerbockers, Rupert Murdoch passed through Darwin with his parents, Sir Keith and Lady Murdoch. Sir Keith became impressed with the design of the Hotel Darwin and engaged its Sydney architects, Stephenson and Turner, to design a house for the *Melbourne Herald* on the Esplanade in Darwin. Built on the ground, the L-shaped building had a six inch thick concrete floor and was built of concrete blocks with 649 louvres, making it a cool house in which to live. Ruth Lockwood said Rupert more or less "lived" in the house when in Darwin and had stayed there while passing through in his Oxford days. He passed through Darwin when returning from London on the death of his father.

Bowditch was not sure how he first met Rupert Murdoch. The initial encounter could have been when Bowditch was running the *Advocate* in Alice. He seemed to remember meeting Murdoch, who was then aged about 20. Journalist Alan Wauchope said he thought Murdoch came to Alice with the English journalist Malcolm Muggeridge and that might have been when Bowditch first met the newspaper proprietor. Bowditch remembered going to Adelaide and being invited home by Murdoch for several meals.

Whatever the first encounter, he became very aware of Murdoch when the rising newspaper magnate came to Darwin and looked over the *NT News*. Murdoch, he said, had laughed at the antiquated set-up and asked him why he put up with such conditions. In those early days Murdoch had spoken about wanting to acquire a chain of country newspapers.

Knowing the paper was really owned by Swan, he eventually told Bowditch he wanted to buy the paper. Bowditch told Eric White who said to tell Murdoch it was not for sale. Bowditch suspected that White wanted to maintain close contact with the brewery for other business reasons. It could also have been a ploy to force up the price of the paper. When told the paper was not for sale Murdoch took quick and decisive action. He went to the NT Administrator, "Cautious" Clarrie Archer, and, according to Bowditch, "conned" him into announcing Murdoch and the *Adelaide News* would be starting a new newspaper in Darwin.

The *NT News* ran a small report about Murdoch's proposal and quoted him as saying he planned to print three editions a week. At the time the *News* was still a bi-weekly. It was pointed out in the paper that Murdoch did not have a building in Darwin in which to start his newspaper. However the tactical move by Murdoch had the desired response. Within 48 hours, Swan Brewery, not wanting to be left holding a paper which would fold when faced with strong competition, panicked and agreed to sell the *News* to Murdoch for 20,000 pounds, the same amount the brewery had paid for the publication. The deal also gave Murdoch control of the struggling *Mount Isa Mail*. At the time the Darwin negotiations were under way it was announced that Murdoch had bought the Sydney daily, the *Mirror*.

Left: front page of the first *NT News* published under Rupert Murdoch's ownership and, below: a two-page spread with a behind-the-scenes look at the paper's production. Courtesy NT Archives.

Within a short time Murdoch's various publications were being produced at the rate of four million copies a week. Once Murdoch had possession of the NT paper he arranged for better equipment to be installed. A Cossar flatbed rotary printing press capable of printing and folding a 24 page tabloid at the rate of 3200 copies an hour was shipped up from Sydney. An electronic engraving machine for making plastic blocks enhanced the pictorial content of the paper. A Ludlow typesetting machine for headings was also provided.

The first edition produced under the new arrangement rolled off the press on 13 September 1960. A special feature to mark the occasion included a picture of young-looking Rupert Murdoch. The editorial was headed: MURDOCH HERALDS NEW PRESS ERA IN THE NORTH, and said the paper would soon be a tri-weekly with a sporting edition to come out early Saturday.

It also said that Murdoch's personal assistant, Ken May, who had been the *Adelaide News* political roundsman, was expected in Darwin in a few weeks to coincide with the visit of Mr and Mrs Murdoch, who would be driving across from Townsville. The Murdochs arrived in Darwin a day earlier than expected and it was said that Rupert had disconnected the speed governor on a hire car and put his foot down. Bowditch said this action had made a favourable impression on him and the *NT News* staff.

On another occasion, Murdoch arrived, possibly from Mount Isa, and Bowditch asked compositor Bobby Wills to drive a hire car to the Fannie Bay Hotel where Murdoch's party was staying. Wills delivered the car to the hotel and Bowditch introduced him to Murdoch. Murdoch told Wills: "You can now say you shook the hand of a man who shook the hand of President John F. Kennedy." Bowditch said that in those early days Murdoch was seen as something of a rebel and at the time was taking on the larger media empires in Australia. Furthermore, when he had been at Oxford University Murdoch had been what Bowditch described as a "lefty".

More office staff were engaged to expand the operations of the paper. There was much speculation about one particular appointee, expected in the near future. The day the man was due Bowditch was drinking with staff in the Vic Hotel and during an animated discussion Jim swallowed some beer which went down the wrong way. Clutching at his throat, he bent over and tried to clear his airway, coughing loudly. People thumped him on the back and guffawed at his discomfiture. Their actions seemed to make him worse. He got so bad that he knelt near the footrest, gasping. Some joker in the group said Murdoch's new man would walk in the pub, ask who was Jim Bowditch and be directed to the man barking at the footrest. That was enough to send Bowditch into another paroxysm.

Kiwi journalist Les Wilson was the journalist sent to Darwin from Sydney. Wilson, who had been a subeditor on the *Mirror* for a year, had been hoping for an exotic overseas posting to England or America, but drew the short straw and got Darwin. He was told to help Bowditch compile radio news bulletins for the Darwin commercial radio station on which Bowditch and Ward were board members, and provide news and feature articles for News Limited papers.

With no experience at all in writing radio bulletins, Wilson had a farewell party in Sydney, arrived suited in steamy Darwin, and nearly died from the heat. He was picked up by the jovial accountant, Murdoch appointee Brian Phipps, and taken to the Parap Hotel. After that, he was driven to the *News* office and found Bowditch and Willey sitting near a pile of empty beer cans. Bowditch had staggered off late in the evening and told Wilson he would see him at six the next morning, which he did.

An interesting observation Wilson made was that "everyone" at the *News* regarded someone sent up from south as a "spy" and he had been so regarded. Even so, Willey borrowed Wilson's blue suit and even a pair of his shoes to wear to Sydney to receive a Walkley Award. Somehow, Willey managed to miss the presentation, saying he had fallen asleep in his room and the hotel had not roused him.

Wilson got along well with Bowditch and enjoyed his time in Darwin, at times saving the editor from being belted. A skilled operator, it did not take Wilson long to slip into the way of compiling radio bulletins, which were delivered to the station by hand, usually by Les or Jim. Delivering the night bulletin was irksome as it tended to interfere with afternoon drinking sessions which induced loss of memory. There was often a frantic dash from the Vic to the radio station with the annoying bulletin which was in somebody's pocket.

One evening Bowditch delivered a bulletin to the station and a pompous announcer read through it and said something should be added to an item. Naturally, Bowditch firmly told the radio man that his job was to just read the news. Tempting fate, the announcer began to argue the toss. Tired and emotional after a hard day at the office, Bowditch slapped a wrestling hold on the fellow. They banged up against the control panel and it was said the station went off the air for a short time. After that the announcer had a clear understanding of job demarcations and never again stuck his beak into the contents of a news bulletin.

Wilson was responsible for starting what became a major Darwin community sporting event, the *NT News* Walkabout, a 15 mile (24 Km) walking race, which became a major community event. The idea for the race came over some drinks in that fertile breeding ground for great stories, bright ideas and enormous hangovers, the Victoria Hotel. One of the drinkers in the pub was affable, pipe-smoking Englishman "Walking" Jimmy Wadsworth, who told Wilson about having taken part in walking races in Singapore and Hong Kong in younger days. Such a race would go well in Darwin, he suggested. Wilson wrote a story with a picture demonstrating Wadsworth's walking style and the *News'* annual Walkabout was born. It became a well-supported event with proceeds going to pensioners.

Another reporter sent by News Limited was Tony Malone, who took over the sports section. Organised, reliable and efficient, Malone seemed surprised at the goings on at the *News*.

Engaged locally as an advertising agent was Percy Burton, who had come to Darwin from Singapore as the ABC regional journalist. He also had experience as a typographer and copywriter, which he used to brighten up the layout of advertisements.

Burton had an eye for the unusual commercial opportunity, and when the Russians shot a dog, Laika, into orbit in a Sputnik

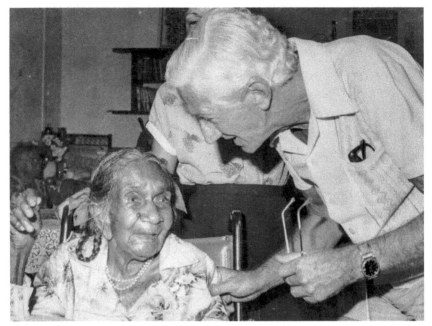

Jim with Nellie Flynn, a famous Territorian and great supporter of
the *NT News* Walkabout, taking part in the event well into her 90s.
Bowditch family collection.

satellite he proposed taking out a patent for a space dog toy. Because
the dog did not survive the flight, manufacturers were reluctant to
take up the idea. Never deterred, he had the same bright idea when
the Americans fired a chimp, Enos, into the heavens. A cartoon
at the time showed a monkey in a US Air Force officer's uniform
smoking a cigar and telling future astronauts they would experience
an uncontrollable urge for a banana once their rocket got to a certain
height. Again, no toy maker was interested. However, his space toy
ideas caused much jocularity in the *News* and Darwin pubs. Percy
was clearly ahead of his time in the toy industry. Another money-
making scheme he outlined was taking photographs of Darwin
houses and selling copies to the occupants who, the theory went,
would send them to relatives and friends down south and overseas.

Before he left the ABC, Burton had been involved in a scrap
with a Cyprus-born tailor who had a shop in the Hotel Darwin.
The tailor was making a pair of white sharkskin shorts for Percy,
who dropped in often to see how they were coming along. During

one of many fittings, Burton spotted a stain in what he described as a "disadvantageous position" the fly and refused to have anything further to do with the shorts. An altercation took place and Burton was hit in the ear. The tailor was charged with assaulting Burton, who appeared in court wearing a monogrammed shirt and a cravat. In answer to a question from defence lawyer George Cridland, Burton denied being used to "grovelling oriental tailors." The tailor was not fined and in a magnanimous gesture, Burton paid the puzzled tailor for the shorts outside the court. The *News* ran a report about the hearing under the heading: THE CASE OF THE SHARKSKIN SHORTS; another witty effort by Willey.

Before driving down "The Track" for a weekend, Burton borrowed a rifle from a gun enthusiast who was reluctant to hand over the weapon. However, Burton assured him he knew how to handle firearms. While driving along the highway he came upon an unfortunate kangaroo which had been hit by a car. The injured animal was flopping about on the road, so Burton got out with the rifle intending to put it out of its misery. Instead of shooting the roo, he used the rifle as a club and began to hit it on the head. Naturally, the creature objected and frantically bounced around. Intending to finish the kangaroo with one almighty blow, Percy missed and hit the bitumen, which caused the stock of the rifle to split. Not only that, he actually bent the barrel. The owner of the rifle was furious when Burton returned the now useless shooter.

When Burton left Darwin he got a job as advance publicity man for a road show. In this role, he lobbed at the *Sydney Morning Herald* one day while I was on duty. He calmly walked up to the subeditors' table and placed a long racy story about his experiences in King's Cross in the basket. It read like the radio serial *Night Beat*. Nobody but staff should place copy in the subs' basket. A copy taster pulled the bulky story out and began to read it, then called out: "Who is this person Burton?" By that time Burton was making free calls to Brisbane from a phone in the interstate reporters' room.

The advertising department at the *News* boasted another exceptional character. A swarthy, good looking fellow, he just lobbed in town from nowhere and began selling advertising space on smokers' stands in hotels. Dapper in dress, even sporting a cravat at times like Burton, he spoke about the psychology of advertising. He even discussed the possibility of having large advertisements painted on the high water towers in town. A relative of his, he said, was a professor in the School of Tropical Medicine, Bombay.

A smooth talker, he often bet he could pick up the phone in Darwin and ring the top man of any leading corporation in America and get him to come to the phone. The reason that captain of commerce would take a call from Darwin, he explained, was that it was human nature for anyone, no matter their rank, to be intrigued by a mystery call from the other side of the world. Nobody bothered to test his theory. A man who knew how the heads of giant US corporations thought would surely be invaluable in the *News* advertising department.

And so he became another member of the staff, carrying out his duties with flair. During one Melbourne Cup some women at the *News* asked compositor Bobby Wills, a keen punter, for a tip. He selected an outsider and when the flamboyant advertising man heard of the choice he declared the horse was a donkey and offered the women odds of 100 to one, which some promptly accepted. Hi Jinx romped home at 66:1, the advertising man paid out a considerable sum and told Wills he wished he (Wills) had kept his mouth shut.

After having been at the *News* for a considerable time, the advertising man decided to travel down "The Track" to Alice Springs to pick up new advertising contracts. As he had become friendly with the head of Commonwealth Police in Darwin, who was deeply involved in the RSL, the advertising wizard said he would sound out businessmen and RSL clubs on his trip and get them to advertise in an RSL magazine he wanted to start. He got a letter of introduction from the police officer, then set off. The only trouble was that he did not stop at Alice and return to Darwin. He just kept going, with money he had raised with the help of the letter from the cop.

Some time later, Bowditch was surprised to receive a reverse charge call from New Zealand the operator saying it was the

"Colonel" (the missing advertising man) calling. With more hide than an elephant, the "Colonel" was seeking a reference from Bowditch for a position he was seeking with a New Zealand airline. Bowditch gave him a firm no and was bemused by the audacity of the fellow.

The newspaper's accountant, Brian Phipps, subsequently went through accounts with a fine-tooth comb and unearthed some fancy bookkeeping by another former employee. It was said that News Limited tracked the man through a bogus job advertisement for which he applied, and demanded he pay back some money or else they would sue him and ruin his career. Apparently, he forked out some money, but it was felt that he had filched considerably more.

The paper soon became a tri-weekly published on Tuesday, Thursday and Saturday. The Saturday edition was made up mainly on Friday. Finding enough local stories to fill the paper in that short period kept everyone working at a frenetic pace. Bowditch invented a person called Mr J.G. Slaggert, a self-employed businessman, who was an eyewitness to many newsworthy events and ever ready to have his views reported on any topic.

The observant Mr Slaggert was quoted in relation to his sighting of a strange object seen in Darwin Harbour which was known as the Mandorah Monster, something akin to the Loch Ness Monster, but some people suggested it was mechanical and even that it was Russian. Mr Slaggert was particularly valuable when you were struggling for a major story to fill a space. Fortuitously, late one Friday night when Bowditch was battling to wrap up the following day's edition, Slaggert saw a flying saucer (shades of Alice Springs) land near the Darwin Golf Course. Of course, he immediately contacted the editor and gave what they call in the trade a graphic eyewitness account of the UFO and its occupants. According to Slaggert, they spoke perfect English, questioned him about Darwin and told him they were Russian.

One problem Bowditch had with this fictitious informant was that he had difficulty in remembering how his name was spelt. "Is it Slogget or Slaggert?" he would ask. At times he would hunt through newspaper files trying to find stories in which Mr S had been quoted to make sure of the spelling. Only a worldly minister of religion, the Rev. Norm Pearce of the United Church, appeared to smell something fishy in relation to Slaggert, and it was not due to Mr S having had a close encounter with the Mandorah Monster. Pearce told Bowditch that this Mr Slaggert, oft quoted, seemed to be everywhere, yet he had never met him. Bowditch laughed, said Mr Slaggert was a very busy man and probably did not mix in the same circles as the cleric. The dubious minister said he looked forward to the day when he would actually meet the fellow.

On top of running the *News*, Bowditch was also involved in managing the Mount Isa paper. While they were exciting times, he was bearing a huge load of responsibility and at times felt worn out.

For a time it looked as if Bowditch's employment with Murdoch would not last much longer. This was because Jock Nelson put a proposition to Jim to return to Alice Springs as editor/half owner of the *Centralian Advocate*. Nelson, still the NT MHR, had become the major shareholder in the paper, having bought out the printer, Ron Morcom. Newspapers attracted Nelson, who had been a paper boy in Darwin. The paper ran into constant staff problems. Nelson described the situation as being left like a shag on a rock whenever somebody left or something went wrong. No member of the staff was a newspaper man who knew what to do to keep things going. The situation was going from bad to worse and they either had to sell the paper or take in a partner. Nelson thought his friend Bowditch could be the answer to the problems. Bowditch regarded the half share offer as tempting. Apart from that, there was talk of the *News* soon becoming a daily which would which put an extra load on his shoulders. As he had never run a daily newspaper, he felt apprehensive.

Bowditch told Murdoch of Nelson's offer. In doing so he said Keith Willey was his logical replacement as editor, and that he would produce a better paper because he had worked on dailies down south. Murdoch asked Jim if he had signed anything committing himself to Nelson's offer. Told no, Murdoch then said to do nothing further until he came to Darwin and spoke to him. Bowditch agreed and told Willey what was afoot. Willey immediately said Murdoch was coming up to talk him out of going to Alice. Bowditch said it would have to be a pretty good offer to talk him out of half share in a paper.

Murdoch arrived with journalist Zell Rabin, who had been the New York representative of Mirror Newspapers, Sydney. Some of his regular reports from America appeared in the *NT News* under the heading: MAIN STREET, USA. While in America, Rabin arranged for Murdoch to meet and be photographed with US President John F. Kennedy. The meeting was seen as a great coup for the rising newspaper proprietor. The photograph of the two together was run throughout Murdoch publications. It also had pride of place in the Sydney boardroom. When Bowditch saw it he was impressed and remarked that Murdoch was on his way to fame and fortune.

Rabin had returned to Sydney in 1962 as editor of the *Sunday Mirror* and became editor of the *Daily Mirror* the next year.

During the visit to Darwin with Murdoch, Rabin took Bowditch aside and told him that Murdoch was going to go a long way in the newspaper game. Unfortunately, Rabin died from cancer in November 1966 at the age of 34 and did not live to see the lofty heights to which Murdoch soared.

Murdoch took Jim and Betty to the Knickerbocker Restaurant and discussed the Alice proposal. Bowditch said Murdoch "got at Betty" by asking some leading questions. Would she like to go back to Alice to live? No. What was up with Jim, why did he want to leave? Jim, she said, was working too hard, there were not enough staff and the plant kept breaking down. Murdoch said he would overcome all of the problems. Betty thought Murdoch "a charming man." He told Jim and Betty that they both deserved a holiday, where would they like to go for a month? Betty immediately nominated Singapore. Murdoch agreed on the spot, and, furthermore, said they could go anywhere they wanted each year for a holiday. Unfortunately, they never availed themselves of annual overseas holidays.

Murdoch doubled Jim's salary and said extra reporting staff would be engaged to ease the load in the transition to a daily. In light of this offer and the promise of major changes, Bowditch decided to stay on. However, he insisted that Murdoch come with him to see Willey and tell him what had happened. Murdoch was reluctant to do so, but went with Bowditch. At the Willey residence, Bowditch got Keith's wife to come with him to get some beer, a ruse to enable Keith and Murdoch to talk. When Bowditch and Lee got back there was a tense situation. According to Bowditch, Murdoch was scarlet, "looking like a piece of beetroot"; Willey was "white with rage." Neither man said a word. Murdoch turned to Bowditch and said, "We are going, Jim," and walked out. There were no goodbyes, no shaking of hands. Bowditch said he never found out what had happened while the two were together.

However, it was suggested that Willey had held high hopes that he was going to be made the editor, a reasonable expectation in view of what Bowditch had told him, and had become annoyed when told by Murdoch that Jim was staying on. Willey maintained his rage, He came to the *News* office, stood outside and demanded that his belongings be thrown out to him. "I will never work for that fat slob (Murdoch), nor will I ever set foot in a building of his," he declared.

Willey went crocodile shooting, an experience about which he wrote a book. For a time he was assistant editor of the *Cairns Post*. Despite vowing he would never work for Murdoch, he went to New Guinea in 1964 as his correspondent and wrote another book, *Assignment New Guinea*. While Willey subsequently referred to Bowditch as "that little, grey-haired bastard," a reconciliation of sorts, arranged by reporter John Loizou, took part in the Don Hotel when Willey returned to Darwin while working for the Department of Trade in Canberra; the pair shook hands.

38. THE STAYPUTS

Resorting to daring and unusual methods, Bowditch played a key part in events that got extensive overseas coverage, challenged the White Australia Policy and worried the federal government. In 1955 he had become aware of the plight of Malays employed as low-paid indentured labour in the pearling industry. One of them was of particular interest, Ali bin Salleh, who had been with him during the dangerous Z Special Unit commando operation on Tarakan.

After being demobbed, Ali returned to pearling as a diver in Territory waters. While working on the lugger *Vivienne*, owned by Darwin master pearler Nicholas Paspaley, a name now world famous for cultured pearls, he was pulled from the deep too fast and suffered "the bends". Instead of being thrown back into the sea and staged, brought to the surface gradually, he endured a four-day boat trip to Darwin. On arrival he was almost dead; after 36 hours in Carl Atkinson's recompression chamber, he was saved, but was crippled from the waist down.

Ali was then sent to Adelaide, where he spent years in hospital. While there he was put into a bath and left alone. Because he had no feeling he did not realise that he was being scalded by boiling water, suffering terrible burns. Placed in a rehabilitation centre, he pined for the north and the people of Darwin banded together to bring him back.

It is believed Bowditch used his connection with Bob Freeden, who did public relations work in Sydney for the airline TAA, to fly Ali to Darwin. Bowditch was at the airport to welcome him home and TAA and the regional manager received favourable mention in an illustrated front page report in the *NT News*. Bowditch was horrified by his wartime friend's physical appearance.

In Darwin Ali was looked after by a well-known couple, Sallum bin Sallik and his wife, Biddy, who were friends of Bowditch. Sallum had also been in Z Special Unit but had not served with Bowditch. Mrs Sallik, "a Broome girl", an Aboriginal-Filipino, with a sense of humour, articulate and friendly, ran a store in the former wartime camp at Winnellie. Her husband and Ali looked so alike that they used to say they were brothers.

An article appeared in the *NT News* about Ali with a picture showing him weaving a basket. Lawyer Dick Ward issued a writ on Salleh's behalf seeking 30,000 pounds damages from the Paspaley Company. ASIO noted the court action and linked it to Bowditch, making an offensive comment about the plaintiff who had fought for Australia and been reduced to a cripple. Attached to a Melbourne *Age* clipping about the court action a secret report contained the following: "It looks as if Bowditch might be behind him in this. [Blacked out] says Ali bin Salleh would not have the brains to take such a course without help."

In what would prove to be a trial run for bigger things to come, Bowditch had become personally involved in vain attempts to stop the deportation in 1955 of Malay diver Yap Ah Chee, also employed by the Paspaley Pearling Company. Angered by the company's refusal to pay for the repatriation of the body of a fellow Malay diver who died while working for the firm, Ah Chee threatened to resign; he was sacked and refused to be repatriated.

The North Australian Workers' Union backed Ah Chee when he took on the pearling company in court. The *News* ran several stories about the diver's plight, one headed: WHY CAN'T I STAY IN AUSTRALIA? At one stage the diver went into hiding.

ASIO records show that Bowditch and a member of the Legislative Council, undoubtedly lawyer Dick Ward, interviewed the Darwin Immigration Officer about the move to deport Ah Chee. One report claimed that Ah Chee, in a statement he made before being deported, said Bowditch had "exerted influence" on him. Furthermore, Ah Chee said he had been "hidden" in the *NT News* office and at the "Bowditch residence" before being found. The weeping diver was deported in June.

When three Malays in Darwin were faced with deportation by the government in 1961, it is thought Biddy Sallik drew Bowditch's attention to the matter and sought his help. In the early stages Mrs Sallik was the spokesperson for the Malays and was interviewed by the press.

The men were Jaffa bin Madun, Zainal bin Hashim and Deraus bin Saris, who had been in Australia ten, seven and twelve years respectively.

All three had been employed in Broome before moving to Darwin in the late 1950s after the pearl shell industry went into a slump due to the impact of plastic on the button market. In Darwin

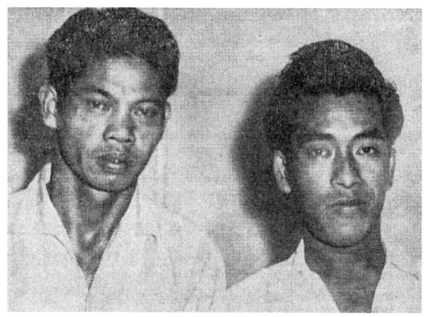

Two of the "Stayput Malays", Daraus Bin Saris (left) and Zinal Bin
Hashim photographed by the *NT News* while their case played out
for weeks.

they were employed by veteran master pearler Jimmy Gomez.
When he indicated in 1960 that he would not be able to employ
the three next season, plans were made to repatriate them. Due
to a complication that bin Madun had been issued British travel
documents in Singapore before coming to Australia, it was decided
to deport bin Saris and bin Hashim.

Both men applied for permission to stay in Australia and a
Bowditch editorial said they had earned the right to citizenship.
Appeals were made to the Queen, Prime Minister Menzies and
Immigration Minister Downer. They were booked to be deported
on a plane departing Darwin on 21 September 1961.

In a surprise development, a class of 42 pupils at Darwin High
School went on strike and held placards which read: DOWN WITH
DOWNER, TWO MALAYS IN DARWIN ARE WORTH ONE
MENZIES IN CANBERRA, MALAYS STAY OR WE STOP,
BOB THE SLOB and STOP BOB THE SLOB. Headmaster Tom
Kissel called an assembly and said the Malay issue was a political

one and not for the school to enter. However, the class which went on strike wrote essays on 'My Views on the Deportation of Two Malays' before going home.

Reports on the school strike were run throughout Australia and overseas. A Mitchell cartoon in Adelaide showed striking illiterate schoolkids in a class carrying placards demanding no more homewerk (sic), smoke time, free choowing (sic) gum and no keeping in.

The school strike apparently had an impact on the Bowditch household as well. Ngaire Bowditch recalled that when she was attending the Darwin Primary School a teacher criticised the *News* and journalists. It could have been in connection with the strike at Darwin High. She enthusiastically told her father what the teacher had said. Bowditch went to the school, lectured the teacher on the role of the press and the issues involved. He then withdrew Ngaire and enrolled her in the Parap Primary School. Ngaire Bowditch was not the only journalist's daughter involved. Doug Lockwood's daughter, Dale, was one of those who went on strike at the High School.

Unionists, including Bill Donnelly, rallied against the deportation. Another activist, communist Brian Manning, an airport fireman at the time, who lived in a former Darwin mayor's house dubbed "The Kremlin", threw himself into the case. A Queenslander, Manning, who also played the saxophone in bands, was something of a young Turk, an idealist "relishing the power of the masses" in the Communist Party.

According to him, during the period from 1959–70, the party membership in Darwin grew from a mere six to more than 40. The party was no longer just "the Red table" at the Workers' Club, but had become a much larger group of activists. The party united on the issue of the Stayput Malays, collecting a petition of 1100 names which went to Canberra demanding the divers not be deported.

The NAWU warned that if the Malays were deported it would call a stoppage and place a black ban on any Darwin master pearler who tried to introduce non-European labour. Watersiders went on strike and the crew of the WA coastal vessel MV *Koolama* held a formal protest in Darwin. Bowditch editorialized that the strike by the watersiders was not a stoppage by "Commos", but a demonstration of rage by men who had no other way of showing their disgust. The Minister for Immigration, Mr Downer, said Bowditch, had let the cat out of the bag by revealing there were so many low-paid indentured labourers in the country. Two nights before the proposed deportation, a large public protest rally was called by the NAWU at the Darwin Oval. The protesters, with Dick Ward, Bert Graham and Mrs Norma Robson in the lead, marched on Government House where a deputation of six spoke to Administrator Roger Nott. Nott telephoned Canberra and held the phone up so that the noise of the protesters outside could be heard. Nott was quoted in the *NT News* as having told the deputation that as far as he knew the two Malays had been good citizens against whom there was not one bad word. Nott also said he had no feeling about colour and added that he had invited Aborigines to Government House functions.

The Malays went into hiding. In an Immigration Department secret report on the case it was said that while it was not known who had concealed the two, "there are grounds for the belief that at this stage Mr Bowditch was personally concerned." Manning confirmed this scenario, saying Bowditch "bit the bullet" and decided to hide them. Journalist Doug Lockwood was taken to interview the Malays in a house set in a lush garden in Phillip Street, Fannie Bay, not far from the Bowditch house, where they were photographed. A front-page story in the *News* next day announced: MALAYS IN HIDING. The hideaway was the abode of "Bluey" and Elsie Jones. Manning said Jones had been the best *Tribune* seller in Darwin but when the communist newspaper ran a nude photograph of Yoko Ono and John Lennon during their "Give peace a chance" campaign, he was so offended that he refused to handle the paper.

Mrs Jones, normally very nervous, almost had a breakdown as the hunt for the Malays hotted up. Bowditch then appealed to Manning to find somewhere else to hide the Malays because Mrs Jones was "terrified".

On 26 September, the two Malays gave themselves up to the Administrator in company with the Mayor, Harold Cooper, the

Rev. Norm Pearce of the United Church, Brother Aidan of the Church of England, Paddy Carroll, secretary of the NAWU, Pat Wood of the AEU, and Lou de Courcy, from Rotary International.

One of the Malays wore a pair of trousers which belonged to Manning as he had been wearing shorts when he went into hiding and thought you should wear long pants in the presence of an Administrator. Taken into custody, they were later allowed freedom of movement about Darwin after signing an undertaking to report daily to the Immigration Officer while Dick Ward made submissions on their behalf. Two days later the men went back into hiding after being tipped off that they were going to be arrested when they checked in with Immigration and would be flown out of the country.

Elaborate plans had been hatched between Canberra and Darwin to get rid of the Malays, who were getting extensive media coverage down south and in Asia. According to a secret Immigration Department report, "The well thought-out plan for the apprehension of the two men was frustrated when, on the night of 27 September, Mr Ward, solicitor acting for the two Malays, was told of the intention to take them into custody. He apparently received the news about 9 pm and either he, Mr Bowditch, or some other members of what subsequently became the Darwin Anti-Deportation Committee, immediately arranged to take the men into hiding. That Mr Bowditch was party to the plan was suggested by the fact that the next morning the Immigration Office was under the observation of a member of the staff of the *Northern Territory News* who reported quite accurately on all that transpired. The association between Mr Bowditch and Mr Lockwood was again suggested by the fact that on the morning of 28 September Mr Lockwood, shortly after 10 am, approached the Commonwealth Migration Officer for information."

How the information leaked out is not clear; there is even a strong inference in Immigration Department files that Administrator Roger Nott might have been complicit. He was seen as pro-Malays and unhelpful at times. Nott was said to have shown Mr Bowditch a teleprinter message from Canberra on the night of the 27th. "In view of the general attitude of the Administrator throughout the whole of the proceedings, this possibility cannot be discounted," the official report stated.

Whatever the real story, Manning was working at the airport in the Civil Aviation fire brigade when he was told the deportation would happen that very day. Immediately he rang Bowditch at the *News* and raised the alarm, asking him to find the Malays, who were in town somewhere, and tell them not to report to Immigration.

There was a flurry of activity at the *News*. Bowditch told me to quickly drive to the Immigration Office, a building on piers, and to stay outside (hence the above report about the office being kept under surveillance by the *NT News*), and warn off the Malays if they arrived. There was no doubting what the Malays should be told if sighted: "Just tell them to run away and hide as they are going to be arrested and deported."

Fortunately, the Malays were alerted and went into hiding again. In answer to a question in federal parliament from Jock Nelson, Downer admitted that it had been intended to fly the men out of the country the day after their arrest. The Assistant Secretary of the Immigration Department, H. Gordon Brooks, was sent from Canberra to supervise the hunt for the Malays. He arrived in Darwin to hear a vehicle with a loudspeaker driving about town alerting people to another "giant" protest meeting that night on the Darwin Oval. Posters also went up about town stating that at the meeting Bowditch and Manning would tell the full story of the Malays. Jock Nelson would also be there to tell the inside story of the fight in Canberra. The mayor, church leaders and Paddy Carroll of the NAWU, would also speak.

As if that wasn't worrying enough, Brooks called on Nott that night and obviously was not happy with what he heard. In his long official account of the case, Brooks devoted a section to the "Attitude of the Administrator", who was also the Commissioner of Police. "My interview with Mr Nott on the evening of September 28 he received me quite affably but almost immediately made two complaints—(a) that "everyone" in Darwin knew of the decision to take the pearlers into custody before he did; and that (b) in making the public statement in Adelaide that Deraus bin Saris had four children in Malaya, the Minister [for Immigration] had been guilty of deliberate misrepresentation and that he, the Administrator, had been seriously embarrassed by arranging publicity in Darwin for the statement, which he knew to be incorrect. He expressed support for the White Australia Policy but indicated that in his opinion the whole matter had been handled badly. He had been swayed by the fact that at his surrender bin Saris had beseeched his, the Administrator's, aid."

At the Darwin Oval meeting that night an Anti-Deportation Committee was formed under the auspices of the North Australian Workers' Union. Brooks listed the members of the committee complete with asterisks indicating persons who were "reported to be members of the Australian Communist Party or known communist sympathisers." The chairman was NAWU president Bert Graham with Brian Manning of the Civil Aviation Crew, Darwin Airport, deputy chairman. Other members were Dick Ward; Pat Wood, secretary of the Darwin branch of the Australian Engineers' Union, and his wife; Des Robson, clerk, Department of Health, Darwin Hospital, and his wife, Norma; Paddy Carroll, NAWU secretary; William Donnelly, waterside worker; Kenneth Stagg, Amalgamated Engineering Union; Mrs Pauline Shah, "wife of an Indian" (he was also a snake expert); Frank Martin, "half-caste boxer"; John Kingsley Banks, member of Meteorological section of Department of Interior, Darwin; Dorothy Ashton, "de facto wife of William Donnelly"; George Gibbs, waterside worker; and James Bowditch, editor of the *NT News*. There were no asterisks next to Bowditch, Ward, Graham, Carroll, Mrs Shah and Martin.

It was claimed that the Communist Party had "engineered" a takeover of the committee, sensing that it could win the fight to keep the divers in Australia. Brooks wrote that Nott had been approached by "some responsible people" expressing concern about the Communist Party involvement. Manning denied any plan to "steal" the Malays; the unions, he said, had strength of numbers and were plainly better organised than Bowditch. A small sub-committee that met each day was set up and the Malays were moved almost daily.

Bowditch's position on the committee was described as being more of an ex-officio member. He had declined to serve officially as he did not want to be seen to be "creating news". Nevertheless, he played a vital part keeping the issue alive in the media. Brooks called on the Administrator the morning after formation of the committee. Nott said that although the meeting had passed a resolution to the effect that it act outside the law if it considered this desirable, he did not intend issuing a statement on the matter in his capacity as Commissioner of Police.

For the record, Brooks wrote: "He [Nott] repeated his criticism of the Minister and his handling of the whole affair, indicated that as Immigration had got itself into the mess, it was for Immigration to get itself out of it, and repeated his allegation that the Minister had resorted to deliberate lying concerning the "four" children of bin Saris. At no stage over the subsequent proceedings did Mr Nott make any public statement, nor offer any assistance."

Apart from not being impressed by the Administrator, the Immigration man from Canberra, it seems, was unhappy with the way Darwin police were handling the manhunt. Brooks said the Darwin force was rather small, numbering about 30 men and two women. While descriptions of the Malays had been issued to all officers, the task of arresting the Malays had been given to the Special Branch, which consisted of two men. "It was clearly obvious that the resources of the Special Branch were hopelessly inadequate for the task," Brooks wrote. Two police women with a radio car were made available to the Special Branch part time. Patrols were made, suspect homes kept under observation, but without success.

With so many people involved in the Anti-Deportation Committee, Brooks said it was impossible for the small band of police to watch everybody. Two additional officers, Sgt McLachlan and First Class Constable Tom Hollow, were allocated to the Special Branch to beef up the squad and, at Canberra's insistence, the entire Darwin force was brought into the hunt. Outlying areas were searched, police stations along the Stuart Highway were alerted, and boats in Darwin harbour were watched. The navy, army and air force were asked to search their large bases for the fugitives. Bowditch scoffed at the size of the manhunt in an editorial, saying it was bigger than any search J. Edgar Hoover of the FBI would mount in such a situation.

Brooks said a "useful contact" was made with a person on the fringe of the "Bowditch-Ward group". Although this person did not provide information about the actual whereabouts of the Malays, inside details of the group's "struggle" with the communists were supplied. However, there was a tip-off that the Malays would be transported to Channel Island, the old leper station, in the harbour. With the help of the naval police, plans were made to arrest the fugitives on the island; at the last moment, "the communist group secured the custody of the Malays, and the island project was abandoned."

The authorities had been optimistic that they would soon capture the men, but Brooks wrote that once the communists got control of them the situation changed. Control was vested entirely in the hands of a small fanatical group, which used the rest of the committee as it felt fit, but gave it no information at all concerning the Malays. While there is evidence to suggest that the Bowditch-Ward group resented matters thus being taken out of their hands, by this time each member of the committee was so far committed that he apparently felt he could not withdraw.

The committee this way became a front body for a small inner communist group which had possession of the Malays and would not disclose their whereabouts to anyone. While the police maintained their contacts associated with the committee these could no longer provide information of the slightest value.

The first stage of the police operations came to an end at this point. Dawn raids were made on 2 October on the homes of committee members and their associates and roadblocks were set up. Brooks that day attended a meeting of the committee held at the NAWU. The meeting suggested that the Minister for Immigration be asked to allow the Malays to stay in Darwin under bond pending examination of legal aspects of their case.

There was a dramatic development on 4 October when a person claiming to be a member of the Anti-Deportation Committee rang police and said a group, not members of the committee, planned to kidnap or injure Brooks. The *NT News* ran a story that said the person who had alerted the police, said to be a well-known and respected member of the Darwin community, had given full details of the "plot" to the paper.

Brooks' account of this extraordinary event was thus: "It was apparently intended that a Malay should come to my room in the Hotel Darwin late one night with a report that bin Hashim and bin Saris wished to see me. If I accompanied this Malayan to a secluded spot I was then to be either assaulted or kidnapped. The police attached some credence to the possibility but while I took some precautions it was extremely difficult to take the threat seriously. In the event nothing happened and it remains a very distinct possibility that the whole matter began and ended merely as a publicity 'stunt'."

Manning confirmed that an over-keen "hard head" had raised the possibility of kidnapping Brooks and holding him hostage to take the heat off the Malays. This extreme proposal had been quickly hit on the head.

Getting further intelligence that the Malays were being shifted about in the homes of people associated with the committee, mass raids were carried out in the mornings. The Bowditch home was searched twice; Mrs Bowditch was home both times and an injunction was sought in the Supreme Court to restrain police from further raids. In all, about 100 homes were searched.

At an Anglican Synod held on Thursday Island there was support for a Darwin resolution condemning the White Australia Policy. Darwin lay member Peter Spillett, the Darwin vicar's warden, called on the government to consider a policy of controlled migration from Asia and Africa. Spillett criticised the cynical attitude of the federal government which did not recognise Communist China yet had trade relations with it.

The government responded by saying that the men had family back home who wanted to see them. It was pointed out the men had been absent from home for up to 12 years, and if the shell industry had remained buoyant they would have been kept in Australia for many more years. Dick Ward was reported saying the government's attitude to the Malays was unnecessarily cruel. Canberra kept in close contact with Darwin, issuing instructions, speaking to Crown law officers, sending teleprinter messages.

One such message was from the Australian High Commissioner, Kuala Lumpur, claiming that the father and brother of bin Hasham were urging him to return home to Malaya. The ABC and the commercial radio station ran the report with a claim by the Anti-Deportation Committee that it was a hoax. The *NT News* ran a story on 3 October claiming to have received the following message from bin Hasham: "I have heard the broadcast over the wireless that said my father asked me to return home. I have not heard from my father for years and cannot see why he takes a sudden interest in me. I sympathise with my father but I am 24 years old and wish to stay in Darwin where I have lived amongst fine people. Please tell Mr Downer this."

Immigration officer Brooks said Bowditch was asked to produce the note; after some delay, it was presented and Brooks commented: it appeared to be a page from a reporter's shorthand notebook, freshly written with a blue biro. Hashim is known to be barely literate in English and the phrasing of the letter was considered not to be that of a barely literate Malayan. Examination suggested that the signature had been forged and handwriting comparisons gave strong reason to believe that it had been written by Desmond Robson, who was considered a member of the "inner" communist group of the Committee, the others being Norma Robson, his wife, and Dorothy Ashton.

Manning's band of activists knew they were being kept under close surveillance. A caravan was parked near the PMG facilities close to the police headquarters in Daly Street throughout the episode. Manning said he firmly believed phones were tapped. One day he picked up the phone at "The Kremlin" and a voice said, "Darwin Police Station."

ESTHER

The true life story of an Australian Country Girl.

Esther Meaney

Activist, Esther Meaney, subject of a book, and her husband, Jack, were willing accomplices in several of Jim's authority avoidance schemes.

In the dragnet for the Malays, police raided a house where the Malay fugitives were staying and one of them hid in a bathroom, armed with a thong. He felt certain that a searching officer saw him reflected in a mirror, but did not make an arrest. At the time of the raid the Malays were hiding in adjoining houses in Gregory Street, Parap. After this narrow escape, Manning held a meeting in "The Kremlin" and it was decided that something drastic had to be done. He consulted Bowditch, who said the Malays should be moved from Darwin to a farm near Batchelor, the former Rum Jungle uranium mine township. The farm, Milton Springs, was owned by Jack and Esther Meaney, mentioned earlier. Apart from Mrs Meaney having been involved with the Peace Council, she and her husband once had a farm not far from the Bowditch house at Fannie Bay. There was a minor problem with the plan: Bowditch was not exactly sure where Milton Springs was.

One or both of the Malays may have actually been lodged in the roof at the Bowditch house before the plan to move them out of Darwin started. Late at night, a convoy of three cars set out from Darwin and headed down "The Track". In the first was Des Robson, of the Anti-Deportation Committee; Manning was in the second and, bringing up the rear with the Malays, was Bowditch. A system warning of the presence of police was devised which involved pumping the brakes quickly three times so that stop lights were seen by the following vehicle.

If they came across a roadblock the Malays would get out of the car, walk through the bush past the police, and then rejoin the convoy farther on. Manning said there was incredible pressure on them "every inch of the way" but they were amazed not to encounter one roadblock. They knew there had been one at the 11-mile during the day, but it was not there at night. If they had been caught by police, Manning said Bowditch would probably have lost his job.

In the tradition of the "best laid plans of revolutionaries", Manning said they missed the turn-off to Milton Springs. The first two cars carried on to Adelaide River, where they had a quick whispered conference on the side of the road and wondered where Bowditch was with the Malays because they could not see his car. The reason his vehicle could not be seen was simple: travelling at 90 mph (134 km/h), Bowditch's car had a blowout and it ran off the road into the bush, terrifying his passengers. Manning, sensing there had been trouble with the car, turned back; his spare tyre replaced the one that had blown.

Still uncertain where their destination was, they were "creeping" about Batchelor at three or four in the morning. They found some Aborigines and were given directions. Milton Springs carried a warning sign which read something like: NO GROG, NO FRUIT, NO GINS, NO TRESPASSERS. Bowditch quickly explained the situation to the Meaneys, who readily agreed to hide the Malays, which they did for several weeks. The springs after which the property was named were a short distance from the house and the Malays camped nearby.

While the Malays were relaxing near the springs the manhunt, complete with roadblocks, continued in Darwin. Jack Meaney was in Adelaide River one day when a policeman said, "I suppose you are hiding those Malays out at Milton Springs?" Jack responded with a laugh, and invited the officer to check the place.

In Canberra, Jock Nelson made representations to Downer, who agreed to stay the deportation order for seven days if the divers came out of hiding and bonds of 250 pounds each were signed by responsible people. Legal proceedings would have to be started within that period to test the validity of the deportation order.

The Malays again came out of hiding. A prominent legal figure, Zelman Cowen, later to become Governor-General of Australia, became involved. At the time he was professor of law at University of Melbourne and made representations to Downer on behalf of the divers. Another large public rally was held when the people of Darwin once more declared their support for the men.

From his report on the saga, it seems clear that Brooks was not impressed with the people of Darwin: "Overall, in so far as it can be judged, the general attitude of the Darwin community is one of apathy. It is an issue which is not fully understood, there have been no public statements of the other side of the picture and there can be no doubt that whatever views are held have been influenced by the very biased news sources available. Some of the more responsible people of Darwin privately expressed support for the Government, while others have indicated that apart from the controversial issue involved, 'direct action' outside the law by a minority group cannot be tolerated. All of such persons, however, have been reluctant to make any public statements in the matter."

He also said that Bowditch had conducted a number of press campaigns against "authority" in the past. In the case of the Stayput Malays, he wrote that the editor's stance had been undoubtedly influenced by the fact that he was "married to a mixed blood girl". An officer in the Prime Minister's Department wrongly asserted that the *NT News* had carried on its campaign against the government because its editor was "partly coloured".

It was announced that leading Victorian solicitor Frank Galbally had been engaged to represent the Malays. Galbally subsequently obtained a writ out of the High Court against the Immigration Minister and the Commonwealth to block the deportation. Mainly based on constitutional grounds, the writ said the Malays were British subjects living in Darwin; sued Mr Downer; sought a declaration the deportation order issued by Downer was null, void, illegal and beyond the powers of the Minister and the Commonwealth Government; claimed the men had never been prohibited immigrants within the meaning of the act; and sought an injunction restraining the Minister or any other person from attempting to deport or compel the Malays to leave Australia without their consent.

The Malays then flew south with Bowditch to confer with Galbally. At Melbourne airport the Malays and Bowditch were greeted on the tarmac by nearly 200 university students waving banners and singing *For They Are Jolly Good Fellows*. The Melbourne University Students' Representative Council also arranged a reception for them next day. At that extraordinary meeting it was unanimously decided to protest against the deportation orders and a deputation of six was appointed to carry the protest to the Immigration Minister. The meeting said the deportation was based on grounds of racial discrimination and also voted to seek a change in the White Australia Policy.

Dr Frank Knopfelmacher, psychology lecturer at the University of Melbourne, said the White Australia Policy cut across Christian principles and Australians believed they were Christian. The *Bible* showed, he said, Christ was an Asian carpenter, the son of Asian parents of no fixed abode. The Malays thanked Melbourne people for their support and Bowditch also addressed the gathering. As the High Court case was not to be heard until February, the two men were given employment by a Melbourne businessman, David Wang, in the furniture industry.

It was the start of a federal election campaign. The Stayput Malays became an embarrassing issue for the government, especially the PM and Downer, with the matter brought up at public meetings. At one noisy gathering Downer faced more than 60 jeering students, their faces blackened with boot polish, who sang to the tune of *Michael Row the Boat Ashore*:

> Old Bob Menzies he ought to know, White Australia,
> That the divers they shouldn't go, No more White Australia,
> Let's be human, let's be bold, White Australia,
> A new world arises from the old, No more White Australia.

The students handed out pamphlets urging changes to the White Australia Policy. During a speech, Downer said the government had played a big part in developing the northwest of Australia and expanding export industries. An interjector responded: "Yes, exporting skin divers to Malaya." A report said the minister lost control at one stage during the meeting. Newspapers and community groups, including the Australian Council of Churches, called for the Malays to be allowed to stay in Australia.

Meanwhile, in the NT the spotlight was focused on another aspect of the manhunt for the Malays in Darwin—the issuing of police search warrants. It was revealed that 57 police, 44 per cent of serving officers in the force, held general search warrants issued by the Commissioner of Police which were in force for six months.

A member of the Legislative Council, Fred Drysdale, moved for the repeal of the section of the Police Offences Ordinance which allowed the commissioner to issue general warrants. He believed a policeman should have to apply to a Justice of the Peace to get a warrant. Under the existing process it was morally wrong and not good for the freedom of the people of the Northern Territory. He said: "It is wrong that a policeman can enter anyone's home, anytime of the day or night, simply because he has in his pocket a warrant issued four or five months ago." At the time the general warrant provision applied in the Territory, Canberra and South Australia.

In late November the Darwin Anti-Deportation Committee launched an appeal for further funds to fight the High Court case. Legal and other costs were mounting. A pamphlet headed:

DARWIN'S CASE FOR THE MALAYANS, bearing the writing style of Bowditch, was circulated down south. It opened saying it was rare that an entire community became a dedicated unit intent on gaining justice for men from another country. The pamphlet contained the statement: "There is a strong objection in Darwin to the 'pushing around' by officialdom of humble and well-respected men because of an outmoded and unwarranted immigration policy."

It is known that Prime Minister Menzies became concerned about the publicity being given to the case nationally and internationally; he telephoned Downer at home offering help, suggesting the issue be placed before Cabinet to ease media criticism on him. Downer declined the offer, saying he wanted to handle the matter himself and that the Minister for Territories, Paul Hasluck, had backed his stance.

As the long, often tense campaign to keep the Malays in Australia now depended on a court hearing, Bowditch expected life would be less hectic. It was not to be. Another major story with international ramifications was about to break. It would focus the spotlight on a European dictator and once more "Big Jim" would be in the thick of the fray.

That exceptional story began the day after the federal election, 10 December, when the Portuguese frigate *Goncalves Zarco* arrived in Darwin from Portuguese Timor to take on fuel. The frigate shuttled around Portuguese possessions showing the flag and its crew of 140 came ashore for a break. Police said they were the quietest group of sailors to hit port in many a year and caused no trouble. Sailors normally had a fling in Darwin, but not the Portuguese. Three lowly ratings who were refused shore leave in peculiar circumstances dashed along the wharf and disappeared in the dark. Police were notified, a search was made, but they could not be found; the ship sailed the next day.

The background to the disappearance was this: the three sailors, on their fourth visit to Darwin, were in a group which included two older sergeants which went to the RSL Club. There they had been entertained by friendly Australians and danced with young girls. When the girls were reluctant to dance with the older officers, said to be in their 50s, they became jealous. The sailors went back to the ship for dinner, intending to head back to the RSL later in the evening. However, one of the "jealous" sergeants issued instructions not to allow the three ashore again as they were trouble makers. Regarding this as unfair, but a clear warning that they were in trouble with superior officers, meaning life could be made very hard for them, the trio decided to jump ship.

The first Bowditch knew of the event was when approached by an obviously anxious, mild-mannered Portuguese clerk, Julio Borges, who was always neatly dressed in white. Borges was an example of the cosmopolitan makeup of the Darwin population. After the war, Borges had worked in the Portuguese Timor capital, Dili, as a government draftsman. There he met the Australian Consul, John Whittaker, and they became friends. Whittaker told Borges he should go to Australia because it was a young country with a future and that he could get a job there. The consul arranged for Julio to fly to Darwin on 31 January 1956, in an RAAF plane. He was picked up at the airport by a car, taken to the Esplanade Hostel and employed by the Department of Works and Housing.

Borges visited the *Goncalves Zarco* when it came to Darwin and was drinking with officers when he was told that three of the crew were missing. If he heard anything about them when he went ashore, the officers asked him to let them know. Borges passed the news around about the missing sailors. He was surprised to receive a call from a Spanish friend who said he knew where the sailors were, that they did not want to return to the ship and were seeking political asylum.

Borges explained what he did when he heard this: "I think Jim [Bowditch] is the man to handle this. If he can't do anything, nobody can." Borges then hurried to the *News*. In a hushed voice, Borges confided that the sailors from the frigate were hiding in the bush. "Please, Jim, will you help them?" Bowditch responded by slapping his forehead in disbelief, and exclaimed, "Oh shit! It can't be true!" But it was: they were Norberto Andrade, Jose da Costa and Joaquim Teixeira, all in their early twenties.

Borges took Bowditch to where the sailors were hiding, in scrub near the Waratah Football Oval, not far from where Jim lived. Bowditch explained that because they had deserted a warship it would be hard to win support for their cause from the Australian government. While there had been strong community support for the Malay stayputs, it would be harder gaining similar backing for deserters. The sailors insisted that if they were sent back to Portugal, then under the rule of the dictator Antonio Salazar, they would be tortured and probably killed.

Warning against over-optimism, Bowditch said he would do what he could to help them. After three days, the sailors came out of hiding and asked the Administrator for political asylum, saying they could not live under Salazar's fascist dictatorship. All three men gained the impression that Nott was a sincere man.

The southern media was fascinated by the story coming so soon after the stayput Malays and wanted to know what was going on in Darwin. In answer to that question, Doug Lockwood wrote that the crusading editor of the *NT News* was the reason so many unusual stories were breaking in Darwin. A report in a southern newspaper ran a photograph of Bowditch with the caption "Zeal."

When the sailors were refused asylum they were arrested and lodged in Fannie Bay Gaol. The close association between Bowditch and lawyer Dick Ward once more came to the fore. Ward's associate Richard Keller began *habeas corpus* proceedings in the NT Supreme Court and deportation was deferred. The men were allowed their freedom providing they reported daily to ASIO while their application for political asylum was examined. When the High Court ruled that the government had the right to deport the men, they were shattered. One said he would commit suicide rather than return to Portugal where they all feared being incarcerated in terrible conditions. Bowditch, however, was not prepared to give in. When Minister Downer said the men had to go back to Portugal, they went back into hiding. Bowditch became involved with another anti-deportation committee.

Once more he was the centre of an international news story. At times in company with reporter Les Wilson, Bowditch would drive out to the bush, call out something in Portuguese, and the three sailors would emerge. He would have a quick talk to them, give them the latest information and ask them if they had any problems.

Borges said Bowditch had been "more than a father" to the three, buying them clothes, giving them money and finding work for them while campaigning down south to keep them in Australia. The three told Borges they could not believe Bowditch was so good to them. The struggle to keep them in Australia focused attention on the Portuguese dictator, Salazar. The International Council of Jurists produced a report exposing the cruel treatment of prisoners in Portugal. With two major news stories attracting national and international attention, Bowditch was under great pressure.

Reporter Wilson was enthusiastically following up an angle in the Stayput Portuguese story when he and *News* photographer Joe Karlhuber drove to the Fannie Bay Hotel at night. When he got certain information, Les drove back into town at great speed in case he was being followed by police, overturned the office car and was trapped by the foot. Karlhuber, who had been thrown about, crawled out and helped free Wilson who suffered mild concussion.

Karlhuber worked under great difficulties and operated in a primitive darkroom at the *News*. He had a refrigerator which was supposed to be used for keeping photographic chemicals, but other people had different ideas. Even when he chained the refrigerator, staff would get into it with bolt cutters and fill it with grog. Because of the fridge, drinking sessions were sometimes held in the darkroom and he often had to clean up a mess of empty cans, bottles and fag ends.

With May Day coming up and plans to give the Government and Downer a real burst with floats throughout Australia, it was announced the Malays and the Portuguese could stay.

It was a stunning victory for all concerned in the stayput battles, especially for the tenacious editor of the ramshackle newspaper in Darwin.

In his capacity as secretary of the NAWU, Paddy Carroll later issued an appeal for a voluntary levy to pay for the two campaigns. Both battles, he said, had run up large legal debts and other expenses. Bowditch, who had led Australia's newspaper campaign, arranged for loans totalling over 800 pounds from his company with the approval of the chairman of directors, Rupert Murdoch. All this money was spent on legal and other costs. The generous gesture from the company carried no interest, but Bowditch was made clearly responsible to see the money repaid. He had personally spent 600 pounds during the campaign, and had written this off to a good cause and experience, but must meet the debt to the *News*.

As he was a wage earner like everyone, he had no chance of finding the money without considerable hardship over a long period. The consequences of failing to repay the money would be obvious. Carroll urged the union to contribute ten shillings a head so the debt to the *News* could be paid.

Betty Bowditch said Jim had no trouble raising money for his crusades. Where it came from, she did not know "he just got it." One likely answer, only revealed in the year 2000, was that Bowditch had a very influential guarantor for an overdraft with the Commonwealth Bank, Ken Waters, the prominent Darwin businessman, former mayor and father of the NT ALP secretary, John Waters, QC. It appears Waters senior had been left holding part of the financial baby in the end.

The Malay Jaffa Madun became a prominent Darwin identity. A chef at the Parap Hotel, he won the title of Australia's best steak cook. It would appear that the thwarted authorities still kept a close and vindictive watch on the Malays. Zainal was deported for petty offences some years later. One related to being in possession of waste lead which he recovered while on a worksite. It was common practice for workers in Darwin to hoard this scrap metal to fund their Christmas parties. The recovery of scrap metal had not been an issue in the past. Another offence was being found on the premises of an illegal gaming house. If playing cards in an illegal gambling den was a major offence deserving deportation, then Darwin should have been reduced to a ghost town. Daris bin Saris is said to have moved back to Broome.

There was a shocking epilogue to the Stayput Portuguese story. Seven years later, da Costa murdered his Greek employer, Andreas Koklas, while they were making a holiday trip around Australia. He drove off in the man's car; from the dead man's bank book he tried to draw a large amount of money to flee the country. At Tennant Creek he tried to sell a camera belonging to the victim to a policeman. He was arrested and brought back to Darwin for trial.

Bowditch went to Borges and expressed his dismay at what da Costa had done, saying he had let down the people of Darwin and Australia. The other two Portuguese stayputs were shattered by the enormity of what da Costa had done. In an expression of regret, da Costa was reportedly "upset" for what he had done to Jim Bowditch.

The court was filled with angry members of the Greek community who wanted da Costa hanged. Judge Blackburn passed the death sentence. Personally distressed by the case, Bowditch nevertheless campaigned to save da Costa from hanging and for the abolition of capital punishment in the NT. Da Costa did not hang and capital punishment was abolished.

Recalling the Stayput Portuguese saga, Borges, still expressing dismay in 1982 at what da Costa had done, letting down so many people, said the then Darwin Portuguese population of about 500 regarded Bowditch as "a great man". Members of this segment of the Darwin community still went to Bowditch for help with problems, even when he was no longer editor of the *NT News*. In 2004, Norberto Andrade still marvelled at the way Bowditch, Dick Ward, unionists and so many other people in the community had rallied to help the trio. In particular, he singled out Bowditch for high praise. "I will never forget him until I die."

When asked what happened to da Costa, who had been saved from hanging, in part due to Bowditch's campaigning, Andrade had this to say: "I heard that he was released from jail in Adelaide and became ill. When told that he was suffering from cancer, he went home and killed himself."

39. THE ROCKEFELLER MYSTERY

In November 1961 Michael Rockefeller, son of Nelson Rockefeller, Governor of New York, disappeared on an anthropological expedition in what was then Dutch New Guinea.

Rockefeller, described as an aesthete, had wanted to study architecture, but was forced to yield to parental pressure and took up economics. While at Harvard University he heard of an expedition of anthropologists and a film crew to the Baliem Valley of Dutch New Guinea to make a record of tribes whose primitive agricultural society was untouched by western culture. He joined the expedition, telling his parents he wanted to do something romantic and adventurous while there were still far away frontiers to explore.

While on the expedition he was told that his parents were going to divorce. He returned to New York, told his parents he was going to be an anthropologist, and flew back to Hollandia, the then capital of Dutch New Guinea. There he teamed up with Dutch ethnologist Dr Rennie Wassing and they went on a two-month field trip gathering material for the New York Museum of Primitive Art. They travelled aboard a catamaran powered by two 18-horsepower motors, collecting artefacts, carved shields, canoe figureheads and shrunken heads. They also planned to record chants and war cries.

A large wave swamped their catamaran offshore near the Eilander River. The two clung to the vessel. Michael decided to try to swim 11 miles to shore. Wassing pleaded with him not to go because of the obvious danger, the waters containing crocodiles and sharks. Despite those pleas, Rockefeller tied his glasses to his head, strapped empty fuel cans over his shoulders for flotation, and swam off. The catamaran was eventually found drifting and Wassing raised the alarm. When Bowditch heard about the disappearance he proposed flying to the area from Darwin to search for him. He felt that because he had served near that area during the war, he might know some of the natives, a very long shot. Murdoch had promised to have the first story from the area and discussed the matter with Bowditch and Ken May.

A major problem was getting approval from Dutch authorities to fly into Merauke, the nearest place to where Rockefeller was last seen. If no quick approval could be given for landing at Merauke, Bowditch suggested he could parachute into the area. "It was my lust to get the story that made me suggest the parachute jump," Bowditch said later. The problem was discussed with light plane operators in Darwin. They indicated a willingness to fly to Merauke, as long as he could get Department of Civil Aviation and Dutch approval for the flight. To prepare himself for a daring and dangerous assignment should the green light be given, Bowditch obtained a parachute and brought it back to the *NT News* office.

During the evening, with the help of many cans of beer, Bowditch demonstrated the technique of parachute jumping to reporter Les Wilson. Bowditch, parachute on back, would mount his desk, jump and roll. Laughter flowed when he said that the parachute canopy, opening with a jerk, would probably snap his old bones. The vision of a fractured Big Jim landing in the jaws of crocodiles added to the madness of the evening. Wilson had a few jumps himself with the parachute strapped to his back.

It was finally decided that Sydney reporter Brian Hogben and photographer Ron Iredale would fly to Merauke via Port Moresby. Bowditch said Murdoch and May probably came to the conclusion that it would have been too risky and possibly very expensive if Bowditch had died carrying out his dare-devil parachute drop.

Nelson Rockefeller flew to Port Moresby with Michael's twin sister in a chartered Boeing 707 and a party of 17 pressmen. A TAA Catalina was made available for the search party at Merauke. A huge land, sea and air search, which included the Royal Dutch Air Force, failed to find any trace of Michael. It was felt certain that he either drowned or had been taken by a crocodile or shark.

The disappearance was front-page news in Australia and America. Zell Rabin reported from New York that Hogben's reports had been given prominence in major American newspapers.

President Kennedy asked the Australian Prime Minister, Mr Menzies, to help in any way he could and RAAF Hercules transports, with helicopters, were sent from Queensland to join the search. An offer was made to send a US aircraft carrier, but Rockefeller said it was not needed. Convinced that there was little hope of finding his son, he returned to America. Before he left he personally thanked many of the people who took part in the search, including the Australians. Many indigenous people had taken part in the hunt and one of the richest men in the world stood with naked locals thanking them for their efforts. Years after the event, reporter Les Wilson got a telex message informing him that he and Bowditch had appeared in a beat up on the front page of a New York publication dealing with the Michael Rockefeller disappearance. The story had Bowditch and Wilson practising parachute drops, not in the office of the *NT News*, but in places all over New Guinea as they searched for Rockefeller.

40. THE MOUNT ISA STRIKE

Because of his involvement in the *Mount Isa Mail*, Bowditch was able to tell of the rare occasion when Murdoch lost a newspaper battle against people with more money and determination. This was during the protracted Mount Isa Mines strike/lockout from August 1964 to April 1965, which was seen as a threat to the Queensland economy. A key union figure in the dispute, Pat Mackie, became a national identity. He was branded "a commo" and described as a "Canadian-Yankee gangster." In defence of the strike, which Mackie said was really a lockout by Mount Isa Mines Limited, he charged that the dispute was manufactured and prolonged to increase world copper prices. At first, the *Mail* had run reports about the strike. However, as it went on and tensions mounted, Murdoch executive Leo McDonald in Brisbane decided to ignore the major event which was receiving nationwide coverage. Bowditch charged that McDonald had been "frightened" that the paper might offend MIM in some way and they would start up a paper of their own. Written instructions were issued to Bowditch from Brisbane not to cover the strike in the paper. So while the bitter strike threatened the Queensland economy and copper prices rose, the *Mail* simply did not report the event. Because of this, Jim said all parties in the dispute turned against the paper. In Bowditch's estimation, the mining company concluded that the *Mail*, by not supporting the company, was clearly not on its side. And by eventually not running anything at all about the dispute, it was really regarded as "a nothing newspaper." Bowditch admitted, however, that had he had his way and fully covered the strike, following certain angles that he felt should have been pursued, especially with Mackie, the mining company would probably have been "dirty" on the *Mail* anyway.

Eventually, MIM offered to buy the *Mail*, but News Limited refused to sell. On being knocked back, MIM then bought out Murdoch's local printer, purchased more equipment and started a new newspaper with the help of Asher Joel, a prominent PR man who had worked for the Victorian Liberal Party. Murdoch decided to fight the new paper and Bowditch was sent to Mount Isa for about three months. Both publications brought out large weekly papers in the small mining town. Bowditch estimated that they were losing 5000 pounds a week. Murdoch went to Mount Isa for a conference with Bowditch and Leo McDonald and a MIM representative. McDonald and Bowditch had a stand-up argument, McDonald blaming Bowditch for the situation in Mount Isa. Bowditch pointed out he had a written directive from McDonald not to write anything about the strike. The MIM company representative agreed that the fact that the paper had not covered the strike was the reason a rival publication had been started. It was impossible for the Murdoch paper to survive in the company-owned and run town. Murdoch eventually cut his losses and sold.

However, he soon had another paper in his sights, the *Centralian Advocate* in Alice Springs, which he bought in 1966. Bowditch said Murdoch, quick on the uptake, had probably formed the intention

The new *NT News* building opened in 1967 was strategically located between the Vic and Darwin Hotels. Photo by Fred Davies Courtesy Library and Archives NT, 0243-0031.

to buy the Alice paper when Jock Nelson offered a half share to Jim if he came back as editor. Nelson revealed he had asked Murdoch in Canberra if he would like to buy the *Advocate*. Murdoch declined, and said he was tied up with other things at the time, but asked Nelson if he needed money. Nelson replied that it was not a money problem at the paper, but a staff problem. Putting more money into the paper would be like pouring money down the drain. Asher Joel, the man who had been in opposition to Murdoch in Mount Isa, had made an offer for the Alice paper, but it had been rejected. Another who expressed an interest in buying the paper had been Colonel Lionel Rose, who had backing from people on the conservative side of politics. Reporter Tony Malone, who had worked at the *NT News*, was appointed managing editor of the *Advocate*. Malone subsequently took up important posts in Sydney and Arizona in the expanding Murdoch Empire.

In 1967 the *NT News* moved into new premises in Mitchell Street, directly opposite the Hotel Darwin, and became a daily. The

Replaced once again, this former *NT News* building is now a series of restaurants. Photo Richard Creswick, 2022.

editor's now salubrious carpeted office had a window with louvre blades through which he was seen to pass money to a number of people.

Cowboy Bill, Bill Garrison, a gravel-voiced character with a large repertoire of jokes and anecdotes, came across from the Hot and Cold bar with two glasses of scotch, went into the editor's room, sat down with Jim and they drank and joked.

Some staff who knew Bowditch from the old Tin Bank days said that with the advent of the daily he spent even longer hours at the office. It got to a stage where it was said he "haunted" the office. Reporter John Loizou, close to Jim, on several occasions tried to convince Bowditch that he ought take life easier and spend less time in the office. With more staff than ever, there was no need for the editor to be as deeply involved in the paper as he had in the past. However, Bowditch did not heed the sound advice from Loizou. He would often be on deck right up until the paper went to press, then continue drinking until early in the morning. In the opinion

Jim, attired typically in shorts and long socks, having a yarn with
Cowboy Bill Garrison outside the new offices. Photo courtesy Barry
Ledwidge collection.

of some, Bowditch began to go downhill from the time the paper moved into modern premises.

A major news story broke in the Northern Territory in 1967 which involved a French couple, Captain Henri and Madame Jose Bourdens, being plucked from a slowly sinking raft north of Darwin. Their yacht had been wrecked on Bathurst Island and after two months, not knowing there was a mission not far away, they made a raft and set sail. Near death, they were picked up by a fishing vessel. The raft had become waterlogged and was several feet under water when they were rescued. Bourdens, 44, a British United Airways pilot and his wife had set out from Singapore on their way back to France, but due to a series of mishaps and a cyclone were washed ashore on the island.

It is suggested Bowditch was absent from Darwin or tied up with something else when the story first broke and Doug Lockwood filed a cover story for Jim. News Limited trumpeted the fact that it had the world rights to the couple's story and it was run at great length in Murdoch papers and overseas. However, a Lockwood version of the French couple's ordeal was also run in Australia and overseas which angered News Limited. A *London Times* article bearing Lockwood's byline said the Bourdens had faced many dangers including goannas. Goannas, the report explained, were "six-foot man-eating lizards" with ridged backs.

Knowing that Lockwood was a stickler for the facts and decried beat ups, there is no doubt that he would not have described crocodiles in this way. In any case, News Limited took court action for alleged breach of contract by Lockwood, but it was dismissed. As a result, Murdoch instructed Bowditch to have no further dealings with "that man Lockwood." Bowditch ignored the directive and the close association continued. Bowditch described Lockwood as a fine reporter and a magnificent feature writer with a vast audience in Australia and overseas. Lockwood's books and newspaper writing, he said, must have been worth millions of dollars to the Australian tourist industry.

41. SHELL-SHOCKED NEIGHBOURS

Living next to the Bowditches was never dull, what with officially forbidden trysts in the banana patch, police raids and other assorted alarums. The Shell Mess was close to the Bowditch house in Georges Crescent and men who lived there had an upright piano for their entertainment, which often resulted in them returning at night from various hotels and engaging in some hearty singing of tunes like *Roll out the Barrel*. About midnight one evening Bowditch, lubricated himself, became annoyed at the noise from the mess, especially the tickling of the ivories and the raucous singing. He stormed up the stairs of the two-storey building and confronted the happy throng. Telling them that only peasants sang community songs, he announced his intention to push the piano down the stairs if they did not stop their infernal racket. To back up his threat, he began to push the piano, on castors, towards the balcony. A very large footballer took hold of the editor by the seat of the pants and the scruff of the neck and, in the words of a popular community song, tried to show him the way to go home. A man of undoubted agility, Bowditch stunned the group when he flipped open the top of the piano and pulled out some of the vital innards. He subsequently received a bill for his unusual piano concerto and paid for the repairs.

Police raids on his house also disturbed the tranquility of the suburb and set dogs barking. One long-suffering neighbour was jeweller Max Tite. Returning home late one night after some heavy drinking, Bowditch went to the bedroom and saw a man in bed. "You bastard!" Bowditch exclaimed, as he kicked the man. "What are you doing in bed with my wife?" Max Tite jumped up and yelped: "This is my wife, Jim, and this is my house. You live two doors away."

Betty Bowditch told of another event involving "that poor man Max Tite." She noticed a receipt for payment for some glass sent to Jim. When she asked him what it was for, he revealed that he had again paid a nocturnal visit to the Tite house. On that occasion, thinking he was home, he had found the door closed and thought Betty had locked him out. He then began kicking in glass panels. Shocked and alarmed, Max Tite had appeared and again told Jim he was at the wrong abode. Without telling Betty of his *faux pas*, Jim arranged to pay for repairs to the door.

After a trip to Bali with some friends, Betty Bowditch returned home with the usual range of electrical goods and gifts. While she was pleased with her purchases, Jim took an instant dislike to them, saying they had been made by slave labour in sweatshops. So vehement was he in his antipathy to the purchases that he threw them off the veranda onto the concrete driveway while she was absent. One of the items thrown over the rail was a stereo. He enlisted the help of daughter Ngaire to heave the stereo over the rail. At the time she thought that dad knew about such things as slave labour and sweatshops, so he must be right. In later years, she realised what "poor mum" had been through. Betty had arrived home to find all her things broken and strewn about the driveway.

Betty endured much over the years and many people said Jim was lucky she remained with him. She constantly remonstrated with him over his drinking and told him he brought a lot of trouble upon himself through excessive drinking. There was a "Dr Jekyll and Mr Hyde" aspect about his personality. Sober, he was gentlemanly, in the old-fashioned way, which saw him stand whenever women got up from or joined a group at a table. And if any male in the group, or nearby, swore in the presence of women, Bowditch would glare at them. Then you had the obverse the drunken, swearing, aggressive editor prepared to fight at the drop of a hat. Though capable of killing people with unarmed combat blows learnt during the war, he would not use them and being of slight build he often came off second best because he mixed it with larger, younger men.

Sleep, he maintained, was a waste of time, so he got by with about four hours a night. Because of his heavy smoking, the home was pock marked with cigarette burns that infuriated Betty. A new teak table she bought soon sported many cigarette burns. Incredibly

Happier times. Jim and Betty at the beach with children Peter,
Ngaire and Steven. 1961. Sharon was yet to be born. Bowditch
family collection.

fast in his reflexes, Bowditch would stalk flies and catch them with
his hand. He said you had to learn the flight paths of flies and
claimed to have studied them while in the trenches of Tobruk.

Jim's sister Mary came out from England and made a surprise
visit to Darwin. Jim arranged to meet her at the front of the Hotel
Darwin and immediately invited her inside for a drink. She did
not drink and Jim said he was surprised to learn that there was a
member of the Bowditch family who did not touch alcohol. She
told him he was just like their father in his behaviour. When he
took her home to meet Betty, Mary sympathised with her and asked
"How do you put up with him?" Betty often explained that she was
kept busy bringing up the children, taking part in their and her own
sporting and school activities, and running the home. Jim had been
on the go all the time, deeply involved in the newspaper, socialising
after work and fighting for various causes.

Both Jim and Betty Bowditch were keen squash players. Betty
was so good that she was employed in a squash court business in
Darwin. The *NT News* had a squash team which included Jim and

In 1972 Steven, (second from the left) was in the NT's junior men's team to the Australian Squash Championships in Brisbane. Also in the team, Desmond Chin (left) and Kieran Jones (right). Team Manager was Alan Nicholls. Photo courtesy Alan Nicholls.

sports editor Dennis Booth. Booth said Jim was fiercely competitive and agile on the court. While introducing compositor Bobby Wills to the game of squash, Jim hit him above the eye with his racquet. Wills reeled back with blood pouring from his wound and Bowditch said, "You are supposed to get out of the bloody way."

When Steven Bowditch was about 12 he joined the *NT News* team and rapidly became proficient. However, while he was learning to play the game, Booth claimed to have beaten him several times, a feat about which he would have cause to boast. A competition was held at the squash courts where Betty worked and Steven won a month's free playing time. Steven became so adept he won the NT Open at 15 and represented Australia as a junior and men's amateur squash player.

Steven went on to become a prominent world-ranked player and was inducted into the NT Sports Hall of Champions and listed as one of the first 100 Aboriginal athletes in the Aboriginal and Islander Sports Hall of Fame, the so-called Black Diamonds or Black Pearls. In 2015 he was also inducted into the Australian Squash Hall of Fame alongside Greg Hunt and Heather McKay.

In 1981 he was captain of the Australian squash team, runners up in the World Teams event and in that year he won the World Individual Squash Championships in Sweden. In 1985 he won the World Open Plate in Egypt, beating the dominant Jansher Khan in the final. He was also twice runner up in the North American Open 1985 and 1986, equivalent to the American Squash World title, and won the US Open.

Appointed to the World Squash Council, he became national coach of Malaysia and Sweden. His squash career took him to 40 countries and he lived in eight of them.

Although Rugby Union player Gary Ella has been credited with being the first Aboriginal to captain an Australian team in 1983, Bowditch captained the Australian squash team which came second in the World Squash Championships in Stockholm in 1981. (Note: Steven points out that Rugby League great, Arthur Beetson was, in fact, the first Aboriginal to captain Australia in any sport.)

Also a top golfer, he won championships at private clubs in Germany, the US and Australia. When it came to sport, Steven had great application which he felt came from his mother. He mentioned the occasion when his father brought home an American Globe-Trotters basketball with coloured panels. Steven, who had not played the game, took the basketball to nearby courts and practised shooting goals from many angles day after day. He was soon so good that he played in a men's A grade side and in 12 months was a referee.

Steven had a high regard for his mother's sporting capabilities. With the right opportunities and coaching he believed she could have been "another Yvonne Goolagong." She had been at the top in three sports in Darwin: squash, tennis and hockey. While claiming to have only played "social tennis", Steven said she was really very good. His mother had those Aboriginal qualities which enabled her to just keep on going no matter what.

As a consultant and business facilitator with wide experience, including time with an American stockbroking firm, Steven Bowditch has played a prominent part in Aboriginal advancement.

Steven Bowditch, speaking at Squash Australia Hall of Fame. Its website describes Steven as one of its 'legends' and prominent on the international scene. Adept at many sports, he is now a consultant and advisor to numerous Indigenous business ventures which he has helped establish. Courtesy the Bowditch family collection.

He was manager of the Regional Aboriginal Business Development, Department in the NSW government. He designed and distributed more than 1700 copies of the widely-used manual *A Guide to Developing Aboriginal Business*. Over the years he has initiated and run many business and cultural events. While based at Casino, NSW, from 1995–7 as Aboriginal Enterprise Development Officer, he helped 5000 Aboriginal individual and community clients with their ideas, facilitating the establishment of more than 30 businesses.

Steven told how the attitude of his father and millionaire Mick Paspalis had influenced his own attitude to money. He said his father had regarded rich people as "evil". As a youngster, Steven had been a paper boy in Fannie Bay delivering papers to the "richest and the poorest."

One of the battlers on his round had been Mrs Hilda Muir, one of the Stolen Generation, with "umpteen kids." She always gave him a big tip. The richest household Steven delivered papers to was that of millionaire Mick Paspalis. When he called there to collect the fortnight's paper money, he hoped that it was Mrs Paspalis or one of her daughters who paid the account because they would include a generous tip, especially at Christmas. However, if Mick settled the account he would slowly count out the exact amount. Sometimes there would be a few pence left from counting out the money, but Mick would smile, and put it back in his pocket.

These experiences, coupled with his father's attitude to the rich, shaped Steven's personal philosophy in his younger days. This attitude to money had limited his "wealth creation" potential, but shaped his sense of right. When he returned to Darwin after travelling for 20 years, he met Hilda Muir and they had an animated conversation, recalling old times. Hilda was still battling and Steven had been delighted to be able to give this woman who had tipped him handsomely when he was a paper boy some money to buy essentials.

In 2001, writing of the paper boy episode, Steven said Mick Paspalis had probably been trying to teach a small boy that money did not come easily—you would have to earn it. It had been a good lesson, "if your dad wasn't Jim Bowditch."

42. CLUMP, SLITHER, CLUMP-WHACK!

One unsuccessful campaign Bowditch fought was against the use of Quail Island, near Darwin, as an RAAF bombing range. Some people came to him seeking his help to stop the bombing. Reporter Les Wilson went to the island and filed a story. The island has a Dreamtime spring and is a turtle breeding ground. The campaign was a long one, but the federal government and the RAAF refused to budge. Bowditch revived the issue in an editorial once again mentioning the Dreamtime spring and its significance to Aborigines. The government and the RAAF were presented as heartless and slow to respond. Then came another unusual editorial headed: TURTLES ARE IN THE SOUP, in which he waxed whimsical and painted a heart-wrenching scene on Quail Island. Mr and Mrs Turtle, he wrote, would never hear the clump, slither, clump of baby turtle flippers. The editorial continued in similar vein, speaking of scrambled eggs, interrupted romances due to bombing and falling birthrates. It raised the possibility of turtles turning to drink, crawling about in bullet-proof vests and childless turtles stealing eggs from other nests.

Out at the RAAF base the editorial was treated like a kamikaze attack on the airport. On reading the paper, the RAAF chief, Group Captain Dixie Chapman, jumped into his chauffeur-driven car and went to the *NT News* office. There he confronted Bowditch in his office over the editorial. Chapman made it clear that he had read a lot of bullshit in his day, but the clump, slither, clump of turtle flippers took the prize. Both men laughed heartily. Bowditch reminded the bemused officer that turtles had mothers too.

Quail Island and its unfortunate turtles were responsible for Bowditch entering another combat zone. A southern journalist said it was not safe to go into the Victoria Hotel beer garden because drinkers there would fight at the drop of a hat. Jim scoffed at the report, and while drinking with Les Wilson at the Vic decided to carry out a survey to show it was not filled with punchy patrons. He went from table to table asking people, sometimes in an offensive way, if they wanted a fight. Most people knew him, and just laughed. Some told him to piss off. Others said they would oblige the following day. But there was a big Irishman who aggressively said he would like a fight because he had read the stories in the *News* about Quail Island and its turtles and they were a load of bullshit. The RAAF, he said, had to practise bombing to be ready for war. At this stage Wilson, who had been watching proceedings like a guardian angel and laughing at the responses Jim got, stepped in. He told the Irishman he had written the Quail Island stories and to come outside and try on somebody more his equal in weight and age. The Irishman was keen to take on Les, also known as "Thrasher" Wilson, and they went to the "bullring" at the back of the hotel. Thump! The Irishman turned turtle and bit the dust.

Despite the valiant efforts of Big Jim and Les Wilson the unfortunate turtles of Quail Island were bombed for many more years until a new range was established on the mainland.

Wilson kept a close eye on Bowditch in hotels and steered him out of many potentially dangerous situations which could have landed him in the cells. There was an occasion, however, when Wilson feared he, his editor and perhaps other people might be placed in the lockup due to a story. This involved a colourful Darwin identity, another Kiwi, Terry Alderton, a Works Department clerk who used to organise boxing matches which were a part of Darwin's way of life in the 1950s and 1960s. The fights were held at various venues, some in the open air, and attracted big crowds, including lawyers Ward and Lyons, who sat together.

Alderton visited the East Arm Leprosarium, where he took boxers to entertain the Aboriginal patients. While drinking with Wilson, Alderton mentioned that there was a sad situation at the leprosarium where a white girl had been admitted suffering from the disease. Sensing it was a good story, Wilson asked if he could go to East Arm with Alderton as his assistant. There was reluctance on both Bowditch's and Alderton's behalf, because the law prevented publication of details about people suffering from leprosy; breaches could result in a prison term. Apprehensive about what might happen, Wilson nevertheless went to East Arm and wrote a touching story about the girl for the Sydney *Sunday Mirror* which included a photograph of her with a nun.

Wilson warned the newspaper's editor, Zell Rabin, in advance about the NT law banning publication of any details about lepers. It had been decided to run the story and after its publication Wilson got calls from angry government officials in Darwin, including the head of the Welfare Department, Harry Giese. Recalling the episode, Wilson said he had packed his toothbrush and razor just in case he was arrested and lodged in the cells. However, the only time he was ushered into the cells during his time in Darwin was to see the editor.

It was no surprise then that Bowditch asked Wilson to extend his time in the Territory by a year. Apart from being a good reporter, Les was handy to have around as a bodyguard for the fragile editor, who got into frequent scrapes. Wilson and Alderton traded blows one night and the fight promoter came off second best.

43. THE WICKED
WHISPERS

When journalist Peter Blake was in Sydney on holiday from the *NT News* about the end of 1962 he met another journalist friend he knew from 1954 in Brisbane, James Arthur Ramsay, also known as "the Evil One". Ramsay was at a loose end at the time. A very good sportswriter, he was banned from future employment on any News Limited publication because something he had written had offended the brilliant Australian international golfer Peter Thomson who had a close association with News Limited which ran the Peter Thomson Golfing Clinic in its publications.

On hearing that Blake was about to return to Darwin to resume working on the *NT News*, Ramsay asked if there might be a job for him in the Territory. Blake, a good all-round journalist with a flair for Runyonesque description, friend of bookies (married a bookie's daughter), and a keen fisherman, rang Bowditch. While billing Ramsay as the best sports writer in Australia, Blake did admit he had one or two problems. One, of course, was that Ramsay was on News Limited's so-called "leper list". When told of this impediment, Bowditch was at first a little dubious. However, noted for helping strays, he relented and said the difficulty could easily be overcome by spelling his name differently in bylines; Darwin being a long way from Sydney, nobody would twig.

Instead of James Ramsay, he became Jim Ramsie. Blake and Ramsay, alias Ramsie, duly arrived in Darwin. The first time the byline Jim Ramsie appeared on a story in the *News* there was a response from Sydney. Is that THE James Ramsay? Bowditch parried such questions by saying it was obviously another person with a similar name. One caller would not be put off, and firmly ordered, "Sack him." Bowditch did not follow instructions. The questions continued from Sydney. Bowditch was asked to send a photograph of this Ramsie, but never got around to it. The bloodhounds kept sniffing. Though Ramsay often appeared grubby

Peter Blake colourful journalist
and sometime bookmaker.

with his shirt adorned with a few stains from drinking sessions and sartee juice, he was indeed "dynamite" as a sportswriter.

Darwin was a free and easy place in those days, but Ramsay was more so and a mite greasy as well. Well-dressed people attending a football club's presentation night complained when Ramsay, who had been drinking all day, turned up to cover the event for the *News* wearing a grubby singlet, no shirt, and a tie. A woman who did his washing stopped doing so because his clothes were always filthy. Ramsay put the ends of newsprint rolls to good use—he took them home and used the paper as bath towels. When it came to tropical hygiene, Ramsay had a special way of preventing the spread of germs from eating utensils: he put all the dirty dishes in the fridge to prevent the growth of bacteria. Of course, opening the fridge resulted in a cascade of contents.

Ramsay and Peter Blake attended a two-storey gambling joint one night. Blake lost all his money, but Ramsay, running hot, won so much the "crown and anchor school" had to close because he cleaned out the bank. Ramsay then went upstairs with his big bankroll and began playing sarlang, a card game, and lost the lot.

Finally, Don McLeod, the Brisbane-based *News* executive who had clashed with Bowditch in Mount Isa, came to Darwin and demanded to see Ramsay. Bowditch warned Ramsay about the looming face-to-face meeting. He advised Ramsay to keep his cool, be pleasant and something might be worked out to keep him on staff.

In a voice both angry and nervous, McLeod told Ramsay that Bowditch had stuck his neck out by employing him and could even have been fired himself for doing so. Ramsay's response clearly indicated he was not destined for a brilliant career in the diplomatic service. Instead of being contrite and demure, characteristics not usually attributed to him, Ramsay told McLeod the *News* could stick his job up "your black arse." In addition, he announced he was starting his own paper in town and would take some of the best *NT News* tradesmen with him and give the paper a run for its money. Needless to say, he ceased working for the paper forthwith, if not sooner.

The shocked executive returned to Brisbane and made uncalled-for derogatory remarks about Bowditch, saying he was living with a "black gin". An advertising man who knew Bowditch rang and told him what had been said. Bowditch immediately rang McLeod and told him what he had said was highly offensive, and that if he ever met him again he would punch the shit out of him. Furthermore, he said he refused to have any further dealings with him.

Ramsay tried to revive the old printing plant at the *Northern Standard* office. He did lure a linotype operator from the *News*, but the plant needed a lot of money spent on it, which Ramsay did not have. However, with the help of Peter Blake and others, he threw himself into production of a zany publication for the Waratah Football Sports Club. Called the *Waratah Whisper*, registered with the Indonesian Bureau of Cultural Affairs for transmission by smoke signal to Bagot, the ramshackle Aboriginal reserve near Darwin airport.

The *Waratah Whisper* had been in existence before Ramsay arrived in town and was originally a free roneoed publication, the name of which had been devised by public servant Geoff Loveday, who went on to become an adviser to the South Australian Labor Premier Mike Rann. In its original form, the magazine had contained items about sporting matches, social events and light-hearted notes.

Ramsay looked at the *Whisper* and said he could turn it into a real money spinner. His inspiration for the new-look publication was a satirical sheet called *Midnight Etaoin* (these being the first six

Jim Ramsay (or Ramsie) hams it up as editor of the *Waratah Whisper*.

letters on a linotype machine keyboard), produced annually for the journalists' ball in Melbourne. That publication sent up people in the Melbourne newspaper world. The Darwin counterpart produced by Ramsay contained pictures of nude women and sent up local identities, businessmen, publicans, politicians and sportsmen. It also had a racy astrology column and risqué jokes. Advertisements were also unusual: Alec Fong Lim, of the Vic Hotel, offered free grog to anyone who could drink 18 gallons of beer an hour. Somewhat foolishly Bowditch agreed to print the *Whisper* at the *News*.

An event took place in Darwin before the first edition which had a startling impact on the content of the new paper. Before an august gathering of Darwin's establishment, the new Supreme Court building had been unveiled. Adorning the facade of the building was a large stylised figure representing the scales of justice. Imagine the shock and laughter which ensued when the drape covering the figure opened to reveal a tea towel on one arm and an empty stubbie on the other. Somebody, believed to be the son of a prominent Darwin law officer, was said to have scaled down the front of the building during the night to turn the figure of justice into a waiter.

The collective brains at the *Waratah Whisper* came up with a better idea for the Supreme Court front—a nude in all her glory. The only trouble was that they had not reckoned on Jim Bowditch being coy about the female figure. Several hundred copies of the newspaper had already been run off when Bowditch saw the nude and ordered the press stopped. Bowditch instructed that the offending bits be covered up with a drawn in brassiere. "I hadn't realised I was such a prude," he said later. "The boys in the factory said the bras made her look sexier."

The head of Douglas Lockwood was superimposed on a woman's body and presented as the Sydney socialite Nola Dekyvere in the report of a social event at Government House.

Lockwood was furious when he saw the publication. Bowditch said Lockwood threatened to sue everybody connected with the *Whisper*. "I had to do a lot of hard talking with Lockwood and pointed out it was just a crazy, schoolboyish paper to raise money for a sporting club. Doug was still cranky with me months after the event." Bowditch was sent up in the same issue, there being a large photo of him with a fag hanging out of his mouth, under the heading: QUEEN HONOURS JIM—Peace in Our Time. It said Bowditch had been raised to the rank of Viscount and given a saloon bar to his OBE. Bowditch had also been nominated for the Nobel Peace Prize. Mentioned in the same honors list was Harry Giese of the Department of Welfare for his services to the growing boomerang trade.

The laughs ceased when the Catholic Bishop of Darwin, J.P. O'Loughlin, spoke out from the pulpit against the *Whisper*, saying it was evil and that no Catholic businessman should support the scurrilous new publication by advertising in its pages. On hearing of this disturbing condemnation of the publication, Bowditch called on the bishop, hoping to "educate" him on the issue. Apart

Queen honors Jim

PEACE IN OUR TIME

A Darwin man has been made a Viscount and two others elevated to the Earldom in the Mardi Gras Honours List released exclusively to Whisper this week.

Well-known journalist James Frederick Bowditch was raised to the rank of Viscount and given a saloon bar to his OBE.

The award was made in recognition of his outstanding efforts for peace in the community.

Viscount Bowditch of Fannie Bay as he will be known from now on has also been nominated for the Nobel Peace Prize award.

The two new earls on the honors list are Director of Welfare, Harry Christian Giese and Legislative Council member Harold "Tiger" Brennan.

Mr Brennan to be known as the Earl of Elsey received his distinction for his "unflagging efforts to aid broken down pensioners.

Mr Giese to be known henceforth as the Earl of Bagot received his award for services rendered to the growing boong hang trade.

Other awards:

- Sir Albert Albany KB, for his work in assisting the diversion of the Manton River to the Ord scheme. OBE
- John Edwards, radio announcer, for ...

VISCOUNT BOWDITCH OF FANNIE BAY.

Jim lampooned in the satirical paper the *Waratah Whisper* with marijuana joint painted in.

from that, Bowditch admitted he was worried that the bishop might urge an advertising boycott of the *NT News* for printing the offending publication. Bowditch believed that the stance taken by the bishop had been very narrow for an intelligent man. During their chat Bowditch told O'Loughlin how he had modestly ordered a brassiere drawn on the naked girl. What the bishop said in reply to this revelation by the prudish editor is, unfortunately, not known.

In light of the response to the first edition, Bowditch advised Ramsay to tone down subsequent issues. What a foolish thing to tell Ramsay. In the next edition there was an elegantly attired woman

Issue 2 of the *Waratah Whisper* doubled down on bare breasts instead of restricting the nudity as requested.

in a topless dress and an article on the front page that focused on breasts and said that the frank and fearless *NT News* had come over faint at the sight of a bare bosom. Somehow, the NT Administrator, Roger Nott, who had only one eye and was nicknamed Roger One Eye, was shown having a close squiz at the *Whisper*. There was also a poem, *A Man Who Was Not*, about the administrator which referred to him having made a big impression on Darwin when he said coats should not be worn at civic functions.

Administrator Nott and usually pith-helmeted member of the Legislative Council "Tiger" Brennan were also depicted wearing Beatle wigs. Another story was written by a special reporter named Argus Tuft. D.D. Smith, Lionel Rose and Harry Giese had their heads placed on cyclists in training. Smith also got special mention for his ability to read "wrongly prepared speeches and make them sound temporarily convincing." The *Whisper*'s radio guide included many programs dealing with the Christine Keeler-Profumo spy scandal in London. Don Whitington's regular Canberra feature was also lampooned.

Much to Bowditch's relief, Ramsay returned to Sydney and in 1964 teamed up with Terry Blake, brother of Peter Blake. Both were short of cash, but Ramsay insisted that they could make a pile of money producing a satirical paper like Darwin's *Waratah Whisper*. He proposed a similar sheet for the annual New Year celebrations in Sydney's King's Cross which saw the streets packed with revellers.

The hard-drinking Ramsay frequently upset Blake's wife when he was staying with them in their small flat. Unbeknown to Blake's wife, the two journos pawned her sewing machine and other possessions to finance the printing of the first *Kings Cross Whisper*. Also hocked without his knowledge was the scuba diving gear and speargun of Terry's youngest brother, Patrick.

The first edition proved a runaway success. They sat in the flat throwing piles of money in the air. Sensing they were onto something good, plans were made for a follow up edition but because of frequent jubilant parties and other excesses, they no longer had the money for the printer. Quick-thinking Ramsay suggested Blake go to the popular bohemian waterhole the Newcastle Hotel, in George Street, near Circular Quay, and put the bite on the publican, Jim Buckley. Blake knew Buckley and it happened that Xavier Herbert, author of the Territory novel, *Capricornia*, was down from Cairns and staying at the pub. Herbert enthusiastically supported the *Whisper* when shown a copy by Blake, who had written an article about Xavier a few years previously. As Herbert had been keen to "stick it up the establishment", he urged Buckley to advance 250 pounds for the second edition, which he did, the money to be repaid within 10 days of publication. The print run of 25,000 sold out so quickly there was a reprint of 20, 000 and leftovers from the first edition were also snapped up. They were sitting on a goldmine.

A growing army of colourful sellers flogged the *Whisper* in streets all over Sydney at two shillings a copy. (At the time the *Sydney Morning Herald* sold for threepence). Compared with some of their motley team of 200 sellers, one of whom proved to be a Nazi and another an undertaker, Blake and Ramsay were like a pair of Mormons—almost. Ramsay and Blake disliked landlords with a passion. Blake, under the name of Argus Tuft, wrote a series in the

Whisper on how to dud landlords. At times he and Ramsay poked pieces of fish and prawns under the carpets of seedy flats in which they lived. Blake even claimed to have hidden a dead cat in a dive owned by a slum landlord.

As the money started to roll in and the *Whisper* print runs rocketed up to 250,000, Blake and Ramsay changed their lifestyle. With his new wealth, Ramsay took up residence in a penthouse overlooking Rushcutter's Bay. Servicemen in Vietnam sent requests for copies of the *Kings Cross Whisper* and patriotic Blake and Ramsay wrote to Defence Minister Malcolm Fraser offering free copies if the government could supply transport. The department wrote back and said there was no room on transport planes to Vietnam. However, Ramsay discovered months later that the reason there was no spare cargo space in the planes was that it was filled with back copies of the *Australian Women's Weekly*. There can be little doubt the troops being shot at in Vietnam would have appreciated the *Whisper* more than the *Women's Weekly*.

On the bravery front, Ramsay regarded discretion the better part of valour. After the *Whisper* sent up a raucous Kings Cross nightspot, he noticed a well-built bouncer from that establishment coming in the front door. Ramsay jumped to his feet and disappeared out the back entrance, fearing the hulk wanted to hammer somebody. Instead, the man just wanted to become another *Whisper* vendor as he had been told it was an easy way to make money.

When the *Whisper* was based in Oxford Street, Darlinghurst, it was a hive of activity. On the ground floor was the Orgy Shop, part of the *Whisper*'s other enterprise: a hugely profitable chain which sold sex aids. A jovial Maori, known as Maori Barry, served on the counter. Barry was full of fun. To get upstairs to the Whisper, you first had to walk past Maori Barry in the sex shop. Journalists and others who came to the building with copy for the Whisper usually received a friendly greeting from him. He would invariably ask them, mock surprise in his voice, if they had already worn out those sex appliances they had bought the week before. People standing about in the shop would leer.

There was a nearby cake shop which found that its business boomed when the Orgy Shop opened. This was attributed to the fact that a lot of people too shy to walk straight into the Orgy Shop, first bought a pie or a cake to justify being in the area. Strategically located nearby was a pub, the Beauchamp, the name Australianised to Beecham's (as in the pills), where many journalists gathered.

The frenetic lifestyle and the pressures of the *Whisper* expansion eventually got at Ramsay and Blake. Both deciding on the same day to get out before they were carted off in straitjackets. So, in an unusual commercial winner-take-all settlement, they tossed a coin. Blake won and the hydra-headed monster was his. Before he headed overseas, Ramsay cleaned out his penthouse and in the wardrobe found 61 shirts and two sacks filled with two-shilling pieces, the proceeds of *Whisper* sales. He went to Hong Kong, where he worked on the *Star*, which over the years employed a gaggle of Australian reporters including Peter Blake, Steve Dunleavy, Roger East and Dennis Booth, the latter being the sports and racing editor. After working in London, Ramsay returned to Australia and worked on the *Sydney Sun*. He suffered a stroke and was taken to the Journalists' Club in a wheelchair, unable to speak. When he died in 1997 at the age of 67, he was described as one of the great larrikin journalists of modern Australia.

Terry Blake was smart enough to channel some of his *Whisper* proceeds into original Australian paintings which covered many of the walls in his Coogee house. While strolling through an Adelaide market in the 1980s, I happened to see Terry Blake, who was in town on an unusual mission, selling the last of the Orgy Shops. Blake colourfully explained that the sale of sex shops was always a cash transaction and on receipt of payment one dashed to the bank with the money before somebody sprang out of an alley and relieved you of the dough. He also said it was a strange commentary on Adelaide, the city of churches, that it had more sex shops than any other capital city in Australia.

In 1988, Terry Blake published *Kings Cross Whisper: The Way It Was*, a hilarious account of the golden days of the publication.

Cover of Terry Blake's book about the *Kings Cross Whisper* phenomenon.

Tragically, Blake received fatal head injuries outside a King's Cross establishment.

Another *Whisper*, the *Fannie Bay Whisper*, was produced in Darwin especially for the Beer Can Regatta in the 1970s and old nude photos from the *Kings Cross Whisper* were used to illustrate it. The zany paper boasted a church reporter with the familiar name of Argus Tuft. Members of a football club were given the job of selling the paper to the huge crowd, but were too shy to be seen pushing a paper featuring naked women, so used the bundles as seats to sit on. Consequently, only a small number of them sold at the beach. However, the remainder sold out at Cashman's Darwin Newsagency.

Then in 1977 a similar publication, *Troppo*, surfaced in Darwin and once again old nude photographs from the *Kings Cross Whisper* graced its pages. As an indication that all naked gals apparently look alike or that pulsating hormones impair the eyesight of men, several eager young bucks in Darwin said they personally knew some of the girls in *Troppo* and were amazed that the publication could get locals to pose naked.

At that stage some of the ladies were nearly grannies and most, if not all, had been photographed in Sydney. An equal opportunity publication, *Troppo* included a series of photographs of male streakers who circumnavigated the Mitchell Street police headquarters in Darwin one night. The streakers included journalists and photographers, some of them later prominent in Darwin and overseas.

To this very day there is a batch of old *Kings Cross Whisper* nude photographs in Darwin and the possibility of using them again in a madcap publication has been discussed several times.

44. RSL WARS

The Administrator noticed a scar on Bowditch's leg. "Is that scar from your war service?" asked Roger Nott. The reply: "No, that's a scar I got kicking in the RSL door." It is fair to say that Bowditch and some of the RSL hierarchy were not the best of friends. He often referred to Colonel Blimp types and RSL club "bullshit". Despite this, Betty Bowditch had fond memories of the old RSL premises which disappeared under a Paspalis multi-storey edifice. In print, Bowditch criticised RSL leaders who backed Immigration Minister Downer senior during the Stayput Malays case. On Anzac Day 1964, Bowditch took part in celebrations and, becoming tired and emotional, flaked out on a table in the RSL. What happened is not absolutely clear. One explanation was that he had become drunk and obnoxious and was asked to leave as it was nearly closing time. He left, but went around the back and kicked in the back door which had a glass panel, badly cutting his leg.

Another version has it that Bowditch passed out at a table and some RSL officials passed derogatory remarks about the slumbering editor. One went over, shook him and told him to get home. Bowditch apparently took umbrage at being told to hit the track and words were exchanged. When he got to the bottom of the stairs, the door was closed behind him so he could not get back in. He then kicked in the glass panels.

After the event Bowditch went to the nearby Workers' Club. Brian Manning was the club's manager at the time and took Bowditch into his office and sat him down. Blood was running down his leg from cuts and he was in a highly agitated state. He berated himself for what he had done at the RSL. Then he admonished himself for the people he had killed during the war. In particular, he recalled with horror how he had killed and mutilated the enemy soldier on Tarakan. At times he cried. Eventually, he fell asleep in the chair and Manning later took him home. Manning pointed out that many people over the years who "went to the rescue" of Bowditch, to prevent him from being arrested or getting into a fight, then drove him home out of harm's way, sometimes faced the wrath of Betty. She, not knowing the circumstances, but furious with Jim for drinking, would sometimes think the innocent rescuer had been in a session with him. The RSL fracas prompted the *Waratah Whisper* story mentioned earlier about Viscount Bowditch and: PEACE IN OUR TIME.

In what can only be described as an unusual, but typical Darwin event, Bowditch was involved in an altercation with three men at the RSL. He left, went to the Workers' Club and enlisted the aid of waterfront vigilance officer, Bill Donnelly. They returned to the RSL and fought the three men. Donnelly, it will be recalled, had been the man responsible for banning the delivery of newsprint across the Darwin wharf when Bowditch refused to drop a story about a waterside worker convicted of pilfering. Yet here he was fighting side by side with the editor in the RSL. The next meeting of the RSL barred him from the club.

One year, concerned that his wild recent behaviour could have adverse consequences for his job, he reluctantly took part in the Anzac Day march wearing his Distinguished Conduct Medal. After the march he got involved in a two-up game which was held in a drained pond which had been donated to Darwin by the Italian community. During the day he remembered drinking with lawyer "Tiger" Lyons, and somehow lost his DCM.

At the *News* office, Bowditch told of the disastrous day and the loss of his DCM. He said that he could not put a classified ad in the paper under LOST asking any person finding a Distinguished Conduct Medal to please return it to the editor of the *NT News*. People would say Bowditch was so drunk he lost his medal. If it had been anybody else who had lost the medal, a report would have been run to help its recovery. The medal never surfaced although many years later a replacement was obtained.

Bowditch was involved in a strange but sad episode involving a drifter who came to Darwin and claimed to be one of Australia's most decorated soldiers. In hotels he spoke endlessly about the war. Inevitably, he met Bowditch and asked him about his war experiences. When Bowditch mentioned the Z Special Unit, the man began rattling off names of men who had served with the commandos. The man was short of money, out of work and had no permanent place of abode. Bowditch took him home from time to time and gave him money. To try to help the man, Bowditch handed him over to a reporter who ran with the line that one of Australia's most decorated soldiers was roughing it in Darwin. It was revealed that the man had never seen active service; his war talk had been fantasy.

When told this, Bowditch said he had suspected all along that there was something wrong with the man's claims. Asked why he had not warned the reporter who had written the story, he said the "poor little guy" had been a "bit bent" and had not hurt anybody, having only "bullshitted" to "RSL types".

Bowditch's open stand against involvement in the Vietnam War brought him into further conflict with RSL members and prompted further ASIO entries. In November 1966 he was reported taking part in a Darwin Vietnam Action Committee display and all-night vigil in the city. Local people "of interest" had included Curly Nixon (NAWU organiser), peace activist Gill Chalmers of the *News*, Jim Bowditch and Bill Opie, manager of the Darwin

Workers' Club. The demonstration, involving about 30 people, was watched by six uniformed police, eight plain-clothes police, two Special Branch officers and two Commonwealth Police officers.

According to the ASIO report, Bowditch, "former C.P.A. member", was in a semi- intoxicated condition and argued fiercely with two men who opposed the demonstration.

When Darwin activist Robert Wesley-Smith began to organise the 1970 Vietnam Moratorium March in Darwin he was strongly criticized by some in the community. He wanted Darwin City Council permission to have tables in Smith Street and Raintree Park at which moratorium pamphlets would be handed out and badges sold. The application was rejected by a council committee and Bowditch sprang to his defence. In an editorial headed: ALDERMEN AS CENSORS, Bowditch said the council, by allowing its committee to refuse the application by Wesley-Smith, had damaged Darwin's image as Australia's most tolerant city. The action was a denial of his democratic rights. A second editorial followed and there was an associated report in which the views of all councillors were expressed, the majority shown to support the application. Alderman Ken Slide, against the application, received special attention. With the name of Slide he not unexpectedly

A slightly dishevelled Jim, sporting a few cuts from a fight at his last RSL visit.

attracted the nickname "Slippery". Wesley-Smith eventually received permission to set up his tables.

Bowditch wrote an Anzac Day editorial saying that despite feelings about Australia's involvement in the Vietnam War, the sacrifices of WWI should not be forgotten. He then took part in the Vietnam Moratorium march organised by Wesley-Smith. It was said that on a population basis, more Darwin people marched against the Vietnam War than any other city in Australia. In 1972 the RSL again saw fit to bar Bowditch from its premises.

Near the end of his life, Jim eagerly went back to the RSL club several times. However, the Anzac Day before his death, Bowditch and another member were asked to leave the RSL because they were considered too drunk to serve. They left and caught a taxi to another RSL club, where Bowditch punched his drinking partner. The man had been quarrelling with the club manager and a witness said Bowditch delivered a "classic punch" which had been "surprisingly good for an old man."

45. THE GURINDJI BATTLE

Many people credited Bowditch with the ultimate success of the battle by the Gurindji to win back their tribal land at Wave Hill, a milestone in the history of Aboriginal land rights.

One of the major players in the campaign, author Frank Hardy, had many dealings with Bowditch during the struggle. Going through a tough time in his life and following the suicide of a close friend, Hardy accepted an invitation from filmmaker Cecil Holmes in 1966 to come to Darwin and forget his troubles. After hitchhiking to Darwin, Hardy became increasingly involved with the Gurindji cause. At times he would go home with Bowditch, puffing on a pipe, and drawing cartoons for the children.

Hardy had served in the Territory during WWII and while based at Mataranka, south of Darwin, editing the camp paper, *Troppo Tribune*, the contents of which he mainly provided, including the artwork. Hardy was an inveterate punter always trying to make quick money on the nags to improve his precarious financial situation. A regular Darwin watering hole for Hardy was the Workers' Club, where activist Brian Manning, involved with Bowditch in the Stayput Malays affair, was the manager for a time. Other people Hardy mixed with in Darwin were communist watersider Jack and Esther Meaney, who had hidden the Stayput Malays. Jack Meaney had a colourful way of expressing things, and said he first met Hardy during the war at Mataranka when Frank was "making a nuisance of himself by trying to organise the camp."

A secret report dated 25/9/66, headed: CPA INTEREST IN ABORIGINALS (NT), covered a social evening under the dual sponsorship of the NT Council for Aboriginal Rights and the Darwin Branch of the CPA. The idea of the gathering, it said, was to foster good relations with the Aborigines, who were invited to have a few beers and a talk, but no mention to be made of politics. Those attending the function included Jim Bowditch, Frank Hardy, Bill Donnelly, Jo Cunningham, Brian Manning, George and Moira Gibbs, Dexter Daniels, Davis Daniels and 10 other unidentified Aborigines. ASIO noted the evening finished about midnight, and "everyone was pretty full." During a later visit to Darwin, Hardy happened to meet Jack Meaney at the Adelaide River Show. The author said he needed somewhere quiet to write a book. Meaney took him home to Milton Springs where the Malays had been hidden. While staying with the Meaneys Hardy worked on the book he wrote about the Gurindji struggle, *The Unlucky Australians*.

Young John Meaney remembered the author pounding out the book on a typewriter and puffing away on his pipe filled with Plum tobacco.

In that book Hardy paid tribute to the part played by Bowditch in the Wave Hill struggle. He described Bowditch as the most colourful character in a city where there were no human beings, only characters. His friend Jim Bowditch, he said, was the last of the fighting editors. Hardy might also have written several of his "Billy Borker" stories at Milton Springs. Some early Billy

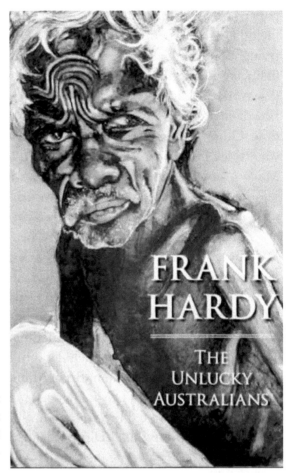

Cover of Frank
Hardy's book about
the Gurindji's fight
for Land Rights.

Borker yarns appeared in the *NT News* and the *Territorian* thanks to
Bowditch's patronage. The yarns were later turned into a popular
ABC TV series.

While Hardy was in the Territory in 1967 in connection with
the Gurindji cause, he became involved in an unusual event—the
Australian Yarn Spinning Championship, an *NT News* promotion.
He was pitted against a colourful local identity, the much tattooed
Tall Tale Tex Tyrell, who had won a Talkathon in Alice Springs
back in 1954, about which Keith Willey had written a lively account.
There were several photographs of Frank, he being billed as "Billy
Borker" Hardy. Hardy boasted a "secret weapon" his pipe, which
he jabbed to emphasise a point. Judges included Cecil Holmes and
Doug Lockwood.

The event was staged in the Hotel Darwin and eventually won by Hardy when Tyrell collapsed after more than three hours of earbashing. A subsequent Swan Brewery advertisement in the *NT News* carried drawings of Hardy and Tyrell which were probably done by Frank. A long article by Hardy said he had become involved in the contest because Bowditch and others in a pub had urged him to enter.

The involvement of "communists" in NT Aboriginal affairs in 1967 and 1968 prompted further ASIO reports. Under the heading: MOVEMENT OF MEMBERS OF THE COMMUNIST PARTY OF AUSTRALIA, it was noted that Harvey Thomas and Frank Bishop had arrived in Darwin by car on 3 August 1967. Thomas was said to be gathering material on the meat and mining industries and Aborigines; Bishop had brought "new party cards for distribution among Darwin members." An agent commented that Thomas wanted to meet Dick Ward, Jim Bowditch, Cecil Holmes, Paddy Carroll and Harry Giese, the NT Director of Welfare.

The case officer's comment in the report said Thomas had asked Harold "Tiger" Brennan, MLA for Victoria River, for information on American exploitation in the NT cattle industry, to which he had replied there was none.

ASIO took an interest in Hardy's book before it was published. A 1968 ASIO secret report noted Hardy had been in Darwin on 26 December 1967 and had gone to Wave Hill. The reason for the visit, it said, was for Hardy to put the "finishing touches" to his book, *The Unlucky Australians*. It continued: "Hardy has shown proofs of the book to everyone who is mentioned in it. The book should have been published in August but has been held up because the publishers are very worried about libel actions. Jim (James Frederick) Bowditch, who is a friend of Hardy's, has read the proofs and thinks that this book may not be published, because of the numerous libellous statements."

The Gurindji saga was precipitated by Aboriginal and a few Whites' indignation at the failure to gain an award giving Aboriginal stockmen equal pay. A poorly prepared North

Australian Workers' Union application for equal pay for Aboriginal stockmen in which not one Aborigine was called to make a submission resulted in Commissioner Moore saying the Aborigines would have to wait for three years before they could get a measure of pay justice.

Graziers indicated they would drive Aborigines off their stations, which they did. Angry activists—black and white— goaded the NAWU into taking protest action and called a strike of Aboriginal stockmen at Newcastle Waters. Manning acknowledged the owner of Newcastle Waters, Roy Edwards, was a reasonable person, but the station was ideal for the NAWU to supply strikers, being next to the highway. One of the stockmen at Newcastle Waters was Captain Major, another articulate Gurindji, who would not only contribute to the Wave Hill victory but later, with Bowditch, confront a large meeting of white residents in Katherine who claimed they were being discriminated against by the Whitlam Government in favour of Aborigines.

Then in August 1966, 22 Gurindji stockmen employed on Wave Hill, led by Vincent Lingiari, went on strike for better pay and conditions. The strikers set up a camp in the bed of the Victoria River near the Wave Hill Welfare settlement. Later they moved to Daguragu (Wattie Creek) and set up a more permanent camp. Daguragu was sacred land, the centre of Gurindji Dreaming, and a short distance from Seal Gorge, where the bones of their ancestors were kept.

News of the strike was telegrammed to Darwin and relayed to Bowditch. About that time, an ASIO secret "Intercept Report" under the heading "Communist Party of Australia Interest in Aborigines", for the period 26–29 August, contained some cryptic information. It said Frank Hardy had contacted communist Laurie Aarons. During the conversation Hardy said a good article had appeared in the *Mirror* and there had been quite a long article in the *Sun*, probably referring to the strike of native stockmen in the NT. A paragraph in the report said Hardy had spoken to one of his native friends who had said "a match is in the spinifex", a highly original way to put it. Hardy, according to the intercept summary, had said he had been speaking to **BADDICH** (phonetic), probably Bowditch, a Darwin journalist, and that there would also be a big coverage in the *Australian* next day.

In another conversation with Aarons, Hardy had indicated he might consider going up, presumably to Darwin. Hardy did visit Darwin and stayed with the filmmaker Cecil Holmes and his wife, Sandra. Bowditch and Hardy drove to Wave Hill and got a hostile reception from whites on the Vestey-owned station. Each man took up the Gurindji cause in their own way while keeping in close contact. Bowditch covered the event in the *News* and made sure it was kept alive in the southern media.

Vincent Lingiari listened closely to advice about running the camp and issued firm instructions. A reporter from the *NT News*, Peter Murphy, flew from Darwin to the Wave Hill airstrip in a plane chartered by the newspaper with Frank Hardy, NAWU Aboriginal organiser Dexter Daniels and others. On arrival, they got a hot reception. They were firmly told they had five minutes to get off

Activist and Gurindji supporter, Robert Wesley-Smith (right) and another supporter with Brian Manning's old truck which took supplies to the striking stockmen and their families. Robert Wesley-Smith collection.

the cattle property by a man who made a show of a firearm and a whip. Ignoring the threats the party spent three days at Wattie Creek during which a supply truck driven by Manning arrived from Darwin.

Murphy was impressed by the strict control that Lingiari had over the camp dwellers who literally tore at boxes on the truck in search of tobacco, they having been without cigarettes for several weeks. Lingiari firmly told them they could not touch tobacco until they cleaned up every bit of paper from around the truck. Murphy went on to become a media adviser to several Chief Ministers of the Northern Territory. In April 1967, the Gurindji petitioned the Governor-General, Lord Casey, seeking to regain tenure of their tribal land in the Wave Hill-Limbunya area. The petition carried the thumb prints of Vincent Lingiari, Pincher Manguari, Gerry Ngalgardji and Long-John Kitgnaari. It explained the document had been transcribed, witnessed and transmitted by Frank Hardy and J.W. Jeffrey, a Welfare Department officer sympathetic to the Gurindji cause, because the Gurindji had never had the opportunity to learn English.

It read:

We, the leaders of the Gurindji people, write to you about our earnest desire to regain tenure of our tribal lands in the Wave Hill-Limbunya area of the Northern Territory, of which we were dispossessed in time past, and for which we received no recompense.

Our people have lived here from time immemorial and our culture, myths, dreaming and sacred places have evolved in this land. Many of our forefathers were killed in the early days while trying to retain it. Therefore we feel that morally the land is ours and should be returned to us. Our very name Aboriginal acknowledges our prior claim. We have never ceased to say among ourselves that Vesteys should go away and leave us to our land.

In the attached map, we have marked out the boundaries of the sacred places of our dreaming, bordering the Victoria River from Wave Hill Police Station to Hooker

Creek, Inverway, Limbunya, Seal Gorge, etc. We have begun to build our own new homestead on the banks of beautiful Wattie Creek in the Seal Yard area, where there is permanent water. This is the main place of our dreaming only a few miles from Seal Gorge where we have kept the bones of our martyrs all these years since white men killed many of our people. On the walls of the sacred caves where their bones are kept are the paintings of the totems of our tribe.

We have already occupied a small area at Seal Yard under Miners' Rights held by three of our tribesmen. We will continue to build our new home there (marked on the map with a cross), then buy some working horses with which we will trap and capture wild unbranded horses and cattle. These we will use to build up a cattle station within the borders of this ancient Gurindji land. And we are searching the area for valuable rocks which we hope to sell to help feed our people. We will ask the N.T. Welfare Department for help with motor for pump, seeds for garden, tables, chairs, and others things as well. Later on we will build a road and an airstrip and maybe a school. Meanwhile, most of our people will continue to live in the camp we have built at the Wave Hill Welfare Centre 12 miles away and the children continue to go to school there.

We beg of you to hear our voices asking that the land marked on the map be returned to the Gurindji people. It is about 500 square miles in area but this is only a very small fraction of the land leased by Vesteys in these parts. We are prepared to pay for our land the same annual rental the Vesteys now pay. If the question of compensation arises, we feel that we have already paid enough during 50 years or more, during which time we and our fathers worked for no wages at all much of the time and for a mere pittance in recent years.

If you can grant this wish for which we humbly ask, we would show the rest of Australia and the whole world that we are capable of working and planning our own destiny as free citizens. Much has been said about our refusal to accept responsibility in the past, but who would show initiative working for starvation wages, under impossible conditions, without education for strangers in their land? But we are ready to show initiative now. We have already begun. We know how to work cattle better than any white man and we know and love this land of ours.

If our tribal lands are returned to us, we want them, not as another "Aboriginal Reserve", but as a leasehold to be run cooperatively as a mining lease and cattle station by the Gurindji Tribe. All practical work will be done by us, except such work as book-keeping, for which we would employ white men of good faith, until such time as our own people are sufficiently educated to take over. We will also accept the condition that if we do not succeed within a reasonable time, our land should go back to the Government. (In August last year, we walked away from the Wave Hill Cattle station. It was said that we did this because wages were very poor [only six dollars per week], living conditions fit only for dogs, and rations consisting mainly of salt beef and bread. True enough. But we walked away for other reasons as well. To protect our women and our tribe, to try to stand on our own feet. We will never go back there.) Some of our young men are working now at Camfield and Montejinnie Cattle Stations for proper wages. However, we will ask them to come back to our own Gurindji Homestead when everything is ready.

In his reply, Casey said the Vestey lease did not expire until 2004. The Gurindji battle went as far as England, where there were demonstrations outside the Vestey headquarters in London. Several television documentaries were made about the case, including one shot by a British team with which Hardy collaborated. Robert Tudawali also supported the Gurindji and took part in the campaign. He was about to go to Wave Hill on a supply truck run from Darwin when it was discovered he was suffering from TB and Captain Major went in his place. Tudawali died a terrible death in July 1967 at the age of 38. In a deathbed statement to police he claimed that he had been drinking a flagon of wine with others near Bagot in Darwin when a row broke out over his 12-year-old daughter. He had been knocked to the ground and grass deliberately lit to burn him. He died of burns to the chest, back and arms.

In a move to ease the Wattie Creek situation which was embarrassing the government and Vesteys, the government in July 1968 said it would build a township on Crown land at the Wave Hill centre in an attempt to meet the needs of the Gurindji and other Aborigines in the district. Most of the strikers remained at Daguragu despite the lack of facilities. Vesteys gave the government an undertaking that the Aborigines at Daguragu would not be disturbed. The Gurindji then began fencing and building on the land. Support flowed in from many sources. Brian Manning said the watersiders of Australia donated $17,000 through a levy, the money to be used by the Gurindji for fencing. About 1970, Darwin activist, agronomist Robert Wesley-Smith, met Bowditch and came under his influence. Bowditch invited Wesley-Smith to drop into the office at the end of the day for a drink and a talk with him and other staff members. Commonly called Wes, he did not drink at the time, but enjoyed the discussions.

Bowditch provided support for Wesley-Smith's campaigns and gave him editorial backing on various issues. Wes and his then wife Jan, both became involved with the Gurindji after reading Hardy's book. ASIO even checked to see that Wesley-Smith was absent from Darwin in Adelaide for two weeks to be married. Wesley-Smith, George and Moira Gibbs were in a group which formed the Murramulla-Gurindji Cattle Company, which after three months was passed over to the control of the Gurindji.

The Gibbs were another example of activists mindlessly condemned by some for their involvement in union work and other issues, closely watched by ASIO. Some of the offspring of Darwin activists interviewed in connection with this book said they had often suffered at school, "copped it" being one expression, due to their parents' activities.

It was not only unionists who were subjected to mindless scorn. Kim Lockwood related an episode at school in Darwin, when he was about 10, at which a pupil came up and told him, "Your dad's a commo." Not knowing what a "commo" was, Kim went home and told his father, who reacted angrily. He told Kim to inform the boy that if he ever repeated that statement he would knock his block off.

When George Gibbs died in 1969, Cec Holmes delivered the eulogy at the funeral service and Sandra performed an electrifying rendition of the stirring union song *Ballad of Joe Hill*. There was an editorial in the *NT News* paying tribute to Gibbs headed: DEATH OF A BATTLER. The communist newspaper *Tribune* said Gibbs had been involved in the movement for Aboriginal rights since the 1950s and in recent times had been closely associated with the struggle of the Gurindji at Wattie Creek.

He had come to the NT in the 1930s and had been a founder member of the Workers' Club. Mrs Gibbs came from a family of union activists, and had been involved in the Peace Council with Esther Meaney. As secretary of the waterside section of the NAWU, Brian Manning inaugurated a $100 annual education bursary to be awarded to an Aboriginal student as a memorial to George Gibbs's dedication to the Aboriginal cause. There being no applicants, the money each year was put towards establishment of the George Gibbs Memorial Collection at the Mitchell Library, Sydney, the repository of all the NT Council for Aboriginal Rights material, his diaries and union memorabilia from the early days. Mrs Gibbs died of cancer in Sydney.

After trips to see the Gurindji, Wes would report back to Bowditch and write letters to the editor. Bowditch ran reports in the paper quoting Wes, described as a human rights activist. These reports kept the Gurindji cause alive and got some improvements in services for Aborigines. In addition, it was educating the white community about the issues. The Gurindji would come to Darwin and at times "a whole mob" travelling on the Wattie Creek truck would go to the *NT News* and talk with Bowditch. One of them was Mick Rangiari, known as "Hoppy Mick" because his pelvis was broken in a fall from a frightened horse. After the accident he had spent several painful weeks lying on a veranda without medical treatment.

Rangiari drove a battered vehicle to Darwin and asked Bowditch to help the Gurindji. There is a suggestion that on that occasion Bowditch bought a complete set of new tyres for Rangiari as the ones on the truck were badly worn.

Wave Hill walk-off leader, Vincent Lingiari (seated) with stockman Victor Vincent and his wife Polly, plus children. Courtesy Rob Wesley-Smith.

Unionist, activist, Communist, Brian Manning was a central figure in some of Jim's most notorious crusades while following many of his own causes. Seen here (left) in 1977 with Sally Wilkins of the *Age* and Rob Wesley-Smith monitoring Radio Maubere, the signal from the East Timorese resistance to supporters in Darwin. The radio operators were constantly being harassed by Australian government officials. Photo: by Cecil Holmes, Rob Wesley-Smith collection.

Wes often returned from trips to Wave Hill with some of the Gurindji and dropped them off at places like Kulaluk and Bagot in Darwin. On one trip Vincent Lingiari came up with his wife and she saw the sea for the first time. Vincent and his wife stayed at Wes's place several times. On one visit they spent several days at Bagot and Wes was ordered off the site when he was seen talking to them on the lawn inside the front gate.

Wes was later commissioned by the Gurindji to buy cattle for them twice and was able to prevail on the government to provide a truck so he could deliver the stock. The government insisted that the Gurindji must have an approved cattle expert to guide them, despite the fact that they said Wes was their adviser. During the long campaign for the Gurindji, Hardy and Carroll had a falling out; Bowditch arranged a reconciliation. At a packed performance in Darwin by American country singer Johnny Cash, Sandra Holmes sang the protest song *Gurindji Blues* written by Ted Egan, later Administrator of the NT, from the floor.

On 30 March 1971 under the heading: ABORIGINAL AFFAIRS IN THE NORTHERN TERRRITORY, ASIO's NT regional director sent headquarters a confidential report about the involvement of NAWU Aboriginal organiser Dexter Daniels in relation to fund-raising on behalf of the Roper River Land Rights Fund. He wrote that Roper River was not readily accessible from Darwin and ASIO needed to rely on [blacked out] to get information on the activities of those of security interest in this area.

Later in the year ASIO said *NT News* employees "taking the *Tribune*" included Bowditch and journalists Peter Cooke, John Loizou and John Meeking, the political roundsman. Cooke was described as being far left in his views, but as yet unwilling to join an "old left" political group such as the CPA.

In 1972, Lord Vestey wrote to Prime Minister Billy McMahon offering to surrender some areas of the Vestey lease to Aborigines. Fifty-three square miles of Wave Hill was given over enabling the Wave Hill centre and Daguragu to be linked by vacant Crown land. When the Whitlam Government came into power the Gurindji leaders were asked to identify their traditional land as well as extra land they would need to make a cattle project.

Then in a symbolic act at Wave Hill on 16 August 1975, Prime Minister Gough Whitlam poured soil into the hand of Gurindji leader Vincent Lingiari to mark the handing over of a 1250 square mile (3200 square km) pastoral lease to Aboriginal control. Mr Whitlam said Australians had much to do to redress the injustice and oppression that had long been the lot of black Australians. The act of restoration, he promised, would not stand alone.

The Minister for Aboriginal Affairs, Les Johnson, said the hand-over of the land to the Gurindji would go down in Australian history as one of the most significant milestones in the 200 years since the white man first came to Australia and began taking the land on which the whole life and culture of the Aborigines depended. Johnson told the Gurindji their great determination and support from many white Australians, the Australian Government and the co-operation of Lord Vestey and his companies, had resulted in them receiving the leasehold title of the land they fought to retain. At the Wave Hill ceremony a representative of Lord Vestey promised 400 head of cattle to the Gurindji and the Department of Aboriginal Affairs set aside $315,000 to help the Gurindi set up their cattle station.

In 2002 Brian Manning presented the Vincent Lingiari Memorial Lecture in Darwin using about 60 of his photos and audio material to illustrate the powerful speech. Lingiari's son, Victor, was present and had given permission for photographs of his father to be shown. Using the latest technology in the auditorium, Manning began with Vincent explaining in his own language, then translated into English, the Gurindji claim to the land. Tears ran down the face of Victor Lingiarai when he heard his father speak. Starting the text, Manning cued in his extensive visuals with other individuals and events. At the end, Paul Kelly's song *From Little Things Big Things Grow* was played with a close-up head shot of Lingiari taken by Manning. During the song, Manning turned up the house lights, nervously waiting for a response. When the song finished, Manning was roundly congratulated. An Aboriginal girl in her twenties told

Manning, "Now I finally understand what the Gurindji strike had to do with land rights."

46. THE LARRY BOY MANHUNT

On 21 September 1968, Aboriginal Larry Boy, tribal name Janba, found his wife, Marjorie, in bed with a white stockman, David Jackson, 21, at Elsey Station, 220 miles (340 km) from Darwin. He took to them with a tomahawk, killing his wife and hacking through the ribs of her lover. After the attack he fled into the surrounding country, which consisted of bush, swamp and sandstone outcrops. A massive manhunt, which included black trackers, dogs, police, many civilians and helicopters was mounted with Constable "Bluey" Harvey in charge. The officer had been stationed at Wave Hill at the time of the Gurindji walk-off and Bowditch knew him well.

Bowditch visited the surviving stockman in hospital. The man told him he could not understand why he had been attacked as sleeping with Aboriginal women was going on all the time. The case brought to light the common practice of white stockmen raping or demanding the sexual favours of Aboriginal women.

Bowditch and a photographer went to the search area to report on the manhunt; a white man shouted, "Here's that boong lover—I'll show you how we deal with black bastards when we catch them!" Bowditch spent five days in the area. The hunt went on for 40 days. On the last day, Constable Harvey was walking by a limestone cliff when he noticed a small cave with cobwebs across the entrance. Because of this, he at first felt that the fugitive could not be inside as he would have brushed the webs aside. However, he noticed the cobwebs were strung like a gate on thin sticks. The fugitive had draped the webs across the entrance to give the impression that nobody could be inside. It was a great piece of detective work for Harvey to notice the deception.

The tenacious constable then crawled into the small recess filled with foul air and found the wanted man flat on his back, his mouth against a small hole through which he was breathing. Harvey, exhausted and suffering from influenza, dragged the man out.

At the trial, Janba was represented by Dick Ward; there were some peculiar aspects of the case, one being the claim that it led to Ward being "sung to death" for somehow, inadvertently, committing a breach of Aboriginal law. There was also trouble over the fact that a person of the "wrong skin" had been used as an interpreter. Ward subsequently developed a kidney disease and received dialysis. Janba was found guilty of the manslaughter of his wife and sentenced to eight years' jail; and for his attack on Jackson he got five years, to be served concurrently. Larry Boy Janba died in hospital just before he was due to be released from prison. It was suggested he picked up a lung disease while on the run after the murder of his wife. Friends of Janba told Bowditch he had willed himself to die because he had killed his wife.

47. BEGINNING OF THE END

It is doubtful if Seattle, Qantas, American hot gospellers and London knew what hit them when Bowditch went on two overseas trips in the 1970s. One was to Seattle, courtesy of Qantas, to see the Boeing 747 jumbo jets and to come back on the inaugural flight of the *City of Darwin*. Before setting out on the trip Bowditch was drinking with Australia's Rock 'n' Roll king, Johnny "The Wild One" O'Keefe, who was performing in Darwin. O'Keefe and Bowditch had clicked the first time they met. Hearing that Bowditch was soon off to the US, he asked him what he was going to wear. Bowditch said he had a pair of long pants and would borrow a jumper and a coat, there being no use for such clothing in Darwin. This was not good enough for O'Keefe; he supplied Jim with a wardrobe of trendy clothes, which included a double-breasted, pin-striped, blue-black gangster-type suit with wide lapels and padded shoulders. There was also a mauve suit, four dress shirts, ties, built up shoes and even floral underpants. O'Keefe also supplied a thousand-dollar Spanish leather overcoat. In addition, he gave Bowditch a pair of gold cufflinks he (O'Keefe) had been given when he appeared on the *Johnny Carson Show* in America. Bowditch had never been so sartorial.

He and other journalists were flown to Sydney by Qantas to join a jumbo for America. The party was accommodated in the Wentworth Hotel; it was erroneously believed by the journalists that the fridge contents, which included French champagne and scotch, were free, so they drained them dry. As a result, on the flight to America the journalists were a bit tired and emotional, especially Bowditch. He slumped down in one of the swivel chairs in the club part of the business section and fell asleep with a cigarette in his hand. Horrified Qantas staff were mesmerised by the cigarette, the ash on which got longer and longer. It was feared he would burn a hole in their nice new aircraft. By the time the plane reached Hawaii he had come to the conclusion that he was the only reporter on board and all the others were high-flying executives. Feeling uncomfortable, he apparently stepped up the intake of alcohol. Arriving in mainland America, he disappeared and somehow became involved with a team of popular African American women hot gospellers, the Clare Ward Singers. Dressed like a suave hit man, he impressed the gospellers with his capacity to do the twist, a rare skill he had acquired which included much stomping of the feet.

Back in Darwin, reporter John Loizou at the *NT News* received a garbled telephone call from Bowditch which left him flabbergasted. The gist of the story was that Bowditch had some terrible disease, was going into quarantine and would never be coming back to Australia. Loizou was asked to pass this astonishing message to Betty Bowditch. Flummoxed by this call, Loizou wondered what to do. However, he did not have long to ponder the situation, because soon afterwards he got another surprising call. It was from Captain Robert Ritchie, the Qantas general manager,

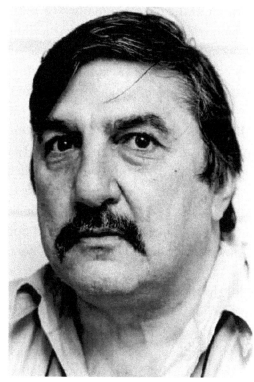

John Loizou, *NT News* reporter, was often called upon to try to get Bowditch out of strange situations.

Captain Ritchie was curt, precise and very clear. He said: "Your Mr Bowditch" had been a menace throughout the trip to America, was now in a Seattle motel with a group of hot gospellers, and the return flight to Australia was leaving in a short time. If "your Mr Bowditch" was not on board he would have to pay his own way home, or swim back to Darwin. The well-informed captain gave Loizou the telephone number of the motel. After thanking Captain Ritchie, Loizou quickly rang the motel, somehow got hold of "Mr Bowditch" and passed on the message. Bowditch missed the return flight. He arrived back in Darwin with very little of his impressive wardrobe and said he had had to leave America in such a hurry his clothes were left behind at the dry cleaners.

Another overseas trip came soon after—not with Qantas—to see the supersonic Concorde. He was so impressed by the jet that it was said he "fell in love with the plane." While in England he saw members of his family, including his brother David who had been a young boy when Jim left England for Australia. Somehow, under the influence, he disported himself at the old Roman town of Bath. In telephone calls back to Loizou in Darwin he spoke of travelling to Switzerland with somebody he had met. Then Loizou got an urgent request to send money to Hong Kong. Loizou and another reporter, Dennis Booth, managed to rustle up the money and wired it off to Honkers.

It is not clear where Bowditch flew back to Darwin from; mystery surrounds what happened to the money urgently sent to him in Hong Kong as he apparently did not get it. When he rolled off the plane, the last to emerge, he was yelling and refusing to cooperate with Customs. After he shouted that he would not be searched, airport officials said he was lucky not to be arrested and to get him off the premises. Bowditch complained of seeing blood covering his arms and cried about murdering a young soldier on Tarakan during the war. In his distressed state, he did not want to see people or go to work. For him not wanting to work was unusual, because he was a workaholic who loved going to the office.

Bowditch was involved in another aviation incident which involved the flight of a Concorde to Australia. The British Aviation Corporation threw a party in the Darwin Travelodge which was attended by southern journalists. At some stage the door flew open, and there was Bowditch, who glared about the room. A BAC official in a cravat standing behind a bar dared to laugh, and Bowditch chipped him. He apologised to Jim for his offensive behaviour. For no reason at all, Bowditch then began to monster the tallest man in the room, the well-known aviation writer, genial John Stackhouse. There was the spectacle of an uncomfortable Stackhouse towering over Bowditch who was threatening him with violence, including throwing him from the balcony. I coaxed Bowditch away from his victim. A Darwin woman who worked with Bowditch described him as being like a tiny terrier which, on entering a room, looked for the biggest dog with which it immediately picked a fight. Many went through the experience of Bowditch, in his cups, threatening to kill them with one or two blows.

The confluence of many unusual events ultimately led to the downfall of Bowditch. In October 1972, Princess Margaret and her husband, the trendy Lord Snowdon, came to town; Bowditch won $40,000 in a lottery; and the richest man in Darwin, Mick Paspalis died in his sleep aged just 56. Add to this the fact that it was the trying time of the year when people go troppo in the harsh weather and the likelihood of something extraordinary happening was high.

The cavalcade of events began with the arrival from Western Australia of the royal party. Travelling with the royals was a Bowditch friend, journalist Jim "Flasher" Oram, of the Sydney *Mirror*. Oram, son of a clergyman, gained his nickname because he had been a notorious dropper of the tweeds at parties, weddings, and so forth in his younger days. An experienced and much-travelled scribe, Oram once went on a bender with Brendan Behan, the Irish author and playwright, which began in England. The well-soused duo flew to Ireland on Aer Lingus and reeled off the plane, the locals greeting Behan like Irish royalty. They headed for the local bars to take in the atmosphere; Behan collapsed and was taken to hospital.

Oram was also a movie buff and hosted a Sydney TV show in which he introduced the evening's film with well-told commentary. When Pope John Paul II was elected, Oram was sent to Rome to interview him. He later wrote a book about the Pontiff which sold in the millions. After the success of his book, Oram went to a ball dressed as the Pope and his companion went as a hooker, representing the book's publisher, which had paid him no royalties. On the way from WA with the royal party the security men got to know that Oram was a man to watch with a few under his belt. Also in the party was David McNicoll, editor-in-chief of Australian Consolidated Press, with whom Oram had had terse words one evening. Naturally, Oram made contact with Bowditch when he lobbed in Darwin.

The royal party stayed at Government House, Snowdon got about in comfortable tropical gear, which included white trousers with an eye-catching pocket near the knee. As if having the royals in town was not excitement enough, Bowditch won $40,000 in the Queensland Golden Casket lottery. First news of the lottery win was conveyed over the phone to the Bowditch residence. Young

Steven Bowditch took the call, got the message, then went out to play, and promptly forgot what he had been told.

Betty was working at the squash centre when the news was phoned through that Jim had won the lottery. She responded with joy and said now they could pay off all their bills. Because of his win, Bowditch took the night off from the newspaper to celebrate. The "True North" column in the *News* next morning led with an item about his lottery win which said Jim had recently been heard say if he had $20,000 he would be off. The only problem about the windfall was that he could not find his winning ticket. On buying a ticket, he would shove it in his pocket and, if it survived the day, throw it into a drawer next to the bed. When he ransacked the drawer, there were plenty of old tickets, but not the vital winning one.

The morning after Jim's lottery win, Paspalis died in his sleep. At a garden party held in the grounds of Government House, and attended by Oram, a colourful band of worthy citizens mingled with the royals. Not far away at the war memorial and watched by police, a group of people campaigning for land rights displayed banners. One read: LAND BEFORE GONGS. Lord Snowdon asked reporters what the sign meant. He was told of a recent event when the Administrator, Fred Chaney, had flown to Goulburn Island to present an MBE to George Winunguj, only to find the islanders had boycotted the ceremony as they were more interested in land rights. When told this, Lord Snowdon smiled and said, "Oh."

Earlier in the day, Sandra Holmes, in a protest at the authorities not including Yirawala, OBE in the list to meet the royals, displayed some of his bark paintings at the front of the ABC, where they would be seen by the princess and her party as they entered the building. There was a picture of Holmes and the Yirawala display at the front of the ABC building in the *NT News*.

On hearing that Paspalis had died, Bowditch went to the *News*. Eventually he and Oram met and went for a drink at the Hotel Darwin. They then returned to the newspaper office and Bowditch dictated a special editorial about Paspalis to Oram, who typed it out. When the job was finished, Bowditch said to Oram: "Well, what do you think of that?" Oram replied: "I'd have used more clichés." Bowditch laughed and responded: "You would, you write for the bloody *Mirror*."

After giving the editorial to be set for the following morning's paper, the two then decided to resume the early wake for "poor old Mick" in the Hot and Cold bar.

When Bowditch returned to the office later that evening he was told of a strange situation. The paper's managing director, Brian Young, had come to the office, read the Paspalis editorial, told the news editor, John Meeking, "it's not good enough", and took it away with him. The contentious editorial supposedly opened something like this: "You can't be the richest man in town and not have enemies. Michael Paspalis was the richest man in Darwin and did have enemies, but he also had many friends and did a lot for the town." Enraged, Bowditch rang Young and demanded the editorial be returned. Young refused, saying he had "total control". Bowditch then rang Sydney and Ken May confirmed that Young did have complete control of the newspaper. Bowditch resigned.

The next morning the staff of 14 reporters and three photographers stopped work and questioned Young. In brief replies, he told them that the staff could not see the editorial; he would not tell them what was in the editorial, nor why he had stopped it from being run. Furthermore, he told the staff there would be no guidelines issued for future interference in editorial matters.

The Australian Journalists' Association in Sydney advised the staff to return to work. Instead, they struck for 24 hours and came back to work with a list of demands. They again asked why the editorial had been withdrawn, saying "the action was so apparently arbitrary and without precedent that it had cast doubt on the competence of both staff and editor." They also said that the action taken was an abnegation of an editor's historical right of free comment. Young replied that he reserved the right to withdraw any editorial matter, at any time and no reasons would ever be given.

Bowditch requested the staff take no further action until he contacted Murdoch, who was in London. A member of the Trades and Labour Council promised support if the staff decided to go out and the printing staff said they would not handle "scab" copy or layout. Bowditch told the staff he would not return as editor unless he continued to have total control of editorial policy, which he had had for 17 years. One southern newspaper report about the situation said May had advised Bowditch not to ring Murdoch over the impasse as he was "a gruff man on the phone." A detailed letter would suffice.

The funeral of Paspalis was attended by News Limited chairman Sir Norman Young, who had handled Paspalis's financial matters for 30 years. A meeting was eventually arranged with Murdoch to decide Bowditch's future at the paper. Bowditch, accompanied by Betty, went to Sydney for the meeting. They travelled via Brisbane because Jim had to produce papers to confirm his identity to claim the lottery prize. In fact, they were so short of money they had to get a bank loan for the trip south. Journalists and others converged on the hotel in Sydney to party on with Jim and discuss the important forthcoming meeting with Murdoch. It was evidently a lively evening as the hotel management next morning asked Bowditch to leave. He and Betty then moved to the Gazebo at Kings Cross.

The Bowditches went nightclubbing with the Freedens. They also met Johnny O'Keefe and Betty remembered going to a Leagues club where O'Keefe was performing and he dedicated a song to Jim and Betty Bowditch. After the performance they went to the Mandarin Club and O'Keefe joined them. It was a hectic time in Sydney and then Jim had to go to the all important meeting with Murdoch. Murdoch reportedly started proceedings by asking what the matter was all about. Young said he thought the Paspalis editorial had not been suitable. Bowditch asked Young to produce the editorial and point out what, in his opinion, was undesirable. According to Bowditch, Young did not produce the contentious editorial and said it had been destroyed. Murdoch, going on Bowditch's account, had looked furious when told this. Bowditch offered to type out the editorial from memory but Murdoch rejected this. At one stage Bowditch was asked to leave the room and it was eventually decided he would return as editor.

While in Sydney on that occasion something "strange" happened to Bowditch. He thought he had a stroke, but did not tell anyone about it, not even his wife. It may well have been a bad hangover or due to the marijuana he and O'Keefe had been smoking. However, when told of this so-called stroke, Betty Bowditch, in 2000, doubted such an occurrence. She suggested that it might have been another instance, through alcoholism, of him seeking sympathy. She told of once being told by a friend how sad it was that Jim was dying from prostate cancer. Not knowing he had cancer, Betty had been shocked and spoke to Jim's doctor. The doctor said he did not have cancer. His claims of being seriously ill might have been a way of seeking sympathy and a cover for excessive drinking. On another occasion Bowditch, after a heavy drinking bout, told me that he had bowel cancer and did not expect to live much longer.

After the meeting with Murdoch, Bowditch and Young both returned to Darwin on the same plane. Although he was back as the editor, he sensed that things would never be the same. Apart from the confrontation with Young, Bowditch knew there were people within the *News* organization who did not like his style of doing things. He had once overheard an *NT News* executive, not Young, saying over the phone that Bowditch was an old-fashioned reporter who did not fit into the modern newspaper office. Bowditch confronted the executive and gave him an old fashioned broadside.

It is fair to say that Bowditch's eventual split with the *News* was inevitable, even of his own making. However, events took place which clearly indicated he was cracking up. Under pressure at work and putting in long hours, he was drinking large amounts of alcohol, especially whisky, which brought back the horror of his wartime mutilation of the young enemy soldier.

After one heavy drinking session he was seen under his desk at work barking like a dog. Clearly, he needed medical help, but was soldiering on in a way which could only lead to another confrontation or a major breakdown in his health. At one stage he joined Alcoholics Anonymous; he even took medication which made him ill each time he touched alcohol. Despite these measures, he resumed drinking. An event took place which appears to have been the last straw as far as News Limited was concerned. Bowditch, who had been drinking, intervened when he saw police arresting some Aborigines and was himself taken into custody. One of the Aborigines was Bobby Secretary, central figure in a Darwin land claim. Released by the police later that evening, Bowditch was again picked up soon after. John Meeking, the *News'* industrious news editor, bailed him out and said, "Bad luck, old mate." Soon after, Meeking announced he was leaving the *News* and went south. Then Young told Bowditch he was no longer the editor. When Bowditch asked why, he was told it was because of his behaviour.

48. THE STRIKE

John Meeking returned from interstate as the editor. On 16 July journalists and three photographers went on strike, saying they could not work with the replacement editor. In fairness, it must be said that Meeking often kept the paper afloat. One reporter there at the time said Bowditch had been lucky that there was someone like Meeking to keep the paper running when the editor was often plainly not capable of doing so. If handled differently, the seemingly inevitable removal of Bowditch might not have placed Meeking in the invidious position in which he found himself.

The dispute also put an English journalist, Eugene "Gene" Janes, in a difficult situation. Janes, like Bowditch, had been born in Lewisham, London, and had also worked in a Queensland lighthouse, near Thursday Island. As a boy he had been literarily inclined and wrote much poetry, urged on by his mother. While working at the BBC as an office boy he contributed to the staff magazine and sold copies of the *Daily Worker*. At the BBC he applied for a job in the Talks Department and spoke to Guy Burgess, who was in the process of producing the longest series of talks put out by the radio station, on unemployment.

Burgess, an expert on Russia, told Janes he might be another Shakespeare, but he was too young for the Talks Department position and had a long way to go. After the war, Burgess, along with Donald Maclean, defected to Russia, followed by Kim Philby. The defections caused great embarrassment to British security. Janes said it should have been obvious to British Intelligence where Burgess's sympathies lay as he wore a hammer and sickle pin in his lapel while working at the BBC.

When the war broke out, Gene, 17, went into the Royal Navy and while operating a Bofors gun in the Mediterranean and squinting into the sun, shot down a RAF Hurricane. Fortunately, the pilot survived. After the war, aged 22, Janes came to Australia, worked at Garden Island dockyard, Sydney, and wrote short stories and radio scripts, mixing with actors and artists. After marrying his English wife, Muriel, who came out to Australia on a trip, they travelled to many parts of Australia. Gene also pounded out pulp fiction paperbacks for Australian publishers at a prodigious rate. These included romance novels. Because he was reluctant to be known as the writer of romances they were published in his wife's name. While the Janes family were living in Townsville, they saw Bowditch on television speaking out about a contentious issue in the Territory. Muriel told Gene that Bowditch was the kind of editor for whom he should be working. Gene agreed, and applied to Bowditch for a job on the *News*. He got the job, so they moved to Darwin. They arrived to find the staff on strike. Janes was in an onerous position. The staff had gone out because they said they could not work with the new editor, Meeking.

Janes had not previously worked with Meeking and pressure was put on him to report while nearly all the regular staff were out. Saying he had no other option, Janes joined the strikers. The strikers put out their own newspaper, *Daily Alternative*. Fortified by flagon wine and slices of watermelon, they put the paper together on a table in a room made available by Dennis Booth. In the 20 July 1973 first issue of the newspaper, staff explained they were not protesting because Bowditch had been replaced as editor. They were on strike because they refused to work with his replacement. They said a newspaper must be produced by a team. This could not be done if the editor and his staff did not respect each other. The declaration said that with Bowditch as editor the *News* enjoyed a freedom rare in Australian newspapers: "We feel that the spirit is now dead."

The lead story in the paper, which sold for 10 cents a copy, was headed: NEWS ROW TO COURT. It said the strike would go before the Conciliation Commission in Sydney on the coming Monday. At that meeting, AJA secretary Syd Crosland made a submission based on a briefing prepared by John Loizou in Darwin. Loizou had remembered Murdoch making a statement that newspaper management had an obligation to shareholders to make sure papers were run properly to maintain viability and strong profits. In a variation on this theme, Loizou took the line that journalists had a similar responsibility to shareholders to make sure management did not take steps which would damage the performance of a newspaper. Early in the hearing Crosland made the submission that this was the first case in Australia of workers wanting to participate in the running of a newspaper. Loizou said this claim seemed to have galvanised News Limited because next day it was represented by a QC.

The strike paper, run off on a manually operated stenograph machine, clearly did not cause the growing Murdoch Empire to tremble. It was delivered by reporter Bob Hobman, clad in stylish beachcomber mufti, who rode a bicycle to which was attached a candle to light his path. Outlets included the pubs and some shops. Loizou was publisher and William Reynolds was editor. As an indication of Bowditch's support in the community, the Darwin branch of the Waterside Workers' Federation donated $130 to the strike funds. An advertisement, headed: A MESSAGE FROM THE WATERFRONT, said that after a meeting on the wharf, Darwin waterside workers had decided to support the principle of the journalists and staff in their protest against the new editor employed by the *NT News*. This was an interesting stance for the watersiders to take since they had once banned the unloading of newsprint for the paper because Bowditch had refused to withhold a court story.

Southern journalists also made donations to the strike funds. To make the strikers feel a little happier, social writer Joy Collins handed out pay packets with a small amount of money in each. In town at the time from Sydney was reporter Les Wilson, who was writing a special feature on the late Mick Paspalis to coincide with coverage of the wedding of Helene Paspalis to lawyer Peter Coombes. At the invitation of Mrs Paspalis, Wilson was staying in the Hotel Darwin. Wilson, who had worked on an Australian Journalists' Association's strike newspaper in Sydney, offered his advice to the *NT News* staff and there was an item about the looming wedding in the *Daily Alternative*.

An extraordinary hearing was arranged in Darwin to try to settle the dispute. Held in the Greek Hall where the acoustics were poor, the proceedings were remarkable for several reasons, not least for the way all seating was gradually moved closer and closer to the industrial commissioner so people could hear what was going on.

A procession of *NT News* staff gave instances of how they had found Meeking difficult to work with in the past. Meeking and Young sat listening to proceedings.

As part of an agreed settlement, the Sydney *Daily Telegraph* editor, Brian Hogben, the man who covered the Rockefeller disappearance in Dutch New Guinea for News Limited, came to Darwin for six weeks to act as adviser to the new editor and the staff. In what was regarded as a major achievement, a standing liaison committee of six was set up comprising Young, Meeking, the journalist adviser and three members of staff. In practice, the meetings were few and the idea of so-called worker participation went nowhere.

An arrangement was made whereby Bowditch would leave the paper, still live in the *News* house in Phillip Street, Fannie Bay, and set up his own media business, North News Unlimited. An item in the *NT News* of 5 September 1973 announced Bowditch's departure from the paper, saying he would set up a freelance features and information service and had accepted a retainer from News Limited (Australia) to give the organisation first right to anything he wrote.

After 18 years of service, during which he had built the paper into a highly regarded and profitable publication, Bowditch was out the door. He left with a payout of less than $5000. In the 1980s, musing about his years as editor at the *News* under Murdoch, Bowditch said they had really been great times, but there had been inevitable changes. For a time, he had regarded Murdoch as "the great white hope" in Australia because of "this great human feeling." But Bowditch felt that as Murdoch accumulated more and more interests and bigger financial obligations, he had turned from a newspaper man who enjoyed the fun of running newspapers into a businessman.

While Bowditch was enterprising and a hard worker, it was a battle from the time he left the paper. Much of the lottery win went quickly as he paid debts and cleared $20,000 worth of bills connected with a failed Pine Creek tin mine venture. He had become involved in the mine in the hope that it would provide an income if he ever got the sack at the *News*, or if he decided to leave the paper. In a typical gesture, he bought refrigerators for an old-timers' home out of his lottery win. In addition, other battlers, worthy causes and hangers-on shared in his largesse.

With help and advice from his friend Bob Freeden in Sydney, Bowditch started a newsletter, *North News*, sold by subscription, which provided economic and political news from the NT. Gene Janes, who had arrived in Darwin only to find himself in the middle of the strike, had a checkered career at the *News*. He broke new ground for the paper by writing a long serial, illustrated by an artist, about Australia being run by an Aboriginal government. Before the story was run, Sandra Holmes read the text and said it was offensive to Aborigines. Nevertheless, it was published.

It is fair to say that Janes did not get along well with Meeking. On one celebrated occasion, Janes, a trencherman of some repute, left a parcel of prawns in the office refrigerator and they disappeared. Angered at their disappearance, he took up the case of the missing crustaceans with the editor, who was not overly interested in the matter. Responsibility for tracking down prawns is not normally listed in the duty statement of editors. Becoming angry at the lack of concern about the prawns, Janes told Meeking what he thought about him, then reportedly chased the departing editor; he was sacked.

This episode rated a mention in the opposition *Star*, in which it was said that in the good old days at the *News* reporters could wrestle with the editor, even try to throttle him, and not get the sack. Mrs Janes made a personal plea to Meeking to reinstate her husband, but to no avail. From then on, Bowditch and Janes were involved in various ventures.

49. THE OPEN DOOR SLAMS

When Bowditch was editor at the *NT News* he had an open-door policy. Anybody could come in and speak to the editor. In the Tin Bank days some callers by-passed the front counter, trotted in through the side door and walked straight into the editor's office. After Jim's departure from the paper close encounters with editors diminished at the *News*. Activist Robert Wesley-Smith, who had almost received favoured son treatment from Bowditch, became persona non grata. Wes, described as a Don Quixote type, dared to challenge an editor about the way he ran the paper and the handling of letters to the editor. The angry editor, reading from a Wesley-Smith letter critical of the way the paper was run, said Wes "must be mad", and instructed reporters not to quote him in any more stories written for the paper. Recalling the ban, which lasted about two years, Wes said it had actually improved his image in some ways. People told him that he seemed to have matured and become less radical because they no longer saw him quoted in the paper.

Former NAWU vigilance officer Bill Donnelly also fell out with another editor at the *News*. According to the unionist, the editor issued a directive not to allow "that goggle-eyed bastard, Donnelly" on the premises. At 82 years of age, as vehement as ever, and able to laugh at having been called a pop-eyed illegitimate, Donnelly declared, "What a great man was Jimmy Bowditch; there will never be another editor like him."

During the time of the Whitlam government there was a strong backlash in the Northern Territory to reforms brought in to improve the lot of Aborigines. In the town of Katherine, which became notorious when it was revealed there was police involvement with the Ku Klux Klan, a movement sprang up called Rights for Whites. Leading figures in the group were Bill and June Tapp of Killarney Station. Mrs Tapp, president of the organisation, maintained that government handouts were encouraging Aboriginal people towards crime, drunkenness and laziness. Bowditch took a personal interest in the issue, sensing that it could split the Territory and create racial tension.

He attended a lively Rights for Whites meeting in Katherine. One of the few Aborigines there was the Gurindji, Captain Major. When a white person said that the people of Katherine had experienced tough times during the Depression, Captain Major said Aborigines had been in a depression ever since the arrival of white people in Australia.

Bowditch strongly urged June Tapp to change the name of the organization from Rights for Whites to Rights for Territorians, which was done. He said with the original name the group could and would be branded racist. Because the supporters of the organisation felt they had legitimate grievances and were experiencing financial and other problems, they would get a more sympathetic ear from Canberra with an all embracing title. He argued that the Federal Government, by spending money on Aboriginal affairs, was, rightly trying to redress a terrible situation which demanded attention. The split in the community was a hot issue at the time and fanned by political groups opposed to the Whitlam government. Some people in high places in the NT secretly gloated over the racial rift.

The situation got nationwide media coverage. The presenter of the ABC's *Monday Conference* program, Robert Moore came to Darwin from Sydney and chaired a debate on the issue between June Tapp and Bowditch. At times the discussion became heated, and Bill Tapp watched proceedings angrily from the wings. After the session, Bowditch said he would not have been surprised if Bill

Tapp had rushed over during the debate and clocked him for giving his wife a tough time.

Bowditch backed the case of a Filipino musician in Darwin, Meno Ella, who was in the country on a visa and had applied to be allowed to stay. The immigration authorities insisted that he and his wife would have to leave. Because Brian Manning was married to a Filipino, Ella was referred to him for help. Manning, head of the NT Trades and Labour Council at the time, raised the matter with Bob Hawke, who was the ACTU leader, and Gough Whitlam. Manning had in mind unionists refusing to fuel the plane the Ellas would board to fly back to the Philippines. ASIO reported on developments.

Meno did not want to become the centre of a major dispute and left. However, when the Whitlam government came to power and Immigration Minister Al Grassby was on a visit to Manila he announced the Ellas could go back to Darwin. Furthermore, Grassby said the White Australia Policy was dead and if journalists gave him a shovel he would bury it.

In 1974, Bowditch helped Darwin lawyer John Waters, secretary of the NT ALP, in his unsuccessful bid to win the Territory federal seat. Waters, who had defended Bowditch, pro bono, or free, in several court appearances, asked him to represent the ALP for the seat of Fannie Bay in the NT elections for a Legislative Assembly which would be the Territory's first fully elected body. Bowditch agreed to do so, and Waters even paid his membership in the ALP to make him eligible to stand. Another Labor candidate was Geoff Loveday, who came from a political family in SA.

The ALP team was headed by Jim's long-time friend Dick Ward. The election was a disaster for the ALP, it failing to win one seat. Some of the reasons for the whitewash were attributed to perceived shortcomings of the Whitlam Government, Territory Minister Kep Enderby's treatment of the Territory as a social laboratory and the dramatic changes in Aboriginal Affairs brought about by Minister Gordon Bryant which had upset many whites.

The appointment of Dr Rex Patterson as Minister for Territories replacing Kep Enderby was popular in the Territory

New Minister for Territories, Dr Rex Patterson (centre) holds a press
conference at Government House. Among the media are Gene Janes
on the Minister's right, the author, Jim Bowditch, Rex Clark (left,
back to camera) and ABC TV Reporter, David Molesworth,
front right.

but not sufficient to overcome the Whitlam Government's wider
;problems.

A great blow to Labor's prospects had been the announcement,
four weeks before the election, that Dick Ward would be appointed
a judge. The announcement was made without any consultation
with the local ALP branch. Bowditch's campaigning was said to
have been negligible. Candidate Loveday used his connections to
get SA Premier Don Dunstan to come to Darwin and help the
ALP campaign. At the official launch of the 1974 ALP campaign
Bowditch kicked in a glass door at the Don Hotel. He was whisked
away by Franky Martin.

The ALP federal numbers man Senator Graham Richardson
happened to be in Darwin and took part in election activities. He
wrote a colourful account of the event in his autobiography *As
Much As It Takes*, which angered Territory ALP leaders. Richardson
said he spent a day at the Bowditch residence working on an ALP
election newspaper and during that time Jim drank a flagon and a
half of white wine.

It did not take long for Bowditch to break another major news story which caused a sensation in Australia and attracted much overseas attention. An Aboriginal girl who had been placed with white foster parents in Darwin, was spirited back to her father in Arnhem Land with the involvement of a white social worker, John Tomlinson. The distraught foster parents contacted Bowditch, who broke the story. There were many wild claims about what would happen to the girl and an American couple offered to "buy" her back.

Bowditch personally felt the removal of the child had been wrong. He said the girl's mother had not been mentally capable of looking after her and the father had been a heavy drinker. Tomlinson subsequently wrote two books in one—*Betrayed by Bureaucracy* and *Is Band-Aid Social Work Enough*—in which he defended his actions and pointed out what he maintained were shortcomings in the NT social welfare system. On the book's cover was a photograph of a struggling and grimacing Tomlinson being manhandled by police. A tongue in cheek caption said it was the author "helping police with their enquiries."

50. CYCLONE TRACY

On Christmas Eve 1974, Bowditch went on a round of parties before driving his VW Kombi van to a party in a printery. As the evening wore on and the rain from Cyclone Tracy bucketed down, Bowditch became an aggressive nuisance. Finally, three men bundled him, struggling and protesting, into a sedan and drove away, the idea being to take him home to Fannie Bay. Along the way he grabbed the driver by the throat. Because of the torrential rain and gale-force wind, it was hard for the driver to see and he missed the driveway at the Bowditch residence, causing the car to sink down in the flooded lawn. Betty put her head out the window and said she did not want Jim home and to take him away. Despite that, Jim was "thrown out", and as the car reversed in a flurry of mud and water, he tried to climb on top. However, he fell off, and the car drove away into the tempest. Bowditch then went upstairs and removed his sodden clothes. Betty and daughter Sharon sought shelter in a downstairs store room as the house began to break up. Bowditch went to rescue their Siamese cat, Sammy, just as the house blew apart. The cat became airborne and wasn't seen for several days. Bowditch went back upstairs and took refuge in the bath where the collapsed ceiling protected him. At daybreak they emerged to view the destruction. The main part of the house with large picture windows had been torn apart.

As all his clothes had been blown away, Bowditch, only wearing underpants, donned one of Betty's dry squash skirts which had been in her car. It was a smart little outfit, white with green piping. Unfortunately, nobody got a photograph of Big Jim in a skirt. Somehow, now clad in a T-shirt and jocks, apparently reluctant to be seen at large wearing a dress, Bowditch was taken to the printery where he had left his van. Like most of Darwin, the printery was surrounded by wreckage and damaged and upturned cars. A scene of chaotic devastation.

However, right side up, little damaged except for a broken side window, was Jim's van. It started without any trouble, and just as he drove off he hit a Great Dane dog, Ollie, which nervously bounded in front of the vehicle. A headlight was broken in the collision. The large dog, apparently unhurt, was verbally abused by Bowditch. He said his van had survived destruction in the fierce cyclone only to be damaged by a dog as big as a Shetland pony.

Bowditch, still wearing underpants, turned up at the house of reporter Kim Lockwood, who had replaced his father, Douglas, as the *Melbourne Herald* group reporter in Darwin. He told Kim that at least 20 people had been killed in the cyclone. Lockwood gave him a pair of shorts. The Bowditches lost just about everything in the cyclone, including irreplaceable photographs and papers. Gone with the wind were title papers relating to grandfather Manning's printery in England. The battered Walkley Award for the *Sea Fox* saga also disappeared.

While Jim insisted on staying on to report the destruction of Darwin, Betty and daughters Ngaire and Sharon drove south in a convoy. With them were the two pet dogs, Fosters and Snoopy, which they smuggled into various accommodation places along the way. After reaching relatives in Port Augusta, they made their way across to Sydney and stayed with the Freedens for six weeks. They also spent some time at North Head Quarantine Station, where people they knew from Darwin had been accommodated.

One of the earliest journalists to lob into Darwin after the cyclone was "Flasher" Jim Oram, who travelled light, in a suit. Once he got to Darwin he abandoned the suit coat and tie and chopped the trouser legs off at the knees. He and Jim were soon working as a team to cover the major story. Bowditch later flew south to see Betty and daughters and then went back to Darwin.

As part of the Whitlam Government's campaign to rebuild Darwin instructions were given to employ as many people as possible in government positions. Due to this directive Bowditch, journalist Peter Blake and the White Hunter, Allan Stewart, were given jobs in the Information and Public Relations section in Darwin. Blake and Bowditch were involved in the production of a magazine for the Animal Industry Branch.

Stewart brought an unusual entrepreneurial flair to the government department. It could be said that he took to the job like a duck to water, but a duck not usually seen on public service ponds. Sent to the Sydney Royal Easter Show to help with the Northern Territory's stand, he was in his element. Leaving the stand to be manned by mere public servants, he made a bee-line for the Members' Bar, where he lubricated his tonsils, met old business associates and rubbed shoulders with top military brass, with whom he got on exceptionally well. From there he arranged for the Royal Australian Navy Band to march up and play at the front of the NT stand. It was so noisy people could not make themselves heard. It was hard to sell the glories of the Territory because of the enthusiastic naval band. An exasperated member of the NT team, Dick Timperley, ex-army, said he would not be surprised if Stewart had organised a band of Scottish pipers to parachute in on the stand.

Because of damage done to the Stokes Hill powerhouse during the cyclone, the supply to Darwin often switched off for some reason which the Department of Works seemed unable to determine. On one occasion, Clem Jones, former Lord Mayor of Brisbane, and Chairman of the Darwin Reconstruction Commission, was in the Travelodge when the power cut out. He drove to the powerhouse and asked for an explanation. Court proceedings were disrupted when the power suddenly went off. The situation was so serious that it was discussed at a special meeting of the Legislative Assembly.

Stewart sat in the public gallery and listened to the debate. Irritated by what he heard, he caused a stir when he called out an obvious military-type solution to the problem: get a submarine to come to Darwin and run a giant extension cord down to the vessel's powerful generator. The Speaker cried "Order! Order!" Stewart, more red faced than normal, apologised, and stomped out.

In May 1975, Bowditch supported an application by Gene Janes for a Literature Board grant to write a book on Cyclone Tracy. The application was also backed by the novelist Ruth Park, D'Arcy Niland's widow, who said she had known Janes's fiction and fact pieces for 15 years. She had admired his firm, craftsman-like grasp of style and form. Janes was a classic example of a fine writer sidetracked by personal responsibilities into too much journalism.

Park wrote he had a terse originality and an intuitive feeling for Australian character. The Calvert Publishing Company of Sydney attested Janes had been one of its most popular authors, who wrote commissioned stories with army, navy and airforce settings. He had also written a detective series and romance and mystery stories. His books had been translated into several languages. Unfortunately, he did not get a grant. (The 2004 collectors' book on Australian pulp fiction covers, published by the National Library of Australia, ran the cover of *Death in a Nudist Camp* by Gene Janes. Author Toni Johnson-Woods, a lecturer at Queensland University, wrote that little was known of Janes except that he was a prolific writer; the book included another action cover of the war thriller *Incident on Shaggy Ridge* by Owen Gibson (another Janes pen-name).

With the sacking of the Whitlam Government, Bowditch got involved in the re-election campaign. The Whitlam appointed NT Administrator, Jim's old friend Jock Nelson, resigned and

Bring your toothbrush. John Waters, lawyer and political activist defended Jim in many of his own court appearances. Always a traveller, after retiring from the law John was able to enjoy his holiday house, La Lunetta in Italy more often.

announced he would contest the NT seat in the federal election. At the request of John Waters, Whitlam had asked Nelson to once more stand for the Territory seat.

Bowditch rallied to Nelson's cause. As part of his efforts, Bowditch conducted a long interview with Nelson on air. He also wrote a front-page story about Nelson for the ALP election paper, the *Territory Times*. At the election Nelson failed to unseat the incumbent, Sam Calder.

Late in 1978, Bowditch was arrested for drink driving. Despite the pleas and evidence that he was haunted by the wartime killing of the young guard, he was sentenced to a total of eight weeks' imprisonment. As he knew he would be going to prison, he took his toothbrush to court the day of sentencing. Nobody, however, had advised him about bringing along spare underpants. In an agitated frame of mind, he rang the Information and Public Relations Branch and asked for some underpants to be bought and delivered to the lockup. Three pairs of "lairy" underpants were delivered to Bennett Street lockup and, at the counter, police were told they were for Mr Bowditch. The police chuckled. Bowditch was taken to Fannie Bay Gaol and then to Gunn Point Prison Farm. While in prison he received a Christmas card from June Tapp of Killarney Station. In good handwriting, the envelope was addressed to Mr Jim Bowditch, Fannie Bay Gaol, and was decorated with hand-drawn holly; the front borders carried continuous lines of Merry Xmas.

Envelope of June Tapp's Christmas card to Bowditch who was first in Fannie Bay Gaol before being transferred to Gunn Point prison farm.

On the back of the envelope were some lyrics from the song *Fannie Bay Blues* illustrated with musical notes. Bowditch appreciated the letter, lost the card, but carried the envelope around for a long time.

After two weeks in prison he was released on appeal against the length of the sentence. He was put on a good behavior bond for a year. When Bowditch was released from Gunn Point he smuggled out in his multi coloured underpants a letter to the wife of an inmate. She had been very pleased to receive the letter. Bowditch was released during the dangerous festive season and went back to work with the government.

It was not only Bowditch who got into trouble in Darwin during the fateful year of 1978. In a dreadful performance, I was involved in a Christmas party fracas in the Hotel Darwin and ended up with my nose painfully buried in a metal cigarette container, resulting in a black eye, a gouged nose and a wonky finger.

Even Rupert Murdoch's nephew, Matt Handbury, working as a sub-editor on the *NT News*, was beaten up, stripped and robbed of $320; he needed 11 stitches and had lumps on his face. A well-known lady in town was pulled over by police and found to be wearing next to nothing, but the gallant lads in khaki allowed her to drive on.

'Twas not the night before Christmas, but very close to that blessed event when guards at Fannie Bay Gaol were alerted by banging on the front gate. They demanded to know who it was knock, knock, knocking at the portal? "Jim Bowditch," was the reply. As if he had uttered that magic incantation "Open Sesame:, a panel in the main prison gate instantly opened. Bowditch had a package, and told the guards it was a chest expander, a bull worker, which he had promised a prisoner at Gunn Point would be delivered before Christmas. The bull worker had been in the Bowditch family for years, used by his son, Steven.

Throughout this period he was still working for the government in the Information and Public Relations Branch. Early in 1979 there was a party to celebrate the 26th birthday of the *NT News* and a group of people, including Bowditch, gathered on the site of the old Tin Bank.

Bowditch cut a "cake" made out of a beer can slab with candles on top. The party continued in the Vic Hotel, where Bowditch managed to smash a glass topped table by pounding it with his fist. Police were called.

1979 Birthday party to celebrate the 26th anniversary of the *NT News*. Jim cuts the 'cake', a Victoria Bitter carton decorated with candles, watched by, among others, Dennis Booth, Joe Karlhuber, Joy Collins and Rex Clark. The ceremony took place on the site of the former Tin Bank.

51. THE MILLIONAIRE'S BOOK

Janes and Bowditch worked together on a proposed biography of millionaire Mick Paspalis. Born in Castellorizo, Greece, in 1914, Michael Theodosios Paspalis went to Port Hedland, WA, as a boy with his family, where they started a general store. He and his brother Nicholas, involved in pearling, came to Darwin in 1927.

Mick had an old Dodge car and started a taxi delivery service for Felix Holmes's butchery.

Holmes was an entrepreneur and an inspiration for Paspalis. Not only did Holmes supply Darwin with its electricity but he owned many other businesses. From the small beginning in Darwin, Mick Paspalis became a very rich man.

After putting in some initial work on the book, Bowditch wrote a four-page letter to Mrs Paspalis, addressing her as Dear Chrissie. In it Bowditch indicated he was "a bit nonplussed", and having some difficulty with the Paspalis family accountant, Sir Norman Young, chairman of News Limited. Bowditch wrote that Sir Norman had several times said the book was a matter between Mrs Paspalis, Bowditch and Janes. Sir Norman had been "non-committal" at the suggestion that Bowditch may have to go to Port Hedland to gather information from people who had grown up with Paspalis. The financial adviser had suggested nobody who knew Paspalis would still be living there.

Bowditch agreed that this might be the case and letters had been written to authorities trying to clarify the point. It was vital to sit down with Mrs Paspalis for an hour or so, Jim said, to get basic family background and details of the early days in Darwin. He went on to quote statements by people who commented favourably about Paspalis.

The book was never written, and it is believed a payment, possibly $1000 each, was made to Bowditch and Janes. With his share of the money Janes bought the first lawn mower the family had ever owned.

Bowditch maintained that Paspalis, for all his millions, was a sad man. While many people called at the Paspalis home on East Point Road, Fannie Bay, he said many of them were only after his money. Paspalis had asked Bowditch how he could get people to like him. Bowditch had suggested that instead of erecting another building which would bring in more money, he should build something for the community.

One suggestion he put forward had been a home for the elderly. Paspalis had thought about it, but came back and said the

From humble beginnings, Michael 'Mick' Paspalis built a substantial property portfolio in Darwin. Two of his shops were the Continental Café and Darwin Super Market in Smith Street, close to the Vic Hotel.

project was something the government should build. "I was getting Mick around to the idea of doing something for the community when the Grim Reaper took him," said Bowditch.

As previously noted, Gene Janes had written war novels. One had been about the Z Special Unit. He was surprised to learn that it had been made into a film, the rights to the book having been bought from the Horowitz Group Pty Ltd, of Sydney, by John McCallum Productions. McCallum was the husband of the stage performer Googie Withers. Janes had received a letter and an ex gratia payment for $200 from the publisher. He returned the cheque and claimed copyright. An official of the Australian Writers' Guild labelled the $200 not only insulting but immoral, $10,000 being the average for film rights.

Bowditch and other journalists wrote about the situation and legal representations were made. The outcome was a settlement of $10,000, half going to legal fees. The joy over the win was short-lived. Janes became involved in an altercation with a Greek neighbour who was making a noise panel-beating a car. The Greek was stabbed and Janes was sent to prison. Bowditch visited Janes during his imprisonment.

During that time the *News* ran stories claiming there were deficiencies in the prison facilities and services. Some shortcomings allegedly related to the treatment of the drug-running pilot Donald Tait. Tait, who had escaped from an Indonesian prison, was intercepted by an RAAF aircraft and crash landed a drug-filled plane near Katherine setting fire to it with a Verey flare pistol. Janes got to know Tait in prison and suggested he write his life story.

It was revealed in the NT Legislative Assembly that stories about Tait had been smuggled out of prison, one inside a book. Bowditch, it was claimed, had helped smuggle out those reports. The close relationship between Bowditch and Janes continued. For a time the two journalists operated out of the Janes' house but a considerable amount of liquor was drunk and production of the business newsletter became sporadic. Subscribers received bogus excuses for non-production of the newsletter, one being a death in the family. Once, while the newsletter was being compiled at the *Star* newspaper office, where it was printed, Bowditch took to an unfortunate restaurant man who used to deliver tasty tucker to the establishment free on Friday afternoons. In the fracas partitions were knocked over. Customers at the counter were shocked to see the place apparently disintegrate.

One day Gene's wife came home to find Bowditch standing over her husband, who was recovering from a recent eye operation, saying he could easily kill him. Mrs Janes tried to ease the situation by making a cup of coffee and handing around a plate of tarts. After asking if she believed in God or the Queen, Bowditch sent the tarts flying when she replied in the affirmative.

She was eventually able to get Bowditch to go home. Later, Jim phoned and asked if Gene was all right as he feared that he had hurt him. Despite being told that he had not touched her husband, Bowditch rang back several more times asking about Gene's wellbeing. Exasperated, she took the phone off the hook. Police then arrived at the front door and said they had been sent by Mr Bowditch to make sure that her husband was all right. Then Jim's daughter Ngaire arrived, saying she had been sent by her father because he feared he had done something terrible to Gene.

52. THE AZARIA CHAMBERLAIN CASE

Life took yet another change of direction for Bowditch when he was engaged as a reporter on the ABC Darwin television current affairs program *Territory Tracks*. He was hired by reporter Matt Peacock, who later became an ABC correspondent in Canberra, New York and London and at the time of writing was back in Australia. Peacock said he employed Bowditch because he felt viewers would appreciate an openly opinionated and knowledgeable editorialist who could put things in a historical context. In this show Bowditch usually appeared side on, typing, and then turned to camera and started talking. The feedback on these appearances was good.

Bowditch became concerned about the Azaria Chamberlain case and expressed the view that Lindy Chamberlain was not

ABC publicity shot taken when Bowditch joined the Darwin current affairs program *Territory Tracks*. Courtesy Archives NT, ABC TV collection, 0416/0118.

guilty. Lawyer Phil Rice, with whom Bowditch had been associated in Alice back in the 1950s, represented the Chamberlains at the Alice Springs inquest in which coroner Denis Barritt found that Azaria had been taken by a dingo, but that there had been human involvement in the disposal of the body. Following this finding, Lindy Chamberlain and her husband Michael, were charged with the death of their baby. Lindy was convicted and gaoled while Michael was convicted as an accessary but avoided gaol time.

Bowditch used the *Territory Tracks* program to air his views on the Chamberlain case. He also wrote about the case in the free weekly *Darwin Advertiser* and the *Star*, calling for an inquiry. During this period he often discussed the case with ALP Senator Bob Collins, who campaigned to have the Chamberlains cleared.

Of the host of theories advanced for what many regarded as a scorched earth approach to the Chamberlains, two were the belief that the NT Government was fearful of being sued for not having acted on warnings that camp dogs were becoming a menace at Uluru and the fear that the tourist trade would take a dive if it were shown a dingo had taken the child. Evidence was given that the head ranger at Uluru, Derek Roff, had been writing to his superiors in Darwin for two years warning of pending tragedy due to the possibility that "camp dogs" might attack tourists, particularly children. This situation was developing, he warned, because people were feeding the animals despite being told not to do so.

Subsequently, new evidence of Azaria's disappearance emerged, there was a retrial and both Chamberlains were acquitted. Some years later the Northern Territory Government issued a pardon and paid compensation.

Other issues which Bowditch covered for *Territory Tracks* included ALP disunity, tropical leave for public servants, Colonel Rose, the impact of missionaries on Aborigines and the White Hunter's contribution to Territory tourism.

At the age of 68, Jim became disenchanted with Darwin and said he was going to leave. His romance with the Territory was over. He was quoted as saying hating things too much was like loving things too much. If things went wrong, you could go mad. He wanted to get out before that happened. For years he had been irked by the way the Territory was developing.

In 1980 Doug Lockwood made a TV documentary for the ABC's *Big Country* series called "Once a Territorian". In it he drove with an ABC reporter up "The Track", seeing old friends again. In Darwin, Bowditch told Lockwood, who had been away for twelve years, that the town had become a "rip-off place".

For some, it was hard to imagine Darwin without Bowditch. Lockwood said it was like Malcolm Fraser saying he would have no further interest in politics and Lou Richards announcing he would have nothing more to do with Aussie Rules. Not long before Lockwood died, he paid a tribute to Bowditch, saying a certain section of the Darwin community hated the *News* when Jim was editor, but they never failed to buy it. Every issue had something provocative, something controversial, something of interest, something to read about even if you did not agree. Bowditch had

1980, two legendary Territory writers, Doug Lockwood and Jim
outside the Darwin Press Club, Hotel Darwin.

stuck up for principles and was a friend of many people, some of
whom did not deserve his attention.

Bowditch contacted author Glenville Pike, who was living
at Mareeba, North Queensland, and sought his advice about
Townsville as a place to live. He told Pike he wanted to get out
of Darwin, and had been told the climate was better in North
Queensland. Pike honestly told Bowditch that in Townsville
he would be unknown and probably lonely. In Darwin he was
well known. Bowditch did, however, leave Darwin and went to
Queensland, where he stayed with people who had right-wing
friends. After some heated arguments, he moved to Brisbane and
wrote feature articles, living in boarding houses. He spoke of
meeting an interesting cross-section of humanity in the boarding
houses, some of whom were "doing it tough". Every Sunday he
would ring Betty and ask her if she wanted him back.

Without advance notice his brother Peter arrived in Darwin
from England on a package flight, wanting to see Jim. Betty said he

For Bowditch, the romance is over

"Hating things too much is like loving things too much. If it goes wrong, you can go mad, and I want to get out before it happens." Such is life for Jim Bowditch — a man who has made headlines almost as often as he has written them.

His name is legendary in the Top End and as one to be reckoned with, and in his 68 years he has forged a reputation as a journalist par excellence, editor,

trouble-shooter and civil rights campaigner. He was also a light-house keeper, door-to-door salesman, a staunch Labor supporter once branded a communist, and an alcoholic.

But Jim Bowditch says his romance with the Territory is over. He left Darwin last week for New South Wales, via Queensland — and says he won't be returning.

Firebrand Jim decides to call it quits

By DEBI MARSHALL

Jim Bowditch is something of an enigma.

He has always been known as a man of principle who would not back down under pressure.

He has also been a self-confessed 'Bad Drunk' who had more than 300 fights, and lost most of them.

His pen was mightier than his punch, but despite his larrikin nature, few who feared his journalistic exposes lost their respect for his convictions.

One of five children, Jim was born in the depression in the 'smut, slime and smoke of the London slum' and left school at 14 to start work in a factory and help support his family.

"I hated the English class system and dreamed of working on the land," he said. "So I jumped on a ship at 17 and headed for Australia with its pound in my pocket."

He was never to realise the dream of being a farmer, but the fighting spirit that came to characterise him was forged in those early struggling years.

"I took advantage of the travelling dole system, moving from place

to place in search of work," he said.

"But there were time limits on the length of stay in one town, and I had many clashes with the police for staying too long."

He once rode 800 miles by pushbike to find work in a goldmine, but he ended up as a different sort of digger.

"World War II started, and I jumped a rattler to Brisbane and enlisted in the 2/9th Battalion," he said.

Jim served for the duration of the war in many fronts and was chosen to join the elite Z-Force.

"I was a wild boy and I think they selected me to get me out of the unit I was in." But his Z-Force training almost ended his army career.

"I landed six miles from where I was supposed to be on a parachute jump, and the local picked me up and dragged me to the pub for two days. When I finally made it back to camp, I had a hell of a lot of explaining to do."

Jim was active in six intelligence missions behind enemy lines in Papua New Guinea and received a distinguished conduct medal and American silver star for his efforts.

"I was very lucky and worked on the principle that fear generates energy into survival," he said. "If you run, you put a bullet in the back, but men who say they came out of war unscathed are lying."

After the war, he had a short stint as a door-to-door salesman, and learnt a great deal from the experience.

Sales

"If I wasn't selling properly, I knew I wasn't communicating with people," he said.

"It stood me in good stead when I later became editor of the Centralian Advocate and the NT News."

He was a lighthouse keeper on Moreton Island for a time before moving to Alice Springs in the late 1940s on the soldiers resettlement scheme hoping to realise his hopes of becoming a farmer.

Instead, he freelanced for the Centralian Advocate newspaper for six months and earned the nickname the 'Instant Editor' when he stepped

those early days, along with his self-taught three-finger typing technique.

"The Territory was a wild frontier in the '50s politically, socially and economically backward," he said.

"If I forged a reputation as a trouble shooter it was because there were many injustices screaming for reform.

"I learned the editorial ropes by hard work, some guts and the luck born of idealistic youth."

After three years at the Advocate, he and his wife Betty moved to the Top End, reduced by the offer of editorship at the NT News.

Drinking

But it was his drinking exploits that often brought him into collision with the law. On one occasion, the magistrate told him that his drunk driving charges "must stop". "I thought that was a little exaggerated," he said, "but I wasn't in a position to argue."

He has the larrikin sense of humor born from the ability to laugh at himself, and many mates to laugh with.

"In those days, marriage between whites and Aboriginals was illegal," he said. "So when they finally wed, it was quite a social landmark."

On more than one occasion, he hid refugees on his own home, and drove the getaway car for three Malayans fighting deportation orders.

Jim was as controversial in his personal life as he was at his position as editor. A staunch left-winger, he was once branded as communist sympathiser and barred from becoming a justice of the peace.

He also won two Walkley awards for excellence in journalism, and left a legacy of reform behind him.

In his position as editor he changed the face of Darwin, and in time, Darwin changed him.

He refused to bow to authority or to change his editorial style, and left the News unceremoniously after 15 years.

"I was worn pretty ragged as much perhaps by my social habits as by the merciless lashings delivered by the tyrants of time and deadlines."

His battle with booze lead him to AA — "It was getting on top of me, and I wanted to get on top of it" — and today, he is a quieter, though no less astute, man.

He is presently writing a book about the people he has met and is finally leaving Darwin.

"I've been here 28 years and am enormously saddened by the change in the place," he said. "But hating things too much is like loving things too much. If it goes wrong, you can well go mad, and I want to get out before that happens."

□ Jim Bowditch: "If I forged a reputation as a trouble shooter it was because there were many injustices screaming for reform.

Newspaper story announcing Jim intends to leave the Territory.
Bowditch family collection.

A Hodgson family reunion: (l to r) Ngaire, her partner George and
Sharon, Betty in front. Betty would not take Jim back but with
daughter Ngaire kept a close watch on his welfare after he returned
to Darwin. Bowditch family collection.

looked just like Jim, and had flown on to Brisbane where he caught
up with his brother. Jim, however, did not want to have much to do
with him. He said he no longer had anything in common with his
brother.

Bowditch resumed contact with the diver Carl Atkinson, who
had suffered a stroke and was living on the Gold Coast. It seems
Jim might have taped Atkinson, trying to get his life story for the
NT oral history records; unfortunately, due to Atkinson's stroke
induced speech impediment, it was hard to transcribe the tape.

During his restless roaming away from Darwin, Bowditch
made contact with Joanna Willey, soon after her mother had died;
he stayed at her house for about 10 days. While there, in what was
described as a "mea culpa" frame of mind, he expressed regret at
the treatment of Keith Willey, saying her father should have been the
editor of the *NT News* because he was a far more talented reporter.
He indicated he would belatedly atone for her father's treatment in

the book he was writing. (In that book he briefly described Willey as one of the best and the fastest writers in early post-war Darwin.)

Among the many subjects he talked about during his time with Joanna was his killing of the enemy soldier on Tarakan, whom he described as "just a boy". In a deprecating way, he spoke of his war service, which resulted in his being awarded the Distinguished Conduct Medal, as having been nothing special, almost a "fraud". He told Joanna that he had left Darwin to get away from drink. It had been impossible, he said, to give up drinking in Darwin because he knew so many people and the pressure was on him all the time to join in.

A religious person, Joanna took Jim, an atheist, to a Catholic rosary meeting. At the time, she was under stress from her mother's death, and was not sure how she would respond at the meeting. She explained to Jim the form of the gathering, which included the chanting of the rosary, and he still insisted on attending. Joanna said she had been thankful for his company. At the meeting he sat quietly listening to all that was said; she had introduced him as a friend of her parents in their younger days when they were in Darwin. Bowditch responded with a moving speech about Keith and Lee.

When Jim's daughter Sharon, a journalist, married Col Allan, managing editor of the Sydney *Daily Telegraph*, called the most feared journalist in Australia, Bowditch and Jim Oram went to the Brisbane wedding. The newlyweds retired to their honeymoon suite in a hotel; Bowditch left as a passenger in a car which was pulled over for a breach of traffic rules. The outcome was that Bowditch gave the police a pay-out, saying they had ruined a perfect evening; he was arrested. The honeymoon was interrupted by the police telephoning to say they had a Mr Jim Bowditch in the watchhouse, come and bail him out.

While visiting Sydney Jim called on the Freedens and was sad to see his friend Bob suffering from Alzheimer's disease. He would look at Freeden and repeat that there was no God. Freeden, he said, had done nothing wrong in his life, yet had been afflicted. Bowditch would say that he (Jim) had done terrible things in his life, including killing many people, and there was nothing wrong with him.

At some stage Bowditch resumed contact with the ex-*NT News* social writer, Joy Collins, who was living at Mandurah in WA, and arranged to visit her. Bowditch subsequently went to Adelaide by bus and called on me. Jim's book manuscript was in a split cardboard box and the suitcase he had was damaged. From Adelaide he flew to Western Australia and stayed with Joy Collins. There he caught up with Italian friends who had run a restaurant in Darwin, the Donatellis. He also called on Z Special Unit members. While in WA he applied through the RSL for a replacement Distinguished Conduct Medal which he had lost in Darwin.

From WA he sent a letter to me and in it mentioned having "already forgotten" the names of some people he had met there who were from the Northern Territory. Later, Joy Collins wrote saying Jim had shown signs of losing his memory while staying with her in Mandurah. He eventually returned to Darwin in 1993 and his book, *Whispers from the North*, was published by the Northern Territory University Press; with a print run of only 500, the book quickly sold out.

While passing through Sydney about 1994, after publication of the book, Bowditch made contact with former *NT News* reporter Errol Simper of the *Australian*. It was arranged they should meet, and Bowditch arrived saying he no longer drank. However, he said the night before he had gone to a pub and when he called a taxi to go home to his daughter Sharon's place, he could not remember the address which had been written down on a piece of paper.

He had instructed the taxi driver to just drive around, hoping to recognise a landmark. With about $30 on the meter, the driver took him to a police station. There the police were helpful and not only got him home but, it is suggested, they might even have paid the fare. If so, it was an extraordinary event for a person who had been arrested many times. Recalling that last meeting with Bowditch, Simper said it seemed as if he was expressly giving him his life's details for an obituary.

Back in Darwin, Bowditch lived on his own in a unit at Nightcliff, not far from what had been the Paspalis drive-in theatre. Betty and Ngaire kept a close watch on him, taking him home for

Above: published in 1993 there was a well-attended launch
for his book, *Whispers from the North*.
Right top: former *News* snapper, Joe Karlhuber with Jim.
Right below: Jim hams it up with daughter Ngaire, her partner
George and family friend, Lois Glaister.
Photos courtesy of the Baz Ledwidge collection.

meals. Although not eating much, and suffering increasing loss of memory, Jim was still attracted to newspapers and had piles of them in his unit. In the last years of his life his memory loss was substantial and he was given to occasional angry outbursts though daughter Ngaire says that when she substituted non-alcoholic wine his angry outbursts stopped.

53. THE LAST MEDAL

In 1995, Bowditch was the belated recipient of the American Bronze Star for an event on 12 September 1945. Strangely, the Americans had not been able to track him down in all that time. The medal was awarded for meritorious service while serving in the Allied Intelligence Bureau.

The citation said his exemplary performance of duty in active ground combat was in keeping with the finest traditions of military service and reflected great credit on him, the Allied Intelligence Bureau and the Australian Army. At a special ceremony in Darwin at the Larrakeyah Army barracks on 26 September 1995, the US Defence Attache to Canberra, Colonel Stephen Barneyback, presented Bowditch with the medal. Colonel Barneyback was accompanied by Sergeant Drew Holliday, who specialised in tracking down undiscovered recipients of American medals although it was actually the late Darwin historian, Professor Alan

THE UNITED STATES OF AMERICA

TO ALL WHO SHALL SEE THESE PRESENTS, GREETING: THIS IS TO CERTIFY THAT THE PRESIDENT OF THE UNITED STATES OF AMERICA AUTHORIZED BY EXECUTIVE ORDER, 24 AUGUST 1962 HAS AWARDED

THE BRONZE STAR MEDAL

TO

JAMES BOWDITCH
(THEN SERGEANT, AUSTRALIAN ARMY)

FOR

meritorious service on 12 September 1945 while serving in Allied Intelligence Force, Pacific Theater of Operations. Sergeant Bowditch's exemplary performance of duty in active ground combat was in keeping with the finest traditions of military service and reflects great credit on him, Allied Intelligence Force, and the Australian Army.

GIVEN UNDER MY HAND IN THE CITY OF WASHINGTON
THIS   18th   DAY OF   August   19 95

Letter recommending Jim for the Bronze Star and medal citation.
From the Bowditch family collection.

Embassy of the United States of America
DEFENSE ATTACHE OFFICE
American Embassy, Canberra
PSC 277, APO AP 96549-5000

U-0210-95   27 April 1995

Department of the Army
US Total Army Personnel Command
ATTN: Military Awards Branch (Major Dagnes)
Alexandria, Virginia 22332-0471

Dear Major Dagnes,

The enclosed WWII award recommendation for the Bronze Star is
forwarded for your attention.

This document is one of a series uncovered in US archives by a
researching Australian professor. The write-ups are for personnel
assigned to the "Z Force" commando group of the Allied Intelligence
Bureau, which ran long-range reconnaissance and behind-the-lines
intelligence missions against the Japanese.   The enclosed
recommendation for Sergeant James Bowdich is forwarded ahead of the
other recommendations partly as a "test case," and partly because
this is the only veteran of this group we've located, and the only
award we've confirmed was not made.

The other "Z Force" recommendations are more substantial than the
one enclosed here. We are researching them with Australian
authorities to determine which, if any, are appropriate to forward
to your office.

As you will note by the enclosed background information, the
Bowdich case has already drawn the attention of the media and
veterans organizations. The February 8 Darwin newspaper article is
incorrect regarding status of the award.

We appreciate your time and attention. Point of contact in this
office is SFC Drew T. Holliday, Operations NCO, 61-6-270-5811,
(fax) 61-6-273-5232. Regards from Down Under.

                                    Sincerely,

6 encls: DAVID C. RYBERG
1. award rec, 12 Sep 45   CWO4, USN
2. award rec cover note, 1945   Operations Coordinator
3. newspaper article
4. ltr, NTU, 27 Feb 1995
5. ltr, Darwin RSL 10 Mar 1993
6. ltr, National RSL 20 Apr 1995

DEPARTMENT OF THE ARMY
U.S. TOTAL ARMY PERSONNEL COMMAND
ALEXANDRIA, VA
22332-0471

REPLY TO
ATTENTION OF
PERMANENT ORDERS 230-1   18 August 1995

BOWDITCH, JAMES SGT Allied Intelligence Force, Pacific
Theater of Operations

Announcement is made of the following award.

Award: Bronze Star Medal
Date(s) or period of service: 12 Sep 1945
Authority: Paragraph 3-13, AR 600-8-22
Reason: For meritorious service
Format: 320

BY THE ORDER OF THE SECRETARY OF THE ARMY:

                                    PETER G. DAGNES
                                    MAJ, GS
DISTRIBUTION: Chief, Military Awards Branch
Mr. Bowditch (3)
ARPERCEN   (1)
Files   (3)

Cover of the *Australasian Post*, Jim with granddaughter Candice and
the story about him being "found" for presentation of an American
Bronze Star. Bowditch family collection.

Powell from Charles Darwin University, who discovered the citation while researching American archives for one of his books and drew it to the attention of the American military.

The story of Jim's discovery, and medal presentation, was covered by newspapers and magazines both nationally and internationally. With headlines including "NT hero gets his US medal", "US honours Z-Force raider after 50 years" and in the *Australasian Post*, for which Jim once wrote, " 'Lost' hero gets his star," with a cover photo of Jim with his granddaughter, Ngaire's daughter, Candice.

Near the end of his life Bowditch would go to the ANZ bank at the Casuarina shopping centre, cash a cheque into $5 bills, go outside and give the money away to passers-by whom he thought were "doing it tough". Once the money was gone, he would return to the bank, cash another cheque and repeat the performance. A bank teller rang his daughter Ngaire and expressed concern. The bank staff were worried that he could be "rolled" as he walked about with a bundle of notes in his hand. Ngaire discussed the situation with her father; he responded by saying he was working to assist the poor, and that it was "my job" to hand out money to those in need. "My father was always a kind and generous man who would give you the shirt off his back," said Ngaire, "so it didn't surprise me that he was giving his money away. I guess with the onset of dementia it was quite reasonable for a compassionate man like my father to see this as his work and social duty. The bank said his largesse left little money in his account upon which to live; it had also feared that people would take advantage of him."

54. STOP PRESS

Two white warriors, each near the end of his life, lay in beds in a Darwin hospice. Like scarred bull elephants, they had both returned from the south to their stamping grounds to die. They were old friends who had not been in contact for years. Now they were practically next to each other in beds, but because of a cruel twist of fate and their afflictions they did not know how close they were. They were Jim Bowditch and Allan Stewart, the White Hunter. Bowditch had been in poor health for some time and suffered from emphysema. Stewart was nearly blind. Visiting her father, Ngaire Bowditch saw the name Stewart and immediately identified him as her father's friend. She introduced herself to Stewart and told him her dad was in a bed a short distance away. Stewart became emotional and cried out: "Jimmy Bowditch! I've searched the country for him, and now I find out he is in the bed next to me!" He began to weep. Ngaire then explained the situation to her father who said, "Don't worry old mate."

Bowditch, 76, died of pneumonia at the Chan Park Nursing Home on 5 October 1996.

That he had lived so long, having led such a hectic life, surprised many, especially his wife. Daughter Sharon rang the Sydney home of reporter Jim Oram, who was suffering from cancer. Oram had given instructions earlier in the day that he would not take any telephone calls. However, when he heard Jim had died he took Sharon's call. Many newspaper tributes were paid to Jim Bowditch. One from Robert Wesley-Smith simply read: "James Frederick Bowditch, HERO-HERO–HERO-HERO."

In a letter to the editor of the *NT News*, one Bowditch admirer said much had been written in the media since his death about his larrikinism over the years. Just one of his wartime experiences— that of sitting in a cramped and stifling submarine with Japanese vessels intent on blowing it up patrolling overhead for 18 hours— would be enough to make anybody a bit bent; allowances should have been made for his subsequent behaviour. Ngaire says that as a result of his submarine experinces, Bowditch never learned to swim and could not put his head under water.

The packed funeral began and ended with the strains of the African-American human rights campaigner and singer Paul Robeson, whose music was seen by the Bowditch family as symbolising Jim's lifelong struggle for the underdog. Bowditch might have met Robeson, who passed through Darwin in October 1960 on his way to Sydney. Because of his open support for communist ideas and a visit he made to Russia, Robeson had been shabbily treated in America. The *News* carried a report which said that during an airline stopover in Darwin the singer and human rights campaigner had spent two hours with unionists Mr and Mrs Des Robson. Furthermore, the newspaper announced that a committee, including *NT News* reporter Jim Kelly, had been formed to try to get Robeson to perform in Darwin on his way back to America. During Robeson's visit to Sydney he sang to workers on the Opera House site. Comments he made about the plight of Australian Aborigines were run in the *NT News*.

Jim's son-in-law, Col Allan, at the time editorial manager of the Sydney *Daily Telegraph* and *Sunday Telegraph*, spoke on behalf of the family at the funeral. He said Jim had been a complex yet simple man who would not have wanted all the fuss and reporting that followed his death. Allan continued: "It is only here that I feel safe saying such things about him, relatively sure that he will not appear in that familiar crouch, hands thrust forward in a combat position demanding that I not eulogise him but instead attack the Labor Party for betraying its ideals."

Bowditch's attitude to life was encapsulated in a poem composed on behalf of the family by his youngest son, Steven:

> A DAY IN THE LIFE OF OUR DAD
> At the crack of dawn
> after his usual four or five hours sleep
> his old typewriter was going rat a tat tat
> we kids heard the racket
> said "Ahhh, Dad, not again"
> and went back to sleep.
> By midday
> You'd see him striding down Smith St
> shorts, long socks, pulled all the way up
> tidy, upright
> racing forward
> on another crusade
> By late afternoon you'd find him at the Parap,
> Vic, Don or some other pub

hammering with words, or fists
about what was right, or what was wrong
By midnight
cigarette singeing mum's new teak table
hunched, elbow propped
pondering in tears
the horrible deeds of war
He didn't need the respect of kings or queens
the wrath of heaven or hell
or the fear of another man to shape his
code
He simply believed in:
equal opportunity
equal distribution of wealth of the land
to treat people equally, and to
think of no man as bigger or smaller
than yourself
We miss you dad
We all love you dad

One of those who delivered a eulogy was the union activist Brian Manning, who had fought many campaigns with Bowditch. In particular, he mentioned the Stayput Malays and the part Bowditch had played in helping to do away with the White Australia Policy. Manning raised an important issue, the counselling of soldiers returning home from horrific wartime experiences. He said he often felt the armed services were seriously remiss in not providing professional counselling to servicemen such as Jim who, although he served with valour and distinction, did not relish war and had great difficulty coming to terms with what he had done.

Much, he said, had been made of the drinking exploits of Jim. "I am sure he caused his family much anguish, as do all who over-indulge," he said. He recalled the incident when Jim had been barred from the RSL after kicking its glass door. In an agitated frame of mind, he had called on Manning in the Workers' Club and admonished himself for his killings in the war.

John Waters, QC said Bowditch had made an indelible impression on the life of the NT for more than 30 years. The Territory's record of racial tolerance during the period from the 1950s to the early '70s had been due to one man, Jim Bowditch. He made reference to Jim's often "half-hearted battle with the grog": "Putting the newspaper to bed was thirsty work, and Jim often had a full and frank exchange of views with police officers on late traffic duty. On more than a couple of occasions it was my job to accompany Jim to have a friendly chat with the local magistrate. On at least two occasions I was so pessimistic about the outcome of these discussions that I advised Jim to bring his toothbrush. While editing the *Northern Territory News* he always had his own misdemeanours fully reported, usually on page 3. Some of his late-night party pieces caused consternation to people newly arrived in the Territory.

"Bowditch," he continued, "had lived life to the full. He was a remarkable man and like all remarkable men had flaws, but would be remembered for producing a sparkling and exciting newspaper."

Another eulogy, faxed from New York, came from journalist Peter Blake and read: "I suspect Jim Bowditch was the last of his kind, the small-town newspaper editor who believed that treading on sensitive, prominent and powerful toes went with the territory and that included those who paid his wages. He edited the paper in bravura fashion without ever looking over his shoulder at the people who owned it. It was a style and philosophy that made the *NT News* a perfect mirror of its community outspoken, brash, cheeky, quirky, and yes, a bit rough around the edges."

He described Bowditch's office in the old Tin Bank as marginally bigger than the lavatory. Of Jim's grog problem, Blake said it had brought him a ton of grief, but he never wallowed in self-pity or blamed his war experiences. "But those who knew and loved him believed the things he'd been forced to do tore him apart."

At the cemetery there was an RSL Honour Guard made up of front-line veterans from WWII, Korea and Vietnam. As a mark of respect for another front-line soldier, a slouch hat and a bayonet had been placed on the coffin. Jim's eldest son, Peter, expressed concern about the items on the coffin. If they did not belong to his father, he said he did not want them on the coffin. There were to be no false trappings at his father's burial.

A wake was held at the Aviation Club and stories flowed. Included in the throng were people who had worked in the old Tin Bank. Betty Bowditch and her close-knit Hodgson family were there in force. A newspaper account of the funeral said because of a clash with parliamentary sittings some "old political friends and foes" were unable to attend. Journalist Jim Oram died soon after on 19 December. Jim's daughter Sharon, expecting a child, went home from the funeral and gave birth to a daughter that night. She named the baby Kate J, just the initial, which stands for the two Jims, Bowditch and Oram.

And true to his Socialist principles to the last, Jim's estate, when probate was granted, amounted to the princely sum of two-dollars and 64 cents. Daughter Ngaire still has the cheque for that amount issued by the NT's Public Trustee.

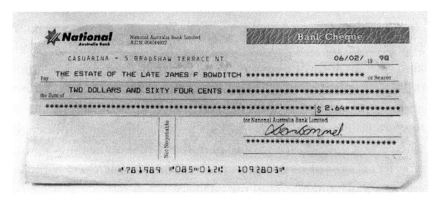

55. FUDGE*

Bowditch's erratic, often outrageous behaviour undoubtedly detracted from his greatness. It also gave his enemies ammunition with which to belittle him and his many achievements. It was only

---

* A fudge is an old newspaper term for a piece of stop press news inserted in a paper at the very last moment.

in 2001, long after Jim's death, that a Sydney doctor presented a plausible explanation for much of Bowditch's wild behaviour over the years. From an early age, the doctor said, Bowditch had evinced a strong sense of social injustice in the world. His bombing of bailiffs and hopelessly challenging his powerful father showed the strength of his feelings. This attitude had seemingly intensified as he grew older and went out into the world. Being bashed by the police sergeant while acting as spokesman for unemployed undoubtedly heightened his dislike of those in power; then he was drawn into the turmoil and trauma of the war.

The doctor said Bowditch's subsequent behaviour indicated he had suffered from unresolved post-traumatic stress brought about by his war experiences. Receiving no treatment for those horrors he, in effect, "self-medicated" with alcohol. Alcohol, outwardly, seemed to be his problem, but it was more complex. His deep-seated antipathy to authority, his crusading zeal, little sleep and hard work combined to put enormous mental, physical and nervous strain on him.

Added to this was the use, later, of marijuana, which Bowditch said relaxed the mind. In his desperation to overcome his complex problems, simply regarded as "alcoholism", he had taken medication which made him sick each time he touched alcohol.

While he did try to come to grips with his "drinking problem", it was hard to stop in Darwin because of the culture. The tragedy is that by trying to overcome this particular symptom, he almost certainly added to his burdens. At some stage he was introduced to Serepax, used to avert seizures when patients are coming off alcohol. It should never be taken by drinkers who are still consuming alcohol. Over-prescribing can result in addiction. Modern thinking is that Serepax should not be prescribed for longer than six weeks. Bowditch was on and off the drug for years, and often used it while drinking heavily.

Side-effects of the drug are blackouts, similar to alcoholic blackouts, which come without warning. The person does not lose consciousness, but part of the memory will just suddenly disappear. Rarer side-effects are dizziness, fainting, vertigo, headache, confusion, hallucination and aggression. Stimulation, excitement and rage can occur.

When Bowditch went to Adelaide by bus to see me on his way to Western Australia, there was clear evidence that he was on a dangerous cocktail of Serepax and alcohol. Having heard on the bush telegraph that Bowditch was "off the grog", and as I was baching at the time, made sure the fridge was devoid of alcohol. However, Bowditch arrived bearing a cask of wine he had been drinking along the way. When the cask was polished off, he ferreted out a forgotten bottle of whisky at the back of a shelf in a pantry cupboard.

About two in the morning, Bowditch threatened to kill me with two blows. Mad eyed, and standing over me with one hand raised threateningly, a whisky glass in the other, he repeated his ability to make a quick killing. Giggling, I tempted fate by saying nervously I was too young to die. At first, Bowditch responded angrily to this jocular response, and said drastic action might have to be taken to "teach Simon a lesson." Then Jim began to laugh, and asked for another whisky.

The next morning, as Bowditch was being driven about Adelaide, he asked several times to stop the car, saying he was suffering from motion sickness. On alighting, he would dry retch. When being driven to the airport, Bowditch became agitated, saying he had run out of Serepax, which he said was for his "anxiety". Spotting a pharmacy, he asked to stop, ran in and was able to get another bottle of Serepax, despite not having a prescription.

At the airport he was concerned that he might have to pay excess baggage as his possessions had been repacked into two suitcases. The airline check-in staff were told "This grey-haired old gentleman is going to Perth, and all his worldly possessions are in these bags." Everybody laughed, there was no excess to pay and Bowditch, less anxious, relaxed somewhat, toying with his Serepax container in the airport lounge.

It is highly likely that another drug he was prescribed to try to help overcome alcoholism had become another monkey on the back of a complex and brave man, the likes of whom will never be seen again in Australian journalism. Bent he may have been, but in a way which undoubtedly benefited humanity.

Belatedly but appropriately on 16 November, 2018 Jim Bowditch was inducted into the Melbourne Press Club's Australian Media Hall of Fame in recognition of his outstanding contribution to Australian journalism. His wife, Betty, daughter Sharon and son-in-law, Col Allen as well as several other family members attended the ceremony. Also belatedly but appropriately, Jim's good friend Douglas Lockwood was inducted into the Hall of Fame at the same ceremony.

This is to certify that

Jim Bowditch

was inducted into the
Australian Media Hall of Fame
on Friday 16 November 2018
in recognition of
his outstanding contribution
to Australian journalism.

Adele Ferguson
PRESIDENT
MELBOURNE PRESS CLUB

Michael Smith
CHAIRMAN
HALL OF FAME ADVISORY PANEL

Certificate advising of Jim's induction into the Australian Media
Hall of Fame, 16 November 2018. From the Bowditch family
collection.

Acknowledgements

At the outset, two comrades Kim Lockwood and Richard Creswick, must be adorned with garlands for finally getting this book on the launching pad. Feel free to shower them with any loose Bitcoins in your pockets or gathering dust in investment portfolios Several times it was on the verge of publication. Then no. One publisher's manuscript assessor said it was an interesting read especially the part where activists against uranium mining in the Northern Territory had suggested Jim Bowditch be asked to use his wartime knowledge of explosives to blow up a bridge and stop the flow of uranium. I was asked if he made a bomb. No. If I had said yes, would it have been published?

Another potential publisher asked why had I dived so extensively into Jim's ASIO file? Why not, I asked with a few expletives? They revealed so much about Big Jim, the times, the Northern Territory, the state of democracy in Australia and the immense pressures upon the man. It seems fashionable nowadays to talk about perceived conspiracies but in my dotage, I often tossed about in bed wondering if a D-notice, issued to prevent publication of information about defence or national security, had been used to prevent the publication.

While this may seem a wild claim, a journalist colleague Pete Steedman, in Melbourne, received a D-notice in the 1960s over a series he started to run about conditions on Northern Territory Aboriginal settlements. In a bid to get the book published, long-time journalist friend, Kim Lockwood, cut 30,000 words out of the manuscript. Ouch! That's about as many words as there are in a bestselling Mills and Boon novel. It was also an indication that perhaps the length of the book was inhibiting its publication.

Communist author Frank Hardy, who in 1968 published *The Unlucky Australians*, about the Gurindji struggle, in which Bowditch was often mentioned, was keen for *Big Jim* to be written. During a session with Hardy, he took me on a tour of the Collingwood area and other places which figured in his controversial 1950 novel, *Power Without Glory*, for which he was charged with, but subsequently cleared of, criminal libel of Ellen Wren, wife of prominent bookmaker and businessman John Wren.

When it seemed unlikely that the book would ever be published, parts of it were run like a serial in my *Little Darwin* blog. From time to time, additional bits of information surfaced and more people were contacted who had information about Bowditch and associated issues of interest. Now that the book has been published, it is time to deeply thank the Bowditch family for their cooperation over the decades.

Darwin's ace photographer, rock sitter and fearless international ice hockey champion, Barry Ledwidge, provided insights and some great snaps from his invaluable collection. Others provided photographs including the Bowditch family and the NT Library and Archives whose staff were always helpful.

Darwin agronomist and activist Robert Wesley-Smith provided a wealth of information about campaigns in which he had been involved with Bowditch including the Gurindjis, the Vietnam War and the Lindy Chamberlain case to name just a few.

Many were those who supplied information and anecdotes about Bowditch's time in Alice Springs during which he, surprisingly, became a newspaper editor of note. Some of them were Jock Nelson, later the NT Administrator; the head of the Alice Works Department, dynamic D.D. Smith; prominent Alice business identity, Reg Harris; the amazing anthropologist who fiercely campaigned for Aborigines, Miss Olive Pink; the head of the South Australian branch of the Federated Clerks' Union, Harry Krantz; journalist Alan Wauchope and the heroic Territory cop and Jim's good friend, Jim Mannion.

Special thanks must go to my wife, Judith, not only for her support over the long flight, but for her encyclopaedic knowledge of the book collection and files which enabled this book to be written. For her massive assistance in this long project she will be rewarded with a large pack of M&Ms now that the Bowditch book has finally landed in Darwin.

Lightning Source UK Ltd.
Milton Keynes UK
UKHW020652251022
411061UK00015B/967